THE LANGUAGE OF FRAUD CASES

THE LANGUAGE
OF FRAUD CASES

Roger W. Shuy

OXFORD
UNIVERSITY PRESS

OXFORD
UNIVERSITY PRESS

Oxford University Press is a department of the University of
Oxford. It furthers the University's objective of excellence in research,
scholarship, and education by publishing worldwide.

Oxford   New York
Auckland   Cape Town   Dar es Salaam   Hong Kong   Karachi
Kuala Lumpur   Madrid   Melbourne   Mexico City   Nairobi
New Delhi   Shanghai   Taipei   Toronto

With offices in
Argentina   Austria   Brazil   Chile   Czech Republic   France   Greece
Guatemala   Hungary   Italy   Japan   Poland   Portugal   Singapore
South Korea   Switzerland   Thailand   Turkey   Ukraine   Vietnam

Oxford is a registered trademark of Oxford University Press
in the UK and certain other countries.

Published in the United States of America by
Oxford University Press
198 Madison Avenue, New York, NY 10016

Library of Congress Cataloging-in-Publication Data
Shuy, Roger W., author.
The language of fraud cases / Roger W. Shuy.
pages cm
Includes bibliographical references and index.
ISBN 978-0-19-027064-3 (hardcover : alk. paper)—
ISBN 978-0-19-027065-0 (ebook)—ISBN 978-0-19-027066-7 (online content)
1. Fraud—Law and legislation—United States—Criminal provisions.   2. Fraud—Law
and legislation—Language.   3. Forensic linguistics.   I. Title.
KF9365.S546 2015
345.73'0263—dc23
2015015279

1 3 5 7 9 8 6 4 2
Printed in the United States of America
on acid-free paper

CONTENTS

1. Linguistics and Fraud   1

2. Government Contract Fraud   26

3. Resource Conservation Fraud   56

4. Corrupt Foreign Business Practices (Fraud)   87

5. Trade Secrets Fraud and Economic Espionage   111

6. Money Laundering (Fraud)   155

7. Securities Fraud   193

8. Art Theft Fraud   221

9. Price-Fixing (Fraud)   251

10. The Effectiveness of Linguistic Analysis
   in Fraud Cases   282

References   295
Index   299

THE LANGUAGE OF FRAUD CASES

[1]

LINGUISTICS AND FRAUD

Virtually everyone has heard of fraud schemes such as the get-rich-quick messages from strangers in far-off places offering to make us rich quickly, emails announcing that we've won a lottery we never entered, bills for medical services we never received, Ponzi scams telling us that our small investment will return fabulous sums of money, or pesky pyramid schemes telling us we can earn a comfortable income if we purchase the product and then recruit our friends and neighbors to do the same.

Even the staid world of academic publishing is susceptible to fraud. Between 2013 and 2014 investigators of a huge, reputable publisher of academic journals discovered fraudulent peer reviews in one of its technical journals. After an extensive investigation, the publisher retracted sixty articles that had been peer reviewed by fake electronic identities, including at least one of which that was created by the journal's own editor. Researchers who fake their own data provide other sad examples of academic fraud.

For most of us, not a day goes by without witnessing some kind of fraudulent behavior. We are bombarded with advertisements offering questionable claims, we blindly sign electronic contracts with tricky wordings that are likely to misrepresent, hide, or pervert the important things we need to know, or we ward off itinerant roof repair scammers who try to cheat us with uncompleted or poor quality work. We have to be vigilant because of the abundance of traps that can make us victims of fraudulent language.

Not all such frauds come to us from outside scammers. Sometimes persons desperate for cash will dream up illegal ways to collect on insurance policies. For example, a woman named Isabel Parker is known as the "queen of the slip-and-fall insurance scam." After her gambling addiction left her penniless, she managed to slip and fall repeatedly in various department stores, supermarkets, and liquor stores. On last count she had flopped 49 times, leading to insurance claims of over half a million dollars. Other individual scammers target public services such as restaurants. Carla Peterson tried to collect on Cracker Barrel Restaurant's insurance by claiming she was served a mouse in her vegetable soup. Other fraudsters have their cars burned up and sometimes even fake their own deaths in order to collect on their insurance policies. These and other claimants are usually caught in their fraudulent schemes because many businesses and insurance companies now employ specialists whose sole job it is to rigorously detect, investigate, and prosecute fraud.

Although many of these events don't lead to a criminal litigation, those that manage to reach that stage often provide analyzable language evidence that gives us clues to the way fraud or alleged fraud works. These examples also demonstrate that accusations of fraud may not always turn out to be completely accurate. This book deals with a range of fraud cases that grew out of complex laws regulating commercial businesses and individuals.

Subsequent investigations often lead to charges of fraud and corruption as the alleged perpetrators carry out government contracts at home and abroad. Others are accused of failing to follow proper federal conservation requirements, buy or sell trade secrets, engage in money laundering, illegally fix the prices of their products, or cheat on their insurance policies. The book includes a chapter illustrating each of these types of alleged fraud and describes how linguistic analysis can be used to help determine whether or not illegal fraudulent language was used and how it was believed to have been used. *Fraud* is a term that embraces a wide variety of deceptive practices, some of which work their way into the legal system as "business fraud," "corporate fraud," and others. By no means do the eight fraud cases presented here cover the entire field of fraud, but they represent at least some of the major types.

Like most of my other books, I wrote this one for two audiences at the same time. One of my goals is for the legal community to learn how linguistic analysis can contribute to their understanding of the language evidence. At the same time it tries to help linguists working on law cases to see how they can negotiate the morass of the legal context and apply their linguistic knowledge and tools to it. There are distinct disadvantages of trying to satisfy two audiences at the same time, but it is my hope that both groups of readers will be patient and even skim through the parts that seem too familiar.

The choice of these cases was prescribed by the ones that I have worked on for the defense. There are many other more prominent fraud cases that didn't call for linguistic help, such as those of Kenneth Lay, chairman of Enron, who cooked the books and cheated his investors during a huge securities fraud that eventually led to the destruction of his huge company. Nor was a linguist used in the fraud case of Bernie Madoff, the titan of Wall Street who is now serving a 150-year sentence for orchestrating the $65 billion Ponzi scheme that he inflicted on more than 1,300 investors.

These and many other fraud cases had plenty of compelling evidence other than undercover tape recordings. It is likely that the prosecutors felt that they didn't need any linguistic assistance to convict these men and the defense attorneys had little or no language evidence that could be analyzed for their defense. In contrast, the cases described in this book contain a great deal of very crucial recorded language evidence, which is likely the reason the defense attorneys thought a linguist might help them discover what could be gleaned from the tapes.

Linguistic analysis can be helpful only when there are reasonable questions about whether the language evidence actually demonstrates fraud. There is little or no reason for attorneys to call on linguists when the evidence is strongly conclusive of either innocence or guilt. The prosecutors in the eight fraud cases described here must have felt that their indictments were overwhelmingly strong, for as far as I know they did not ask for any linguistic assistance. This is not surprising, because in the hundreds of criminal and civil law cases I've worked on over the past four decades, only about 1 percent of them were brought to me by the prosecution and in only one such case was I asked to testify at trial. Four of those prosecutors who retained me explained from the start that they sought linguistic help in order to discover whether their intelligence analysis had missed something important, a perspective that I consider prudent. Since my analysis demonstrated that the language evidence justified their charges, there was no need for them to use me at trial. In contrast, two other prosecutors later admitted to me that they had retained me only to prevent me from working on the defense side of the case.

Although I have testified at trial in many civil and criminal cases, the lawyers in the eight fraud cases described in later chapters did not ask me to testify. Only retaining lawyers make that decision, and there are many reasons for it, some of which are never explained to the experts they retain. My approach is that the best thing I can do for retaining lawyers is to inform them as much as possible about the linguistic issues involved in the language evidence and to help them use it in their preparations for trial. Often it can be useful for their examination of witnesses, in their opening and closing statements, or in their negotiations with prosecutors. Only when the lawyers think they can't communicate the linguistic analysis effectively enough by themselves have they asked me to testify at trial.

I have found the best way to begin an analysis of the language evidence is to first view it in its holistic context, providing snapshot views of the speech events, schemas, agendas, speech acts, and conversational strategies used by the participants, and then assembling these snapshots into a panoramic picture of the entire event. I have found that in most such cases prosecutors focus on small and contextually isolated bits of language that comprise what they believe to be convincing smoking gun evidence. Sometimes these purported smoking guns can wither away when they are contextualized by the analysis of the speech event, schemas, agendas, speech acts, and conversational strategies in which these alleged smoking guns are nested. Since these linguistic procedures will be used throughout the book, it is prudent to begin with some definitions.

The development of linguistics, like the history of many fields, began with the study of smaller units of analysis—the sounds, morphemes, and words of language. Eventually linguists began to study increasingly larger language units, such as phrases, clauses, and sentences. In more recent years linguists have begun to examine the structure of units of language larger than a sentence in what is now called discourse analysis, conversation analysis, and sociolinguistics. They have found that just as there is structure in the sound systems, grammar systems, and semantic systems of language, the systematic structure of the continuous language behavior found in large chunks of language within an identifiable social context also reveals important information.

This study of the predictable structure of larger units of language bears strong influences from other academic fields, including anthropological linguistics, psychology, philosophy, and sociology, but it is by no means a new idea for linguists to think that linguistics is not autonomous. As early as 1867 William Dwight Whitney had pointed out, "The whole development of speech, though initiated by the acts of individuals, is wrought out by the community" (404). By 1924 Ferdinand de Saussure had pointed out that language contains variability growing out the social context in which it is used, and Leonard Bloomfield (1933) in his monumental book, *Language*, devoted an entire chapter to speech communities. These were precursors of the more modern developments of sociolinguistics and discourse analysis, both of which today form an integral part of the discipline of linguistics.

SPEECH EVENTS

In contrast with the tendency of many modern linguists' view that the major role of linguistics is to discover the internalized rules of language (called language competence), Hymes (1972) argued that speakers' language competence is discovered not only by their grammatical competence but also by the way they use language, which he called communicative competence. This type of competence included the degree to which language was socially feasible, appropriate, and actually accomplished.

Included in the many features of communicative competence is the speech event in which that competence is revealed. Gumperz (1982, 9) described speech events as recurring occasions that have "tacitly understood rules of preference, unspoken conventions as to what counts as valid information and what information may or may not be included." Gumperz then identified some recognized speech events such as job interviews, committee negotiations, courtroom interactions, and formal hearings, noting that there were many others as well. Anthropological linguists were quick to analyze the speech events in tribal contexts (e.g., Joel Sherzer's [1974] study of Cuna speech events) and I have more recently described the structure of various speech events in the legal context, including business transaction speech events, courtroom testimony speech events, solicitation to murder speech events, police interview speech events, and others (Shuy 2013, 2014).

As the cases described in this book will demonstrate, it is critically important that the participants first understand what speech event they actually are in. Not doing this can create a "trains passing in the night" type of misunderstanding and confusion.

SCHEMAS

From studies in the psychology of language came the construct that participants in a conversation bring to each new encounter their already existing information, attitudes, ideas, values, and beliefs to help them interpret and organize any newly presented information. Bartlett (1932) called this their schemas. Somewhat similarly, Goffman (1989) used the term "frame analysis" to refer to the study of the way people organize their past experience. Other scholars have developed this construct over the years, but it remains a recognized mental framework that enables conversational participants to confirm their pre-existing beliefs and ideas. Schemas also can be dangerous if and when they lead to misperceptions of the new information.

Not surprisingly, the cases described in this book demonstrate that participants' schemas are heavily influenced by the perceived speech events in which they participate. The obvious predictable schemas of the police and prosecutors are that their targets are guilty. Otherwise they wouldn't be accused. This schema is only natural for jurors as well, since the defendants already have been charged by law enforcement. Even linguistics experts can have the same schema when they begin to analyze the language evidence, and no doubt readers of this book will hold a schema of the subjects' guilt as they begin to read about the cases here. The language used in a criminal law case provides evidence of participants' schemas that helps explain why they said what they said. Yet it is important to note that it is easy for initial schemas to become biases that are difficult to overcome. When our schemas about what is going on are not accurate, misunderstanding and confusion are very likely to follow and this is potentially true for experts as well as for law enforcement officers, lawyers, and jurors.

AGENDAS

People engage in everyday conversations because they have some-thing to contribute either through the conversational topics they themselves introduce or through their responses to the topics introduced by other participants. Conversation is a cooperative endeavor in which its basic principles include saying what is nec-essary, true, relevant, and unambiguous (Grice 1975). There is no way to get into the minds of speakers to know precisely what their intentions may be, but the topics they introduce in a conversation and their responses to the topics of others gives as useful a picture of this as we can get. In this sense, language is indeed a window to the mind, as psychologists have pointed out. Careful description and organization of all the topics in a conversation introduced by the speakers and all the responses to the topics of others can pro-duce a structured linguistics finding that is often a very useful way to assess the possible intentionality and predisposition of partici-pants. When speakers recycle their topics, this can be even clearer (Shuy 2013, 2014).

SPEECH ACTS

After identifying the speech events, schemas, and agendas of participants, the next step is to examine their speech acts. A speech act is an illocutionary act performed by a speaker who uses this linguistic means to communicate a message to a hearer (Searle 1969). A perhaps oversimplified way of saying this is that a speech act is a way of getting things done with language. Each speech act has its own felicity conditions, the criteria that must be satisfied if the speech act is to achieve its purpose. The number of possible speech acts is long, but the ones most relevant to fraud cases include those of promising, admitting, advising, agreeing, denying, offering, and reporting. Speech act analysis has played an important role in many civil cases (Shuy 2008, 2010) and criminal cases (Shuy 1993, 2011, 2012, 2013, 2014).

CONVERSATIONAL STRATEGIES

Speakers use conversational strategies consciously or unconsciously in order to accomplish their purposes. Hansel and Ajirotutu (1982, 87) describe the conscious strategies as "ways of planning and negotiating the discourse structure over long stretches of conversation." Some such strategies are simple positive plans about what to say and when to say it, but others are more negative, such as blocking what the other person is trying to say, using the hit-and-run strategy (introducing a topic and then changing it quickly before the other participant has a chance to respond), camouflaging the meaning or intent of what one is saying, and being ambiguous. These and other conversational strategies used in undercover police operations are described and illustrated in *Creating Language Crimes* (Shuy 2005).

These analytical procedures are carried out in the above noted sequence: first describing the speech event, then observing the attendant schemas that flow out of that speech event, next describing the agendas, then the speech acts, and then the conversational strategies. These snapshot views are then assembled to provide a panoramic picture of the conversations.

Often, however, there is also still more linguistic work to do at the level of the smaller language units of sounds, grammar, and semantics. This is the level of analysis in which the alleged smoking guns tend to appear—the words, phrases, or sentences upon which prosecutors often base their charges and to which defense lawyers often cower in fear. As this book demonstrates, it is most useful to contextualize the alleged smoking gun passages within the larger language units, for what may appear to be a smoking gun may be shown to not be one at all.

This is virtually all that linguistics can do for criminal cases, including fraud. Linguists should never even come close to approaching the questions of the guilt or innocence of the clients because that is the sole province of the triers of the fact. Nor should linguists succumb to the temptation of emotionally joining on one side or the other when they work with attorneys. This can be difficult whether experts are retained by either the prosecution or the defense, for the experience of working side-by-side naturally engenders bias. But the temptation to win the case must fall outside the scope of any expert and the analysis must be as neutral and objective as humanly possible. Unfortunately, not all experts are neutral and unbiased. Even those experts who are not considered mere "hired guns" may unconsciously succumb to the agendas and schemas of the retaining lawyers and their clients, which can color their analyses in spite of even the best of intentions to avoid doing so.

THE MEANING OF FRAUD

In order to discuss fraudulent language, it is first useful to say what is meant by *fraud*. It is defined as a physical action characterized not only by other physical actions, such as "taking unfair advantage," "deceitful practice," and "depriving someone of something of value," but also by language that law characterizes as "intentional deception," "false representation," and "perversion of truth." These characteristics involve complex phenomena that are dealt with in ethical, semantic, pragmatic, psychological, social, political, and cultural terms.

Lying is a communicative act controlled by contexts in which the speaker knows that what is said is not true but uses compliance-gaining strategies to manipulate the hearer about the truth or falsity of the information. Lies are a part of the family of communicative acts that fraudulently violate the conditions of previous knowledge. Linguists and psychologists have written a great deal about the language of lying and deception (including Bolinger 1980; Bok 1989; Ekman 1985; Puzynina 1992; Miller and Stiff 1993; Shuy 1993; and most comprehensively by Galasinski 2000). Their general conclusion is that it is much easier to define lying than to detect lies while they are taking place. Many commercial programs currently are made available to law enforcement agencies that are eager to improve their skills in detecting lies made by their suspects. Despite the claims of these programs, they fall far short in many ways (Shuy 1998). No linguistic analysis is able to detect lying, but it is possible to demonstrate how it can't be done by programs claiming to identify individual liars.

Except for Eggington's (2008) brief chapter on deception and fraud, linguists have said relatively little about fraud in the legal context. There may be good reasons for this, because fraud is perhaps more readily recognized by written records and physical actions that are judged to be illegal, while the spoken language elements that contribute to the act of fraud seldom rise to the level of criminality outside of the contexts of perjury and fraud laws. As the statutes indicate, fraudulent language is that which makes illegal use of lying and deception but the statutes provide no advice about how to detect this.

A Federal Statute on Fraud

First, we consider what the laws of the United States consider fraud. The federal statute deals with it in the context of defrauding by governmental officials:

18 USC § 1001

Fraud

(a) Except as otherwise provided in this section, whoever, in any matter within the jurisdiction of the executive, legislative, or judicial branch of the Government of the United States, knowingly and willfully—

(1) falsifies, conceals, or covers up by any trick, scheme, or device a material fact;

(2) makes any materially false, fictitious, or fraudulent statement or representation; or

(3) makes or uses any false writing or document knowing the same to contain any materially false, fictitious, or fraudulent statement or entry;

Of particular interest in this statute are the adverbs, *knowingly* and *willfully* that preface the verbs *falsify, conceal,* and *cover up,* and the nouns *trick, scheme,* and *device.* We will see these words often throughout this book. The nouns in this statute—*statement, representation, writing,* and *document*—indicate that language is a primary vehicle through which fraud can be conveyed and discovered. And this points to the potential usefulness of analyzing the way these terms are used in the real-life contexts of purported fraudulent actions.

One example is found in laws that relate to various types of fraudulent behavior that include antitrust violations indicating anticompetitive collusion such as intentional price-fixing, bid rigging, restraint of trade, monopolies, and schemes used for market division or allocation. The Sherman Antitrust Act of 1890 was enacted to protect consumers from artificially and fraudulently raising prices and from business arrangements that could lead to unfair competition and obstruct or misuse interstate transportation, such as restraints on the competitive system created by unfairly designed monopolies and agreements that have the characteristics of cartels.

The Clayton Antitrust Act of 1914 focused on intentionally created price discrimination when such action knowingly and willfully creates a coercive monopoly, exclusive dealing agreements, tying arrangements, mergers or acquisitions that substantially reduce market competition, and domination of the market through misconduct. Here the legislation uses the nouns, *schemes, discrimination,* and *misconduct* along with the adverbs *intentionally, knowingly,* and *willfully.*

On the surface, the meaning of *knowingly* and *willfully* may seem fairly obvious, but these words are not easy to define. Decades ago, G. W. Patton, in his *A Textbook of Jurisprudence* (1972, 313n2) suggested that *willful* not be used at all because of its ambiguity. We can assume that Patton was referring to law's inability to define what *willfully* means. Tiersma (1990, 60-61) makes the same point about *knowingly,* the partner of *willfully* in this statute, saying, "the scope of the adverb *knowingly* is virtually always ambiguous . . . and has spawned endless litigation." Words describing mental states such as *intentionally* also are virtually impossible to define without viewing them in much larger contexts (Searle 1983; Shuy 2013). But first we consider existing definitions of fraud itself.

Desk Dictionary Definitions of Fraud

Interested laypersons may try to rely on dictionaries when attempting to pin down the meaning of *fraud*. *Merriam Webster's Collegiate Dictionary* (11th ed.) supports the defining terms and expressions used in the federal statute:

> **Fraud: 1a.** deceit, trickery, intentional perversion of truth in order to induce another to part with something of value or surrender a legal right **b:** An act of deceiving or misrepresenting, trick **2a:** a person who is not what he or she pretends to be: imposter, cheat.

Although this and other common dictionary definitions say nothing about criminal or civil fraud, fraudulent language can be understood to relate to the use of fraud in the everyday activities of life. However distasteful such acts may be, some deceitful perversions of truth are deemed legal and some are not, and this naturally requires a definition that specifies what illegal fraud is. And this is where definitional problems seem to reside.

Dictionaries cannot be expected to outline and describe all the instances and circumstances indicated in their definitions (Landau 1989, 153–216). This is particularly problematic in efforts to describe mental states. Definitions in dictionaries or statutes can only serve as templates or guidelines for understanding specific actions such as *lying* and *deception* that purportedly exemplify their lexicographic entries. Such templates are particularly relevant for terms such as *lying* and *deceit* when used to define *fraud*.

One might expect the statutes to be more comprehensive, clear, and precise than the entries found in common dictionaries. But this task is no easier for writers of statutes than for lexicographers. In his century-old book, *Manual of Equity Pleading and Practice*, Eugene Jones complained, "Courts refrain from defining *fraud* lest they be confronted by their own definition and it be found too broad or too narrow to cover cases that may subsequently arise" (1916, 43–44). His opinion suggests that there may be some apparent value in the vagueness found in some statutes.

Law Dictionary Definitions of Fraud

Have fraud laws managed to become clearer in recent years? One place to seek the answer is in the two most respected dictionaries of law, *Black's Law Dictionary* (2004) and Bryan Garner's *A Dictionary of Modern Legal Usage* (1995). *Black's* says that fraud is usually a tort, but in some cases, especially when the conduct is willful, it may be a crime, also called *intentional fraud*. *Black's* provides the following list of fraud types (key defining terms are emphasized):

> *Bank fraud*, which is the criminal offense of attempting to execute a **scheme** or **artifice** to defraud a financial institution by means of **false** or fraudulent **pretenses, representations, or promises** (18 USCA § 1344).
>
> *Bankruptcy fraud (criminal bankruptcy)*, which is the act performed **knowingly** and fraudulently in a bankruptcy case, such as **concealing** assets or **destroying, withholding**, or **falsifying** documents in the effort to defeat bankruptcy-code provisions (18 USC § 152).

15

Civil fraud, which is distinguished from criminal fraud in that civil fraud is **intentional** while criminal fraud is **willful**. Civil fraud carries only monetary penalties (such as tax evasion).

Criminal fraud, which relates to fraud that is illegal by statutes. It is subject to penalties of fines and imprisonment, such as **willful** evasion of taxes by filing fraudulent tax returns.

Garner defines *fraud* as follows (key terms are emphasized):

Fraud . . . is a chameleon hued word. It may mean: (1) a tort consisting in a knowing **misrepresentation** made with the **intention** that the person receiving that **misrepresentation** should act on it; (2) the **misrepresentation** resulting in that tort; (3) a tort consisting in a representation made recklessly **without any belief in the truth,** but made with the **intention** that the person receiving that **misrepresentation** should act on it; (4) a **misrepresentation** made recklessly **without any belief in its truth**; (5) **unconscionable** dealing short of actionable **deceit** at common law; (6) in the context of conspiracy to defraud, a **surreptitious** taking of property without deception; or (7) in the law of contract, an **unconscientious** use of **power** arising out of the relative positions of the parties and resulting in an unconscionable bargain. Because fraud occupies shifting ground, it is best braced with a modifier.

After Jones's 1916 complaint (mentioned above) that the courts don't define fraud because any definition may come back to haunt them, more recent statutes apparently have tried to delve more deeply into the meaning of *fraud*, and Garner points out that types of fraud now are distinguished in a number of ways (key defining terms emphasized):

Fraud in fact, which is what is known as actual or positive fraud—a **concealment** or **false representation** by means of a statement or conduct that **causes injury** to another. It occurs when a legal instrument as actually executed differs from the one **intended** for execution by the person who executes it, or when the instrument may have had no legal existence because the substance of the document was **misrepresented** to a blind signatory.

Fraud in law (legal fraud), which is fraud that is presumed under the circumstances, as for example when a debtor transfers assets and thereby impairs the efforts of creditors to collect sums due. Legal fraud is potentially ambiguous.

Bank fraud, which is the criminal offense of attempting to execute a **scheme** or **artifice** to defraud a financial institution by means of **false or fraudulent pretenses, representations**, or **promises** (18 USCA § 1344).

Bankruptcy fraud (criminal bankruptcy), which is an act performed **knowingly** and fraudulently in a bankruptcy case, such as **concealing** assets or destroying, withholding, or **falsifying** documents in the effort to defeat bankruptcy-code provisions (18 USC § 152).

Civil fraud, which is distinguished from criminal fraud because civil fraud is **intentional** while criminal fraud is **willful.** Civil fraud (such tax evasion) carries only monetary penalties.

Criminal fraud, which relates to fraud that is illegal by statutes. It is subject to penalties of fines and imprisonment, such as **willful** evasion of taxes by filing fraudulent tax returns.

Note that both Garner's and *Black's* dictionary definitions of fraud rely heavily on the terms, *intentional* and *willful* in their efforts to distinguish criminal fraud from civil fraud as separate behaviors. Of this purported distinction, Garner reports elsewhere in his dictionary that time and again *willful* is used to mean only intentionally or purposely, contrasting with accidentally or negligently, and that *willful* does not necessarily convey impropriety. Garner adds that some argue that *willful* is not appropriate because of its ambiguity. Based on the above definitions, it is not difficult to agree that *willful* is ambiguous, but it also appears that clarity is no better for *intentional* and that the efforts to determine any differences between them appear to be vague and sometimes even circular.

From the statutes and dictionary definitions we learn that fraud consists of (1) the physical acts of tricks, schemes, artifices, abuses; (2) the language of lying, deceiving, misrepresenting, concealing, withholding, cheating, destroying used to accomplish these physical actions; and (3) the mental states of knowingly, intentionally, willfully, unconscionably, unconscientiously, surreptitiously that accompany physical actions and language of fraud.

Some Difficulties with Adverbs Defining Fraud

Because these adverbial modifiers set the stage for identifying fraudulent language, it is first useful to mention briefly the range of their meanings in contexts of law.

Unconscientious [Use of Power]

Competent leaders can use their power conscientiously, as when legislators enact laws to benefit constituents or when employers provide benefits to their employees. Parental power also is often conscientious. A person's lack of a proper moral or ethical conscience can't be determined with certainty by mind reading or guesswork, but it can be more readily divined and evaluated, however, by the language in which it occurs. That is, we are usually better able recognize it when we see language evidence of it rather than from an abstract definition of it.

When asymmetrical power exists, it enables one person to cheat or take advantage of another. Such power comes from knowing something the other person doesn't know, from having a social status advantage over the other person, and from the observable qualities of superior social and language skills. For example, in the courtroom, many witnesses and suspects resort to what O'Barr (1982, 65–71) calls the speech register of "powerless language," which is characterized by hedges, hesitation forms, intensifiers, and other features, all of which tend to cast doubts on the user's convincingness, truthfulness, competence, intelligence, and trustworthiness. Such qualities can be best observed by the language context in which the purported "unconscientious use of power" is said to exist, for a single definition of power can't account for the more complex notion of power.

Intentionally and Willfully [Deceive/Take/Use/Conceal/Misrepresent/Cheat]

Abilities to detect intentional and willful lying, deception, and fraud share similar problems, mostly about what it means to be intentional and willful without enjoying the power and skill to reach inside another person's mind. In the legal context, fraudulent language contains the features of both lying and deception even though people can honestly say things that are untrue without willfully knowing or intending to utter falsehoods. In fact, we judge some intentional deception in life to be socially and morally acceptable, as in dramatic presentations, fictional novels, and even in the ways people select makeup and clothing to try to make their bodies appear more attractive than nature provided. In addition to such socially sanctioned intentional deception, in some circumstances people can deceive without even meaning to do so.

A major problem in identifying fraudulent intentional lying and deception is that no science has the ability to delve into the minds of the people in order to determine their true intentions with accuracy. The best and perhaps only windows that reflect a speaker's mind are the language clues that people use to express what they intend (Shuy 2014). The only other alternative is to infer or guess at their intentions. This is not to say that it's always wrong to infer intentions, for contextual circumstances sometimes provide fairly evident clues of guilt, as when the police catch a man holding a gun as he stands over a recently murdered victim. But even this apparently strong inference can be challenged if later we learn that the victim actually had committed suicide and the accused man had merely picked up the gun afterward. Because it is entirely visually based, this may not be the best example, but evidence in many cases of alleged fraudulent behavior comes from the spoken or written language relevant to an act that has occurred in the past. Language leaves useful trace evidence that is perhaps more helpful and convincing than that of many of the crime reconstructions based on contextual visible circumstances.

At least part of the problem of determining a person's mental state of intentionality arises when we try to isolate alleged intentionally fraudulent statements from the discourse contexts in which they occur (Husserl 1965; Tyler 1978). Levinson (1983, 15–16) observes, "only those inferences that are openly intended to be conveyed can be properly said to have been communicated." That is, the intended meaning must be mutually understood by both the sender and the receiver of that communication. Tiersma

(1987, 305) supports this postulate, pointing out that receivers must understand the illocutionary effect of what the sender is communicating. But even this understanding can introduce a problem. When a bad thing happens, those who are offended by it assume that the offender had bad intentions even though that offender may have had something entirely different in mind—possibly even something benign.

In contrast, there can be little doubt about intentions when the offender uses a performative (Austin 1955, 4–6), such as "I intend/plan/promise to cheat you out of your money." But most people tend to not use such performatives very often. It is clear that people have intentions when they talk or write, because language is a social phenomenon that, as Searle (1983, 79) points out, derives from the intentionality of the mind. If this intentionality is to be understood at all, the best indicator to reveal it can be found in the language in which it is conveyed.

Knowingly [Deceive/Cause/Use/Represent/Withhold/Destroy]

In order to know something, a person must believe it to be true, have good reason to believe it to be true, and have a substantial probability that it is true. Importantly, Garner differentiates *knowledge*, which requires awareness of a fact or condition, from *notice*, which requires merely a reason to know of a fact or condition. This important differentiation came home to me in the mid-1980s, when I was helping the US Social Security Administration (SSA) revise millions of notices that it sent out to recipients. The belief held at SSA was that informing recipients about something would result in their knowledge about it. But even when we improved these notices to make them clearer, many SSA recipients still didn't give evidence of knowing what was in the messages. The old classroom principle was confirmed: telling someone something does not mean that they know it. A good example of this is seen when the police read suspects their Miranda rights. This recitation may be thought to inform these suspects (although even this often can be doubtful), but it says little or nothing about what the suspects then know about their rights.

Surreptitiously [Cause/Conceal/Use/Misrepresent/Withhold/Destroy]
Surreptitious conveys the meaning of unauthorized, clandestine, and stealthy, all of which can occur in non-legal as well as legal contexts. For example, a baseball player can steal a base surreptitiously, even without authorization from his coach to do so. Similarly, in order to surprise our family, we may act secretly and surreptitiously to give them a surprise birthday party. We then wrap up presents in ways that misrepresent and conceal their contents in the hope that the gift will fool them into thinking it was something other than what we actually bought, an act of deliberate deception. And it is common for people to surreptitiously withhold or destroy old love letters from a previous lover in order to protect their current partners from becoming unnecessarily hurt or jealous. These illustrate only a few of the many acts that we do surreptitiously without violating any laws. In the legal context of fraud, surreptitiously doing something sometimes may add little to the definition.

Falsely [Conceal/Cause/Use/Misrepresent/Withhold/Destroy]
Any of the noun phrases modified by the adverb *falsely* can occur in contexts that involve no intention to deceive. A person who conceals something may have benign intentions and a person who misrepresents something may do so out of ignorance. *Withholding information* can be a tactic that has no bad intent, as when we don't inform our terminally ill loved ones that they are actually near death. We accidentally and unintentionally may *destroy* important

things. Similarly, *cause* is a verb we use in hundreds of contexts that are perfectly legal.

Without Belief [in the Truth of What Is Said and Done]
Saying something that you know is not true is the same as intentional deceitfulness. Galasinski (2000, 18) speaks of "information manipulation" of two kinds: omission and commission, both of which are intentional. But some messages that are unintentionally misleading simply can be described as mistakes or gaffs (Buller and Burgoon 1994). One problem with accusing someone of saying something "without belief in the truth of what is said" is, once again, that nobody is able to dig into the minds of speakers or writers to determine with any degree of certainly what their beliefs and intentions really are.

These definitional issues illustrate problems that arise in trying to define fraudulent language in the context of law. We are left with either trying to infer it or carefully examining the spoken or written language for evidences of it. Inferring is not always bad, but when language evidence is available, it's prudent to examine it carefully before leaping to any inferential conclusions. And this is where linguistic analysis can help.

This book describes how linguistic analysis can be used to help determine whether or not illegal fraudulent language was used and how it was believed to have been used. In the following chapters, the analyses of the language evidence in each fraud case uses the same linguistic tools in the same sequence that I've emphasized in my previous books (Shuy 2012, 2013, 2014): speech event → schemas → agendas → speech acts → conversational strategies → smaller language units of sentences, phrases, words, and sounds where the smoking gun evidence usually occurs. Each of these linguistic tools can provide individual snapshots of the language evidence. Then, when these snapshots are assembled, they can produce a panoramic picture of the conversations. That is, the speech events, schemas, agendas, speech acts, and conversational strategies are important parts of the whole that often can help illuminate the alleged smoking gun snapshots, which lawyers usually isolate as discrete and independent units of language divorced from their holistic context.

All of the fraud cases described in this book illustrate how these snapshots can be assembled into a panoramic view of the evidence. The eight cases deal with the ways the prosecution has charged fraud in cases of government contracts, Environmental Protection Agency (EPA) regulations, foreign corrupt business practices, trade secrets, money laundering, securities trading, art theft, and price-fixing. Although fraudulent language and behavior appear to have been significant in the investigation and prosecution of these cases, the word *fraud* is not always included in all of the criminal statutes. Even though *fraud* does not appear in the names of the relevant statutes of money laundering and the Foreign Corrupt Practices Act, I chose to include these cases because their prosecutions relied heavily on allegations of fraudulent language.

This book can provide only the most relevant samples of the language evidence used in fraud cases. The vast amounts of language of the emails, telephone calls, faxes, and face-to-face meetings in these cases make it impossible to provide all of it within the limitations of book form.

As I've said in my previous books on language in legal contexts, there are many cases in which the charges are completely justified and therefore provable. I write here only about those cases that are found on the margins, where there is a reasonable dispute about whether the fraud charges could be justified. Although I was not asked to testify in these cases, I consulted with defense attorneys in all of them and was paid for my services. I provided my analyses to the retaining lawyers, however, and as discussed in the final chapter, some attorneys were able to use it more effectively than others in the defense of their clients. Because more than one defendant is normally involved, conspiracy is virtually always charged in such cases.

[2]

GOVERNMENT CONTRACT FRAUD

One type of government contract that is administered by a government agency is called the US Foreign Military Financing (FMF) Program. It is under the direction of the State Department's Bureau of Political-Military Affairs, a government agency managed by the US Defense Department. The FMF program is a foreign policy tool for promoting US interests around the world by funding arms transfers and providing military training through its Foreign Military Sales (FMS) program to specific friendly, democratically elected governments in foreign countries that are authorized to receive such aid. It provides grants for the acquisition of US defense equipment, services, and training intended to promote US and global security while at the same time furthering the interests of domestic American businesses.

In 1997 the government charged David O. Smith, president of the American Eurocopter Corporation (AEC), a Texas-based manufacturer of military helicopters, with conspiracy using false statements and fraud (18 U.S.C. § 371) while he and two codefendants engaged in illegal wire fraud (18 U.S.C § 1343) and conducted interstate commerce with unlawful monetary transactions (18 USC § 1957). Also indicted were Patrick Rudloff, sales manager of AEC's French parent company, Eurocopter International (EIC), and Ori Edelsburg, an Israeli businessman who, among other things, brokered contracts in connection with sales to the Israeli government.

At that time Israel was one of the largest importers of weaponry and military equipment from the United States under the FMS program. In November 1993, European Helicopter Corporation (EIC) entered into a $63 million contract to produce and sell four Panther maritime helicopters to Israel, contingent on the US government's approval to fund only portions of the cost of the helicopters produced in the United States, as authorized under the FMS program. Approximately $35 million of the contract was to be paid to Smith's company (AEC) with funds provided by the FMS program. The contract also specified that no commissions could be paid to people who solicited, represented, or served as agents for the contract, and Smith's company certified that no such persons would be paid.

The US conspiracy statute obtains when two or more persons can be demonstrated to have formed an agreement to defraud the US government out of money or property, to have interfered or obstructed legitimate government activity, or to have made wrongful use of a governmental instrumentality. The defraud clause requires proof of an overt act following an illegal agreement that has criminal intent. To "defraud" means to have the knowledge and intent to cheat the government out of money and to interfere or obstruct a lawful governmental function by deceit, craft, trickery, misrepresentation, or overreaching the governmental intention. To be considered a conspiracy, there must be an overt act to further the agreement after that agreement was reached.

The government brought the criminal indictment charging Smith, Rudloff, and Edelsburg with overt acts of illegally violating the regulations relating to FMS policies, and while doing this together they violated the federal conspiracy law,

18 U.S.C. § 371. The indictment claimed that the three defendants "did knowingly conspire, combine, confederate, and agree with each other and with other persons known and unknown by impeding, impairing, obstructing and defeating the federal government functions of the Department of Defense FMS program" with "trickery, dishonesty, deceit, and fraud for obtaining something of value and thereby denying DOD the right to control the expenditure of FMS funds" (*U.S. v. David O. Smith, Patrick Rudloff, and Ori Edelsburg*, Virginia Eastern District Court, Case No. 1:97-cr-00022-JCC). David Smith's fraud case provides an example of how linguistic analysis assisted Smith's criminal defense lawyers.

BACKGROUND

Two separate trials were held. The first trial against the parent French company (EIC) and its subsidiary American (AEC) was based on the prosecution's inspection of the two company's files and records. As a result Smith's American company agreed to pay a fine of nearly $11 million for making false statements in its reports concerning its part of a sales scheme for which its parent company, Eurocopter International, was primarily responsible and was assessed a fine of $13 million.

At that trial the government did not attempt to determine which individuals were specifically responsible for the false statements. A month prior to this settlement, however, Smith, Rudloff, and Edelsburg received criminal indictments on one count of conspiracy, three counts of false statements, three counts of fraud by an interstate carrier, and four counts of unlawful monetary transactions. Since the jury found both Smith's company (AEC) and its parent company in France (EIC) guilty of misusing FMS funds, the remaining question for the second trial was whether Smith, Rudloff, and Edelsburg were the persons responsible for conspiring, orchestrating, and contributing to the fraud. By that time Rudloff and Edelsburg already had become fugitives, leaving only Smith to be present at trial.

Complicating the matter in this case was that the French parent company also produced parts of the helicopters in that same contract with the Israeli government. It is common for brokers to act as intermediaries and negotiators between the participants and to receive commissions for their successful efforts, except for restrictions about paying them for the American portion of the contact. Ori Edelsburg was an Israeli businessman who was responsible for brokering this helicopter contract for Smith's parent company in France, where American FMS restrictions against paying brokers does not exist. For the French parent company's part of the contract, Edelsburg was legally entitled to a commission for doing the legwork of seeing to it that the contract was awarded, in contrast with the American company that was forbidden to use FMS funds for this purpose.

The prosecution strongly suspected, however, that part of Edelsburg's commission was paid illegally by Smith's American company. His company's billings to the government were required to reflect only the costs of the portions of the helicopters produced in the United States and no part of that billing should include Edelsburg's commission. The US government investigators believed that Smith's company had falsely documented the amount of FMS money to which his company was entitled by including Edelsburg's unauthorized commission hidden in it, which if true would amount to fraud, deceit, trickery, and false representation. Now the government's task was to try to prove which individuals in both the American and French companies were responsible for this.

THE INVESTIGATION

My past experience in working on investigations of this type is that it is a common strategy for the prosecution to start by trying to turn lower level employees rather than by beginning with the more highly suspected corporate executives. If the lower level employees verify that illegality was going on, the next step is to move up the corporate ladder to identify the sources responsible for it. And this is exactly what the investigators did in this case. First, the FBI agents contacted Ron Tolfa, Smith's employee in charge of AEC's contract with Israel, and they either got him to admit his own guilt in the matter or convinced him that someone else orchestrated it. Perhaps out of fear of being implicated himself, Tolfa agreed to cooperate with the investigation by tape-recording his meetings, phone calls, and discussions with Smith and persons at the French parent company. These tape-recorded conversations formed the major evidence used against Smith when he was charged with conspiracy to fraudulently violate the FMS requirements.

Like all other cooperating witnesses who work as undercover agents, Tolfa's only task was to elicit and capture on tape any evidence of Smith's knowledge and awareness of his company's illegal payments of commissions to Edelsburg, for such evidence would be likely to prove that Smith had conspired to violate FMS requirements and therefore knew or should have known about what his company was doing.

From June 1994 through July 1996 Tolfa provided seventeen tape-recorded conversations to the government, five of which were long meetings and the rest were shorter telephone calls. During these conversations, Smith and others talked with Tolfa about the Israeli contract and its relationship with the French parent company with whom Edelsburg properly could be paid a commission. Tolfa's specific task was to capture on tape any evidence of Smith's knowledge that Edelsburg was improperly paid a commission out of FMS funds.

Complicating matters considerably, at the same time Edelsburg also had other contracts with the parent French company (EIC) that were totally unrelated to American FMS funds, for which he was receiving legitimate broker's commissions. One difficult task in the linguistic analysis of the tape-recorded conversations was to try to keep straight the confusing network of contracts for which Edelsburg was or was not receiving commissions.

Complicating matters even further, Edelsburg also had brokered a separate deal for Israel that did not involve the sale of helicopters co-produced by Smith's company and its French parent company. This was his private deal with the Israeli government for the sale of its old military equipment to Chile, for which his commission from the Israeli government was perfectly legal. Therefore, when the word *commission* was used in the many tape-recorded conversations, listeners had to be clear about which commission was being discussed.

As usual, the linguistic analysis began with a description of the speech events, the schemas of the participants, their agendas as revealed by topics introduced and responses to the topics, the speech acts used by the participants, and the conversational strategies used by Tolfa, the cooperating witness who recorded the conversations. These analyses contextualized what the prosecution represented as the smoking gun evidence that it believed demonstrated that Smith knew and facilitated the fraudulent use of FMS funding to pay Edelsburg a brokering commission.

SPEECH EVENT

As described in my previous books (Shuy 2013, 2014) and in other chapters of this book, speech events are the largest patterned language structure in conversational communication and the ones that are prudent to begin with before analyzing any other patterned structures that are nested within them. As noted in chapter 1, Gumperz (1990, 9) described speech events as recurring occasions that have tacitly understood rules of preference with unspoken conventions concerning what counts as valid and predicts what information and in what sequence that information may or may not be introduced during the conversations. Examples of commonly recurring speech events are interview events, courtroom hearings events, and various types of business transaction events (as seen in the different types of fraud cases described in this book), and many others.

The critical speech events in the undercover recorded conversation were primarily business progress report speech events, where it is common for lower level employees to report progress and problems to their superiors for their knowledge and agreement, disagreement, or suggestions. The specific topics relating to such problems and progress vary, but the speech event framework and sequence follows a rather simple three-stage process of "report/plan/agree."

There is nothing inherently fraudulent about this speech event unless the participants report, negotiate, plan, or agree upon something untrue, if an act of fraud was agreed upon, or unless one or more of the participants was defrauding one of the other participants during this speech event.

However simple and obvious this three-stage process may seem, unless stages 2 and 3 are knowingly accomplished, the

The Business Progress Speech Event

Stage	Employee	Both	Superior
1	Reports past progress		Requests clarification and new information
2		Negotiate/plan next steps	
3		Agree or disagree about how to accomplish next steps	

business progress report speech event normally fails to provide evidence of an inchoate crime. Upon completion of this speech event, the participants typically carry out any actions that were planned, negotiated, and agreed upon, which would constitute the overt act that accompanies whatever was agreed upon. As in all speech events, the participants must reach a mutual understanding concerning what they are reporting, requesting, negotiating, and agreeing or disagreeing about. Without such mutual understanding, the three stages are not felicitously accomplished, and without mutual understanding that any fraud was involved, the target's illegality can be seriously questioned. In cases such as this one, the prosecution's charges of Smith's alleged fraud can be questioned if the employee did not report past progress accurately and if Smith did not agree with any questionable following steps that should be taken.

Resolution of ambiguity by both participants is often a critical part of the speech event. This case centered on whether Ron Tolfa, the employee cooperating with the FBI, reported progress of the contract accurately, whether he made his suggestions clear and unambiguously to Smith, and whether the two participants agreed about taking the following steps they discussed. The primary focus of this linguistic analysis was on the five business progress report meetings tape-recorded by Tolfa, although telephone calls made throughout the investigation also occasionally offered bits of supplementary information.

Since space does not permit reproduction of all of the conversation evidence in this case, only those parts that were considered relevant by the prosecution and defense are represented in the following analysis.

Stage 1: Reporting Progress

The stage 1 reports of progress in this case began on June 14, 1994, when the parent and subsidiary companies were planning the proposal with the Israeli government during their meetings and phone calls with the relevant executives. When Smith participated, his role was to ask questions while Rudloff, from the European parent company, and Tolfa, in charge of the American company's part of the contract, answered them. For example, when Smith asked what parts of the proposal were eligible for FMS funding, Rudloff told him that nothing was eligible, to which Smith responded, "That's right." Rudloff continued to talk about FMS saying, "We have dropped the budget outside of FMS because it's making EIC a lot of problems for the transfer price." After this Rudloff then said, "I think our silent partner is going to be in America next week," apparently referring to Ori Edelsburg. The government inferred that this was smoking gun evidence showing that Smith knew that

Edelsburg would be paid an illegal consulting fee by his American company (this issue will be discussed in the following section on smoking guns). During stage 1, Tolfa and Rudloff reported progress while Smith asked questions. It appeared to be very clear that Smith understood that his American company was not entitled to FMS funding and that the Israel contract for helicopters would not include it.

Similar progress reports were made during the following months until February 1995, when Tolfa telephoned Rudloff complaining that Ori Edelsburg was continuously asking him about whether the Israeli government had made a milestone payment so that he could be paid his commission. Tolfa then taped a call to the French parent company asking about how the commission works and was told, "You don't have to know (laughs)." When Tolfa asked, "Isn't it 10% for Ori?" the French executive answered "yes," but there is no tape-recorded evidence that Tolfa ever reported this to Smith. Nor was it made clear which company was paying that 10 percent.

When Tolfa met with Smith a few days later, he reported that Ori was calling him all the time to ask about his commission. Tolfa did not mention and therefore left ambiguous what Ori's commission was for or who was to pay it. Then Tolfa immediately changed the subject and began reporting on their progress in building the helicopters and some problems with the mechanicals, after which Smith asked, "What's holding things up?" After Tolfa dropped the topic of Ori, they remained in the stage 1 progress report for the rest of the conversation.

Their stage 1 report of progress speech event continued in a meeting between Tolfa and Smith on May 19, 1995, when Tolfa reported to Smith about the FMS guidelines saying: "We can't have direct commercial contracts any more"; but again, he changed the topic immediately to the progress being made in producing the helicopters until later he recycled the previously brief topic of Ori:

> TOLFA: He's beating us over the head about his payment . . . he thinks we're stupid because he's not getting his payment and he's looking for his money. He wants his commission out of this whole thing.
>
> SMITH: So he gets paid when we get paid? Is that how it works?
>
> TOLFA: I guess when European Helicopters gets paid, it triggers Ori's payment. Now we are working out the payment.
>
> SMITH: That's about future contracts? What, is he panicking a little bit?
>
> TOLFA: He's a little bit obsessed. We are talking about the payment. I told him to calm down, he was angry with me. He's probably gonna be in town sometime in the next two weeks or so, he'll probably call you.
>
> SMITH: Okay.
>
> TOLFA: Now we are working out the, the, the payment.
>
> SMITH: I'd like to keep your team going after Mantra [a new contract]. I'd like to grab off another program, maybe on the Australian program. I know that Ori has set the irons in the fire.

Smith treated this meeting partly as a stage 1 report of progress and partly as the stage 2 planning future steps for the company, while Tolfa tried to embellish it with vague hints that Ori would be getting a commission out of FMS funding. Even though once again Tolfa did not clarify who was paying Ori the commission, the prosecution considered this smoking gun evidence that Smith was knowledgeable about Ori getting an improper commission out of American FMS funds.

Curiously, a following telephone conversation between Ori and Tolfa on June 20, 1995, made it clear that Ori did not expect to get commission paid out of American government FMS funds:

TOLFA: Did Patrick [Rudloff] explain to you what your situation as far as commission payment and all that stuff is working?

EDELSBURG: He knows about me.

TOLFA: I don't wanna make a mistake and jump into all that stuff.

EDELSBURG: I don't think you should and it's not your business. I don't know what commissions you're talking about. You don't have to do anything.

This exchange gave the clear impression that Edelsburg didn't even expect to get a commission from the American company.

Stage 2: Negotiating and Planning Next Steps

Now that progress had been made in producing the helicopters, the participants were at stage 2, negotiating and planning the next steps. In their progress report meeting on October 3, 1995, Tolfa explained to Smith that they should make plans for a government auditor who would be coming to visit AEC as part of a survey about what government contractors thought about the existing governmental controls:

TOLFA: They have the right to examine subcontractor's books, documents, papers or other records involving transactions related the subcontract. Uh, EIC [the French parent company] has, you know, Ori's contract. I'm assuming, 'cause I know Ori's, in fact, he's over there today.

SMITH: Um-hmm.

TOLFA: My concern is, do they, can they get access to EIC [French parent company] records? Because if they do, they can get—

SMITH: No, I don't think so. They're investigating AEC [us].

TOLFA: Okay, uhhh, because if this, if they can get their hands on that, then we have a, we have a problem with the, uh, certifications. Because, uh, and, uh, that was another question he asked, you know, who, who signed the certifications. What he, he had concern, is why the CEO didn't sign. I said, "he did."

SMITH: I signed the contract. We didn't want the same signature on the cert as on the main contract. That was a check and balance.

TOLFA: If they can get into EIC's documentation and find out that Ori's getting a commission on it—

SMITH: Well yeah, we have to be careful but we're allowed to have representatives. We're allowed to have outside consultants. But we did not have one on this contract. And so everything you said is correct. EIC can have a consultant there. They will tie Ori to the Chilean transaction, which is totally unrelated to this contract. It's fine.

Tolfa obviously was fishing for Smith to admit that their company was violating FMS requirements, first about signatures on the certification to the government and second about Ori's commission. His fishing effort failed when Smith explained why different signatures were on the contract and certification. As for Ori's commission as consultant, Smith clearly pointed out that their American company "did not have one on this contract." Again Tolfa's fishing effort failed.

The next day Tolfa called Ori Edelsburg and told him about the government's upcoming visit:

TOLFA: If they can get into their books, they will see something about your relationship with EIC and Telephonics.

EDELSBURG: First of all, there's no commission paid to me by
EIC [the parent French company]. Not for this deal anyway,
that's for sure.

TOLFA: Okay, good. I didn't wanna get in the situation where if
they got access to EIC's documents, they would have traced
back to us.

EDELSBURG: No, no, no. I want to be legal and that's the way
I've always been. My contribution to the program has been
in Chile. Nothing to do with you guys and my relationship
with Eurocopter France has been always connected with
the Chilean deal and not with you. And that should be very,
very clear to everybody if it's not by now. I never collected
any commissions on this deal. Plus, you know, the other
thing, your, your program is only partly funded by FMS.

TOLFA: Yeah, that's true.

EDELSBURG: First of all, your program is not funded 100%
by FMS.

TOLFA: No.

EDELSBURG: I have no access to what you've done with other
people, I have no access to what you're doing, but at least my
involvement has been and is only with the Latin American
part that's really not something that you guys are getting
involved in. Everything I've done up-to-date has been legal,
a hundred percent legal. I will not get in trouble for shit. You
need to sit down and tell the truth. And the truth is very simple. I brought the Chilean deal. It was one of the ways for the
government of Israel to finance the deal. But I was acting on
behalf of the government of Israel. I have been paid by the
government of Israel also. Just for you to know and please
don't share this information with everybody, I've been paid
by them and whatever I've done with Eurocopter is in context
with the Chilean deal.

Here Edelsburg again made it very clear that Tolfa's American company had no part in his commission payments. He clarified that whatever confusion exists about who paid his commission, he was paid by the French parent company for his brokering the Chilean deal for Israel in order for Israel to have enough money to purchase the helicopters in this contract. Tolfa's fishing effort failed again.

Stage 3: Agreement about How to Accomplish the Speech Event

It is also clear from all of the language evidence that despite Tolfa's efforts to discover illegality, nothing on tape indicated that either Smith or his American company agreed to use FMS funds to pay Edelsburg's commission. In fact, both Smith and Edelsburg clearly denied this. Therefore, Tolfa's effort to twist the stage 3 agreement to make it look as though the American company was paying Ori a commission was not successful. Smith's take on stage 3 remained the same throughout. He was focused on completing the contract with the Israeli government to produce four helicopters for them.

On July 26, 1996, Tolfa got one last chance to capture illegality on tape. Production had gone well and by now Israel was talking about a new contract for one more helicopter. This face-to-face meeting with Smith gave Tolfa another opportunity to capture him saying on tape that FMS money was being used to pay a commission to the broker.

Smith now explained to Tolfa that representatives of the parent French company, Eurocopter, had told him that Ori was concerned that in this new contract the French parent company might involve their American subsidiary company, AEC:

TOLFA: But how does Ori get involved in this?
SMITH: Well, Ori is gonna have to be paid through ECI, because I'm sure I'll have to sign that there's no agent involved.

Tolfa got nothing from this, but he continued to talk about the new Israeli contract for an additional helicopter. Smith answered that the contract doesn't yet have clearance from the Israeli air force and that Ori was spreading the idea that the contract might again involve his American company as a subcontractor. Smith added that Ori is going to have to be paid by the European parent company, not by the Americans: "I can't sign because I'm sure I'll have to sign that there's no agent involved. It's gonna have to be the Vice President of EIC in Europe." Once again getting nothing inculpatory out of Smith, Tolfa then asked if it is going to be handled the "same way as it was handled through EIC" on their past contract. Smith agreed: "Um-hmm." Smith's agreement might have been considered bad for him if personally he had handled anything illegally in the previous contract, but it had no usefulness to the FBI if he didn't.

It is clear from the recorded evidence represented in these three snapshots of the business progress speech event that Smith did not agree to pay Ori's commission for the American company's part of this potential new contract. Based on the same evidence it remains unclear whether it was the French parent company that disguised Ori's improper commission for the American company's portion as part of the parent company's work on the contract. But this was probably why both the American and French companies were assessed $24 million dollars in fines during the earlier civil case judgment. Whether or not this was true was not the issue in Smith's current criminal fraud case. Instead, the question was whether Smith knew about it and even orchestrated it.

SCHEMAS

Throughout all of the recorded phone calls and meetings, Tolfa's language made clear that his schema was that Smith already knew that the American subsidiary was paying Edelsburg a commission in conflict with the requirements imposed by the US government for FMF contracts. Smith's schema, as revealed by his language evidence, was very different—that his American company was following the rules and not paying a commission to Edelsburg. Tolfa tried many times to taint this continuing business progress speech event by making it appear to be an illegal plan for the American subsidiary to pay Edelsburg illegally, but the language evidence of this snapshot of the consistent schemas did not support Tolfa's efforts.

AGENDAS

Tolfa had two very different agendas, one given him by law enforcement as an undercover agent trying to capture illegality on tape and the other agenda of playing his proper role of informing his superior about the progress of their joint contract with Israel. Smith stayed with his own agenda, trusting Tolfa, his subordinate in charge of the contract, to do the work properly and supervise the production. Edelsburg's agenda, as he said it himself, was to do everything legally, in contrast to the way Tolfa represented it as an effort to find out when Israel made payments to the French parent company so that he could be paid his improper commission for the American portion of the work.

Tolfa's representation of Edelsburg's agenda came into question, however, when Tolfa taped their conversations together. On those occasions the broker denied that he was paid either by the American company (AEC), or by the French parent company (EIC), claiming instead that his commission from the French company related to the Chilean deal that he independently brokered for Israel. It was left unclear whether the French company paid him a commission for anything, but clarification of this didn't matter in terms of the charges against Smith, because FMS funds related only to American companies and the tapes provided no evidence that Smith agreed to use these funds illegally. The agendas of the speakers added another snapshot view of the entire case.

SPEECH ACTS

The speech acts of reporting, asking questions, agreeing, promising, and denying are central to all fraud cases, including this one. Following the proper role of the superior party in this speech event, Smith asked many questions about the progress of the proposal, the contract, and the eventual production of the helicopters. He also agreed and made it clear that his company was not paying a commission to Edelsburg because this was not permitted under FMS regulations. He was never given the opportunity to deny this because nobody, including Tolfa, ever explicitly accused him of it.

Tolfa reported information about the company's progress in writing the proposal, in completing the contract, and in producing the helicopters, hinting vaguely all the while that something may be illegal about how they were doing it. In cases like this I often produce charts displaying the fishing expedition of the undercover agents. I made many such charts in this case, citing the exact words of what was said during Tolfa's fishing efforts noted above and concluding that Tolfa's fishing efforts failed to catch Smith saying anything illegal.

Tolfa seldom tape-recorded Edelsburg and Rudloff, but in the few times they can be heard on tape, they denied the government's accusations that there were any secret payments to Edelsburg made from FMS funds and they also denied that Smith knew about any such transactions. In fact, the two men strongly denied both accusations. These speech acts added another snapshot view of the entire panorama of the investigation.

CONVERSATIONAL STRATEGIES

Tolfa used three conversational strategies in his recorded conversations with Smith: the ambiguity strategy, the hit-and-run strategy, and the strategy of withholding crucial information that Smith needed to know.

The Ambiguity Strategy

Reprising one of the major conversational strategies described in my 2005 book, *Creating Language Crimes*, I pointed out that Tolfa's major conversational strategy was his frequent use of ambiguity. In fact, most of the passages in which he used ambiguity were considered smoking guns by the prosecution. Tolfa's most prominent use of ambiguity occurred when he used the word, "commission." This word has multiple referential meanings, depending on their context, which Tolfa carefully omitted. In this complex case, the prosecution interpreted the word as a reference to a commission that Edelsburg got improperly from FMS funds. "Commission" also could refer to Edelsburg's commission paid by the French parent company, which would not have violated any US regulations unless EIC disguised it in some way. Or the word could refer to Edelsburg's commission growing out the deal he brokered between Israel and Chile, which had no legal significance to this case.

Since ambiguity invites inference, Smith's language indicated that he inferred that Edelsburg's commission referred either to his commission from the French parent company's portion of the contract or to the Israeli government's commission to Edelsburg for the deal he brokered to sell French arms equipment to Chile. Both Tolfa and the prosecutor inferred that whenever "commission" was mentioned, it related to a violation of US regulations preventing commission payments made to brokers.

The Hit and Run Strategy

When Tolfa dropped vague hints about possible illegality to Smith, he frequently changed the subject immediately to his proper role of reporting progress. Assuming that Smith even caught the hint of illegality, the quick topic shift would have discouraged him from responding to Tolfa's hints. The recency principle took over, because listeners tend to respond to the most recent topic presented to them. When spoken language is rendered into a written transcript, such responses can even more strongly encourage and mislead later readers of that transcript to think that the respondent had understood and agreed with the hints, largely because no negative response is present. Unless all the details of the spoken expressions are pointed out, the absence of denial can give the false appearance of an agreement.

The Withholding Crucial Information Strategy

Tolfa was co-opted by law enforcement early in this investigation. During his recorded interactions Tolfa knew or thought he knew that the French parent company was hiding Edelsburg's improper American part of his commission in the costs reported by the French parent company. Although Tolfa's undercover assignment was to capture on tape that Smith knew this, the tapes make it very clear that he never came close to reporting it to Smith.

This snapshot of Tolfa's undercover strategy provided another dimensional snapshot to the overall investigation. I have discovered in many past undercover operations that when the agents discover that chances of capturing illegality are slim, they often to resort to the conversational tricks of ambiguity, hit-and-run, and withholding information that can obscure matters for the target. This in itself is a clue that the target was so unpredisposed to commit the crime that the agent had to resort to trickery. And when even that trickery fails, the agent's case is made even weaker.

SMOKING GUNS

As noted in other chapters of this book and in many government investigations using undercover recordings, the prosecution placed great emphasis on what it considered the smoking gun evidence pointing to Smith's knowing and willful participation. One of the central issues in undercover investigations is that both parties must have mutual agreement about the alleged illegality, including the words and expressions used to describe it. The prosecution could locate surprisingly few smoking guns in this investigation, their most hopeful ones being the way the participants used and understood the expressions, *commission, payment, silent partner, certifications, paid through EIC, handled the same way EIC handled it*, and *you don't have to know*. As the following analysis demonstrates, the meaning of these expressions is conveyed by setting them in the context of the speech event, schemas, agendas, speech acts, and conversational strategies used by the speakers, and also by analysis of the grammar and semantics of the expressions themselves.

Commission

As noted above, the prosecution inferred that when the word *commission* was used, it referred to Edelsburg's commission for being paid improperly with FMS funds for his work as a broker for the American company's portion of the helicopter contract with Israel. Tolfa reported that Ori was asking him about his commission without mentioning where Edelsburg was getting it. When this ambiguous reference is seen in the context of the business progress report speech event in which the word occurred, it becomes clear that Tolfa and Smith were on two very different wavelengths created by two very different schemas about what they were talking about. As noted earlier, the word *commission* can refer to Ori's improper commission paid by the American company on its portions of the contract, to Ori's proper commission paid by the French parent company for its portions of the contract, or to Ori's commission paid by the Israeli government for brokering a deal with Chile. Since Tolfa did not specify which commission he was talking about, there was no reason that Smith's schema would lead him to suspect that Tolfa meant that an improper commission was paid. Lack of specific references can give the appearance of agreement that simply may not be there. At that point the participants' schemas take over, leading them to different understandings of the word's reference. One of the FBI guidelines for undercover operations such as this states specifically that agents must make the illegal nature of the enterprise clear and unambiguous to their targets and that there must be a mutual understanding of the alleged illegality.

Payment

Tolfa had discussions about Ori's commission payment with several representatives of the French parent company, but there was no taped evidence that Smith was involved in any of those conversations. In February 1995 Tolfa reported to Smith that Ori was "beating him over the head about his payment." Here *payment* clearly referred to Ori being paid a commission, although Tolfa omitted references that would clarify who was making the payment and which payment was in question. Tolfa may have realized his lack of clarity when he followed up with, "I guess when European Helicopters gets paid, it triggers Ori's payment. Now *we* are working out the payment."

Here the pronoun *we* is ambiguous in itself, conveying several possible meanings:

- the speaker and the person present;
- the speaker and unspecified persons not present;
- the speaker's organization and the listener's organization;
- the speaker and an unnamed organization; and
- the speaker and other unspecified persons present or not present.

The prosecution failed to recognize this ambiguity and was forced to infer that Ori's *we* referred to the speaker, Tolfa, and Smith, the listener. But Smith's lack of uptake from Tolfa's ambiguous use of *we* is evident by his quick return to his schema of what listeners can expect in stage 3 of a progress report speech event: "I'd like to keep your team going after Mantra. I'd like to grab off another program maybe on the Australian program." Smith's company was the subcontractor with the parent French company, in which context Tolfa's *we* can easily refer to that combined effort, meaning the speaker's organization and the listener's organization rather than the other possible meanings noted above.

Here Tolfa's use of the grammatical ambiguity strategy failed to elicit an inculpatory response from Smith, also illustrating that what is not said can be as important as what is said.

Silent Partner

The prosecution made much of Tolfa telling the representative of the French parent company, Rudloff, that he had asked another representative of his French company how Ori's commission worked and was told, "You don't have to know (laugh)." Smith was not a part of this telephone conversation and there is no taped evidence that Tolfa ever told Smith about it. Nevertheless, the prosecution apparently inferred that *silent partner* was a code word meaning that a secret plot was afoot to pay Edelsburg an improper commission. Ambiguity usually leads to inferences based on the participants' schemas that are colored in turn by the speech event in which the ambiguity took place. Since Smith was not even a participant in this conversation, the prosecution had to infer that at some point Tolfa must have related it to Smith. There is no taped evidence that he did so.

Certifications

I have found that when undercover cooperating witnesses and agents consistently fail to get their targets to admit guilt, they often move to a different topic suggesting possible illegal behavior. In their final recorded meeting, Tolfa tried to elicit Smith's knowledge that the American company should worry about the visiting government auditor because he might discover that their records could reveal that the French parent company disguised Ori's improper brokering commission in such a way that he was improperly paid for brokering the American portion of the work in addition to the proper French portion. After Smith evidenced no anxiety about the government audit, Tolfa became a bit clearer, saying that two different people signed the contract and "we have a problem with the certifications." Smith dismissed this, saying, "I signed the contract. We didn't want the same signature on the cert as the main contract. That was a check and balance." Apparently this was standard contract procedure, since Tolfa didn't pursue that issue further.

Failing at this fishing effort, Tolfa made one last effort to reprise Ori's commission, hinting to Smith that the company's documentation might lead the auditors to discover that Ori was getting an improper commission. This time Smith caught Tolfa's hint and assured him: "AEC did not have one on this contract. They will tie Ori to the Chilean transaction, which is totally unrelated to this contract. It's fine." Tolfa's fishing efforts failed again.

Paid through EIC [the French Parent Company]

Also in this final meeting, Tolfa desperately tried one more Hail Mary pass. When he reported to Smith that Ori had told him that the French parent company might include its American subsidiary in a new contract, he asked Smith how Ori might get involved in this. Smith's simple answer was, "Ori is gonna have to be paid *through* the French parent company," adding "I'm sure I'll have to sign that there's no agent involved." The preposition, *through*, is also ambiguous, with several possible meanings, including:

- direction—in one side and out the other (went through the tunnel);
- location—between or in the midst (walked through the garden);
- process—by way of (climbed through the window);
- cause—by means of (ordered through a catalogue);
- origin—first owner (purchased through a dealer);

- distribution—here and there (a tour through France); and
- inclusivity—up to and including (the movie runs through Friday).

The prosecution inferred that Smith's *through* was associated with the process (by way of) and further inferred that Smith meant that Ori's commission for the American work would be hidden in the process of passing it through the French parent company. To derive this meaning, however, the prosecutors would have to make two analytical leaps of faith. First they would have to ignore all of the many contexts in which Smith, Rudloff, and Edelsburg had denied this very assertion and had clearly stated that there was no commission paid out of the American company's portion of the helicopter contract. Second, they would have to reinterpret Smith's causal "by means of" as a process "by way of." Smith's meaning of *through* here is consistent with every time in the tape-recorded evidence that Smith, Rudloff, and even Edelsburg referred to the origin of broker's commission. It conveys that the French parent company was the causal means by which Edelsburg's got his commission and that the American company was not the causal means by which it was paid.

Handled the Same Way

Building on Tolfa's apparent inference that when Smith said "through ECI" (the French parent company), he meant that Ori's commission for the American company's allegedly hidden portion of the work was caused by Smith's company, Tolfa fished with a bit more clarity by asking if it was going to be handled "the same way as it was handled through ECI on their past contract." To this Smith said "Um-hmm." If the prosecution's schema was that the first *way* it was handled was improper, then the *same way* obviously would be equally improper. When he asked this question, Tolfa apparently was seeking confirmation of this. In contrast, Smith's schema throughout the tapes, made evident by the language he used, was that since the first *way* was proper, *the same way* was equally proper. Rather than confirming impropriety, Smith actually was consistent in his denial that he had done anything improper.

You Don't Have to Know (Laugh)

This was probably the government's weakest smoking gun of all, because it came from a phone call that Tolfa made to a lower level representative of the French parent company. Tolfa told this person that Ori had been pestering him for his payment and so he was wondering how the commission works. The representative replied, "you don't have to know" and laughed. Then Tolfa asked if it was 10 percent and the representative said "yes." The prosecution apparently believed that the representative's laughter implied that something improper was going on. Perhaps it was, but it gave no indication that it involved Smith's knowledge or willingness nor that of his company. There also is no recorded evidence that Tolfa told Smith about what was said in this exchange or even about the telephone call itself. Even if the prosecution was correct about the French parent company's illegal action, this did not implicate Smith, because paying Ori a commission was legitimate for the portion of the work done in France.

CONCLUSION OF THE CASE

I met with the defense attorney and corresponded regularly about my analysis, showing how the progress report speech event set the framework for the language evidence within it. My report demonstrated how Smith was consistent in his assumption that their entire conversations were in that speech event which, like all speech events, had tacitly understood rules of preference and unspoken conventions about what counts as valid and that it predicted the information and sequence that could be introduced. Tolfa followed the conventions of this speech event but at the same time tried to accomplish his own agenda of capturing illegality on tape.

Even when both parties stay within the same speech event, there is an inherent asymmetry in conversations in which one participant is not aware that the other person has a different disguised agenda. Such asymmetry disadvantages targets since their lack of awareness of the other person's different schemas and goals makes them less careful than they would be if the other speakers' roles were open and transparent. When targets are aware of this asymmetry, they can be more vigilant and perceptive about hints and fishing expeditions and under such conditions their denials of illegality can be expected to be stronger. The fact that the person who tape-records another person is the only one who knows that the tape will become a permanent record to be used in an investigation heavily disadvantages the person being covertly taped, who might otherwise strive harder for clarity.

In spite of the facts that Smith was unaware of Tolfa's hidden goal and that he was being tape-recorded, it was difficult for the prosecution to make a case. As shown above, Smith's contributions consistently demonstrated that even if the French parent company was acting improperly, he was unaware of it. His schema, growing out of his perception of the speech event, was that his company wrote a proposal, entered into a contract, and was producing helicopters for the Israeli government. It was his role to check on the progress of these various stages of the work. And that's what his language demonstrates that he did.

Although Tolfa stayed within the predictable stages of the progress report speech event, he tried many times to give it the color of impropriety, fraud, and conspiracy. As noted above, each of his fishing efforts went down in flames as Smith responded only with language conveying that he had no knowledge of impropriety or fraud. In spite of the prosecution's attempt to find smoking gun evidence, Smith revealed his agenda through the questions he asked and the responses he gave to Tolfa, none of which were inculpatory, Smith provided no speech acts of agreement to anything illegal. He, along with Rudloff and Edelsburg, provided many denials that Edelsburg was receiving a commission for the part of the contract and production of helicopters that related to work done by the American company. Even Tolfa's use of the conversational strategies of ambiguity, hit-an-run, and withholding crucial information had no effect on Smith's consistent position of propriety and legality.

Despite all this, Tolfa soldiered on as a cooperating witness for the government in his effort to capture on tape Smith's knowledge of fraud. All that the government had to go on were the seven alleged smoking guns, none of which were convincing at Smith's subsequent trial, where the defense attorney told me that he used my analysis without needing to call me as an expert witness.

Reprising the adverbial modifiers that identify fraudulent language noted in chapter 1, the prosecution was not able to prove that Smith used his power as chief executive unconscientiously, that he intentionally and willfully withheld, concealed, or misrepresented information, that he knowingly deceived, that he acted surreptitiously, that he falsely concealed anything, and that he spoke without belief in what he said. The same could not be said about Tolfa, the cooperating witness.

The jury acquitted Smith on all counts of conspiracy to commit a fraud upon the government.

[3]

RESOURCE
CONSERVATION FRAUD

Until 1976, legislators paid little attention to the effects on human health and environment caused by hazardous wastes, used oil, and underground storage tanks. In that year the 96th US Congress reacted to the growing amounts of industrial waste by passing the Resource Conservation and Recovery Act (RCRA) (42 U.S.C. § 6901) controlled and managed by the Environmental Protection Agency (EPA). The law focuses mostly on the management of hazardous wastes at their point of origination and their transportation, treatment, storage, and disposal in what is sometimes called a "cradle to the grave" system. Subsequent amendments and related legislation dealt with the legal liabilities of four "Superfund" projects concerning abandoned waste sites, clean water, radiation control, hazardous incinerators, and land disposal of certain wastes.

In September 1994 the government indicted Hardcoat Inc., a metal finishing business in St. Louis Park, Minnesota, along with its owner, Kenneth Heroux and his environmental consultant, George Miklasevics, for conspiracy (18 U.S.C. § 371) and making fraudulent statements (18 U.S.C. 1001) in their communication with designated EPA officials (*U.S. v. Hardcoat, Inc., Kenneth Irving Heroux, and George Erik Miklasevics* CR 04-205 DWF/JSM).

BACKGROUND

Hardcoat was a small company in Saint Louis Park, Minnesota, owned by Kenneth Heroux with George Miklasevics as his environmental consultant. The company plated various objects with heavy metals such as chromium by dipping them in a series of open vats containing chemical solutions, some of which were highly acidic or caustic. This process generated industrial waste liquids and sludge. Hardcoat discharged its waste through a sewer pipe that ran under the floor of the shop building and into the city's sanitary sewer, which then carried it to the Metropolitan Council Environmental Services (MCES) treatment plant.

Under the authority of the US Environmental Protection Agency, regular inspections were carried out by the Minnesota Pollution Control Agency (MPCA), which had the power to require a facility to investigate potential contamination from spills or discharge of industrial waste onto the owner's property. In Minnesota, MCPA delegates some of its authority in Hennepin County to the Hennepin County Department of Environmental Services (HCES), which promulgated its own hazardous waste ordinance to industrial facilities in that county.

On May 29, 2003, HCES inspected the Hardcoat property for compliance with its regulations. Eleven days later, HCES sent Hardcoat a letter telling Heroux to hire a sewer inspector who should use a video camera to check for breaks, holes, and other damage in the sewer line. If any breaks were found, Heroux was told to hire a repair company and have it report a summary of its findings and make a videotape showing how the line was repaired.

Three weeks later Heroux hired Alto Sewer Company to inspect his sewer line and document any problems with a video camera. Alto found two breaks in the sewer line through which it was possible for industrial wastes to leak into the environment. After completing the inspection, Alto Sewer Company gave the required videotape to Hardcoat's secretary/receptionist who signed a receipt for it and passed it along to Heroux, who then contacted the owner of Alto, asking him to recommend a company to repair his sewer line. On Alto's advice Heroux then contacted Atco Utilities to do the repair work.

Until the repairs could be made, Hardcoat continued to use the sewer line. Atco Utilities promptly got the required city permits to repair the line and began excavation on July 23, 2003, discovering that a section of the bottom of the sewer pipe had been eaten away, possibly allowing waste to be released into the environment. Heroux told Atco Utilities to replace the sections of the pipe that needed to be replaced and as it did so, Atco's workers discovered two more breaks that the previous video made by Alto Sewer Service had not revealed. Atco Utilities then told Heroux that most of the pipe needed to be replaced. Heroux subsequently authorized Atco Utilities to replace what was needed. Upon completion of the repairs, Atco then videotaped the sewer line again, showing that it was now fully intact.

After this work was done, Miklasevics (Hardcoat's environmental consultant) sent a letter to MCPA enclosing the inspection report done by Alto Sewer Service and the second videotape made by Atco Utilities of the repaired sewer line, but he did not enclose the video of Alto Sewer's initial inspection. Two weeks later an HCES investigator called Alto Sewer and learned of the existence of the two videotapes—the first one made by Alto Sewer Services before the repairs began and the second one made by Atco Utilities after the repairs had been completed.

When the HCES investigator called Miklasevics to ask about the videotape, he sent them, Miklasevics explained to her that he was told that there was some sort of blockage in the sewer pipe but now it had been fixed. The investigator then called Heroux about the results of the inspection and Heroux told her that all was good now. The subsequent indictment reports that the HCES investigator asked Heroux two times whether there were any problems encountered during the inspection and Heroux said, "No, all went well, everything is fine."

Based on the above, the indictment charged that Heroux and Miklasevics "conspired and agreed together and with each other to knowingly and willfully falsify, conceal, and cover up by trick, scheme or device a material fact and make materially false, fictitious, and fraudulent statement or representation, in violation of Title 18, U.S.C. 371 and 1001."

THE GOVERNMENT'S EVIDENCE

The indictment relied on the written documents, the HCES investigator's tape-recorded telephone conversations and interviews with various participants, as well as the notes and reports made by the investigator that purportedly summarized various conversations.

Document Evidence

- A letter sent by HCES to Hardcoat on June 9, 2002
- A Work Order by Atco Utilities to repair the sewer pipe on July 10, 2003
- The permit application filed by Atco Utilities on July 23, 2003
- George Miklasevics's written report to HCES on August 12, 2003

Tape-Recorded Spoken Evidence

- George Miklasevics's telephone call with HCES on September 4, 2003
- Kenneth Heroux's telephone call with HCES on September 9, 2003
- HCES investigator's tape-recorded interviews with Heroux on September 9 and September 17, 2003
- HCES investigator's two-minute tape-recorded telephone conversation with Miklasevics on September 24, 2003
- Heroux's meeting with HCES and an agent from the EPA Criminal Investigation Division on September 26, 2003

Investigator's Written Report Evidence

Activity Reports in the form of notes taken during interviews with Miklasevics (September 15, 2003), Heroux (September 17, 2003), Mrs. Susan Heroux (November 3, 2003), Hardcoat's secretary/receptionist (December 3, 2003), Bruce Bethiaume, supervisor for the city utilities division (October 1, 2003, and January 16, 2004), Brad Dvorak, city sewer inspector (October 1, 2003, and January 24, 2004), Timothy Carver, owner of Alto Sewer Service (September 11, 2003, September 15, 2003, and September 23, 2003), and Andy Carver of Atco Utilities (September 26, 2003, and November 21, 2003).

SPEECH EVENT

The first step in analyzing the evidence is to identify the type of speech event (or events), because speech events determine the "tacitly understood rules of preference, unspoken conventions as to what counts as valid and what information may or may not be understood to prevail" (Gumperz 1982, 9). Analysis of a speech event also provides a useful snapshot of the evidence it produces. Although a speech event often consists of a single discrete occasion such as an interview or conversation, in this case the single speech event continued over some fifteen months and embraced various forms of written and spoken evidence with many participants. Throughout, it followed the following five-stage structure of a business evaluation speech event, in this case one that continued over a period of seven months.

In this case, Hardcoat representatives tacitly agreed that a problem might exist (stage 1), although they claimed to have

Business Evaluation Speech Event

Evaluator	Company
1. Reports a possible problem	Agrees (or disagrees) that problem exits. If agrees, go to stage 2
2. Sets requirement for solving the problem	Agrees (or not) to follow evaluator's requirements. If it agrees, go to stage 3
3. Checks on progress of company's response	Provides evidence of required progress (or fails to do so). If evidence is provided, go to stage 4
4. Checks on final result	Provides (or not) evidence of successful result
5. Approves (or not) evidence provided by the company	

been unaware of it. In stage 2, Hardcoat agreed to the evaluator's (the government investigator's) requirements and had the sewer line inspected for possible damage. Hardcoat also provided the requested evidence that the problem had been fixed (stage 3), by first hiring a sewer line inspection and then hiring a recommended contractor to fix the sewer problem that had been discovered by the company that performed the initial inspection. Although the HCES investigator checked on the final result (stage 4) and agreed that the problem had been fixed (stage 5), a legal issue emerged after the speech event was over when the investigator came to believe that its two representatives, Heroux and Miklasevics, had made fraudulent statements to the investigator when they reported the progress and completion of the repairs in stages 3 and 4.

In criminal investigations, it sometimes happens that aberrations of the structure of the speech event can enlighten the meaning of the evidence (Shuy 2013, 2014). Even though there were no aberrations in the structure and sequence of this speech event, the prosecution placed its focus on the alleged fraudulent manner by which the required steps in this speech event were accomplished. It claimed that when Hardcoat's representatives presented evidence of successfully repairing the sewer in stage 4, the company fraudulently disguised the problems discovered in stage 3. She believed that Heroux and Miklasevics knew that their sewer line was broken and that it had been transmitting dangerous chemical waste into the environment.

SCHEMAS

As in most law cases, the schemas of the participants grew out of the nature of speech event. Hardcoat and its representatives were told by the government office that their shop building was suspected of having a leak in its waste sewer. As evidenced by Hardcoat's representatives' language, their schema consistently was to comply with the government's request that they determine whether HCES's suspicions were true and to fix the problem if any problems were found. Following these requirements, Hardcoat hired a company to perform the inspection. When the inspectors found leaks in the drains, Hardcoat complied again by having its sewer line repaired. It was the way they reported their compliance that purportedly created the HCES investigator's schema that Hardcoat knew from the beginning that their sewer line had been leaking toxic waste into the environment and had done nothing about it.

In addition, the investigator's schema, as evidenced by her own spoken and written language, as well as by the language of the subsequent indictment, was that although Hardcoat through Heroux and Miklasevics had complied with the investigator's demands, they violated the Resource Conservation and Recovery Act by conspiring to provide false statements about the extent of the original damage. This snapshot view of the participants' schemas provided a direction to understand the conversations that took place.

AGENDAS

In most investigations, whether by law enforcement or by monitoring agencies such as HCES, investigators introduce a vast majority of the topics during their interviews with company representatives, while the dominant normal speech role of those investigated is to answer the investigator's questions. In this investigation the only exception to this was a letter written by Miklasevics to HCES after the repairs to Hardcoat's sewer line were completed, in which he introduced all of the topics that explained what Hardcoat had done to comply with HCES demands.

It was clear that the investigator's agenda was to uncover misdoings by Hardcoat, while the agenda of Hardcoat's representatives was to explain what they had done, whether or not they actually perceived that the investigator was fishing for evidence of misdeeds. This produced an asymmetry of power in their exchanges, in some ways similar to that of a police interrogation in which the interviewees can be very aware that they are suspected of a crime but different from it because in this situation the interviewees were unaware that they were under suspicion and reported only what they had done in response to the requirements that the HCES investigation had placed upon them. Persons who are unaware that they are under suspicion are less conscious of their need to avoid the appearance of dissembling and they usually don't expect to be asked ambiguous or tricky questions.

This snapshot of the agendas of the participants provided a context that helped understand the issues in conflict.

SPEECH ACTS

As noted above, Hardcoat's representatives used the speech acts of agreeing to the HCES request by complying with its demands. Both Heroux and Miklasevics reported facts about the past and current condition of Hardcoat's sewer line and denied knowledge of any breaks in it before the inspections were made, adding that if there had been any visible leakages, they would have noticed them. The investigator's speech acts were to complain about Hardcoat's purported sewer leaks, to request information, to request clarification, to request confirmation, and subsequently to complain that Hardcoat through Heroux and Miklasevics had fraudulently conspired to violate the requirements of the Resource Conservation and Recovery Act. Interestingly, the investigator never used the speech act of accusing to Heroux or Miklasevics, leaving this for them to try to infer.

This snapshot of the speech acts used provided another view to understand the conversations.

CONVERSATIONAL STRATEGIES

Rather than accusing Hardcoat of violating EPA regulations, the investigator chose instead to use expressions that had two or more possible meanings, leaving it to Heroux and Miklasevics to figure out what she meant. HCES originally notified Hardcoat about the need to have its sewer line inspected, but that notification said nothing about any potential environment damage. The agency may have suspected such damage but it obviously couldn't accuse without evidence. Nor did the subsequent inspection by Alto Sewer and the repair work done by Atco Utilities describe any environmental damage, for it was neither their expertise nor responsibility to do so. Therefore, after the repairs were completed, HCES investigator Tanya Maurice used the conversational strategies of indirectness and ambiguity as she tried to discover evidence that Heroux and Miklasevics knew that leaks had existed that had been causing environmental contamination.

In cases where undercover agents try to elicit a target's illegality or knowledge of illegality, they have been known to use various conversational strategies to elicit it (Shuy 2005). In her conversations with Heroux and Miklasevics, inspector Maurice used some of these strategies in her effort to elicit the targets' knowledge of environmental damage stemming from Hardcoat's leaking sewer pipes. If she could establish that the two men knew that the company was violating environmental laws, she could provide evidence to the prosecutor of a conspiracy to commit fraud.

Maurice's interview methods were similar to the fishing for guilt techniques used by undercover agents in criminal investigations such as bribery or murder. Her fishing approach began by offering vague opportunities for the targets to inculpate themselves. She carefully avoided making explicit and direct accusations, however, instead using ambiguously worded questions. Four of her ambiguous words were *results, problem, fixed/took care of,* and *you.* These are very commonly used words in most conversations and do not stand out as potential smoking gun expressions. But when the apparent intended meanings of these words differs from the targets' apparent understanding of their meanings, the words can convey the appearance of illegality to later listeners such as prosecutors, judges, and juries.

Results

Maurice first used the ambiguous term, *results,* probably hoping that Miklasevics would say something about the repairs stopping some existing environmental problems:

> MAURICE: I just thought I'd call and ask you what the results of the inspection were.
>
> MIKLASEVICS: Well, they had a broken tile so they replaced that. Evidently there was a blockage, they couldn't get through so they fixed the problem.

For Maurice to have been explicit in her question, she might have said something like "What environmental damage resulted from the break in your sewer line?" But Miklasevics's answer indicated that he understood *results* to mean what everyday dictionaries say it means: outcome, desirable consequences, or effect. To Miklasevics, the *results* of the repairs were the outcome, desirable consequence, and effect of the work just completed on the repaired sewer line. Maurice's fishing apparently tried to go beyond the immediate context of repair work to something far more dangerous—environmental contamination and damage. But that's not what her question asked and Miklasevics's response showed that her fishing effort failed.

The investigator was no clearer in her same ambiguous question to Heroux:

MAURICE: I was just hoping you could tell me what the story is, what were the *results*.
HEROUX: All good. All went fine and everything's fine.

Like Miklasevics, Heroux apparently assumed that the investigator was asking about the results of the repairs while she apparently was fishing for his awareness of previous environmental damage to the environment. It would have been easy for her to have asked what she really wanted, but again she didn't.

Problems

When asking questions, it behooves the skilled interviewer to clearly identify the topic of the question. When talking about a "problem," the reference to the specific identity of that problem has to be clear to both parties if any meaningful conclusion can be drawn from the response. The following exchanges illustrate how Maurice was not clear:
To Miklasevics:

MIKLASEVICS: Well, they had a broken tile so they replaced that.
MAURICE: What do you mean, broken tile?

MIKLASEVICS: Well, uh, evidently there was a blockage.

MAURICE: What kind of a blockage was in the pipe?

MIKLASEVICS: I really don't know.

MAURICE: So it was a block and not a breach? Was there any holes or fissures in the piping?

MIKLASEVICS: That I don't know. I think the sewer company took care of the whole problem, whatever it was.

MAURICE: They ran another camera through a second time?

MIKLASEVICS: Well, after they took care of the problem.

To Heroux:

MAURICE: Okay, so you didn't have any problems?

HEROUX: No. All went well, everything's fine.

MAURICE: No problems at all?

HEROUX: Nope.

MAURICE: Some metal finishers have had problems.

HEROUX: Oh, I know. There's a guy in St. Paul, I know. I hear you.

MAURICE: I'm glad you didn't have any problems at all.

To Miklasevics and Heroux, the investigator's use of *problems*, similar to her use of *results*, referred to what was needed to get the sewer line fixed. Maurice was not specific about what her word, *problems*, grammatically referenced, leaving this for Miklasevics and Heroux to infer. The immediate grammatical context was the repair work, so if Maurice wanted them to tell her whether they found any environmental damage, she could easily have asked that question clearly and explicitly. Instead, she chose to fish for the targets to bring it up themselves and her fishing efforts failed.

Fixed/Took Care Of

Investigator Maurice was even more inefficient at eliciting any environmental problems from Miklasevics:

> MIKLASEVICS: So they fixed the problem.
> MAURICE: A blockage in the pipe?
> MIKLASEVICS: Yeah.

This too would have been an opportunity for the investigator to address the topic of Miklasevics's knowledge of environmental damage, for after all, he was Hardcoat's environmental consultant. Again she didn't do this, but she kept on fishing:

> MAURICE: You seem to think that the sewer company just pretty much went ahead and fixed everything?
> MIKLASEVICS: Yeah.
> MAURICE: They ran another camera through a second time?
> MIKLASEVICS: Well, after they took care of the problem.
> MAURICE: All right.

Again despite her fishing effort the investigator didn't manage to elicit either man's knowledge of any environmental damage.

You

It is well known that the second person pronoun *you* is innately ambiguous because it can refer, among other things, to the person being addressed, to the group that the person being addressed represents, or to plural parties present or not present. Here Maurice was interested in discovering how Hardcoat handled Atco Utilities' summary report about the repairs that it performed. Atco had reported that their repair people left this report with Hardcoat's receptionist/secretary. She reported that she passed it on to Heroux, which he verified. Now Maurice tried to learn whether Hardcoat's environmental consultant, Miklasevics, also was knowledgeable about the report, inferring that if anyone at Hardcoat knew about environmental damage, it would be their environmental consultant Miklasevics. If he knew about it, he could also be accused of knowing that there was potential environmental impact of the sewer line problems.

Again without specifically mentioning her goal, the investigator asked Miklasevics the following about Alto Sewer's initial inspection videotape:

MAURICE: Okay, all right, they didn't give you a copy of that?
MIKLASEVICS: No.

Since in context Maurice's line of questioning had focused on Miklasevics's personal involvement in the matter, he could understand her *you* to refer to him personally rather than to Hardcoat in general. Instead, it appeared to inspector Maurice that Miklasevics was telling her that nobody at Hardcoat ever got a copy of that tape, an answer that could be taken as evidence of fraud, because it was clear that the receptionist and then Heroux had received that tape from Alto Sewer. However, there was no recorded evidence that Miklasevics ever got it or even saw it. It is possible that investigator Maurice was merely an inept interviewer, but otherwise her continuous use of ambiguity appeared to be part of her conversational strategy of using this strategy to fish for guilt.

Further evidence of the government's use ambiguity can be seen in the letter sent to Hardcoat by HCES on June 9, 2003, concerning the findings made by Alto Sewer after initially inspecting the sewer. This letter said, "have them provide you with a videotape and a brief written summary of their findings." This letter did not say that Hardcoat should also send HCES a copy of the videotape that Alto Sewer made. The HCES investigator seemed to think that Hardcoat was hiding something by not including Alto Sewer's first video when Hardcoat reported the results of Atco Utilities' repairs, even though the HCES request did not specify that they should include Alto's initial video. As will be seen throughout this book, what is not said can be as important as what is said in investigations such as this.

This snapshot of the speaker's agendas reveals the influence of their understandings of the speech event and shows how their schemas were carried out. Agendas are the best reflections of what the participants are thinking about.

SMOKING GUNS

Armed with the panoramic view provided by the snapshots of the participants' expectations derived from the structure of the speech event, the language evidence of their schemas, their agendas as revealed by the topics they introduced and their responses to the topics of the other speakers, their speech acts, and the conversational strategies employed by the investigator, we are now prepared to address what the prosecution considered to be the smoking guns. Since the indictment specifically laid out the prosecution's case against Hardcoat, Heroux, and Miklasevics, the prosecutor's alleged six major smoking guns are addressed here. Some of them already have been mentioned as part of the other snapshot views above.

Fraudulently Withholding Information

The indictment charged:

> Miklasevics committed fraud by not mentioning to HCES that there were two inspections and that the first inspection indicated that Hardcoat's sewer lines needed repair.

For comparison, the following is the relevant portion of the investigator's initial report to Hardcoat:

> Hire a sewer inspection company to put a camera up your sewer line, from the pretreatment unit's drain to the city sewer to check for breaks, holes, root infiltration or other damage. Tell me who you will hire and when it will be done. Have them provide you with a videotape and brief written summary of their findings. Tell me the frequency you will have the sewer line inspected in the future and include a copy of the amended inspection schedule showing the inspection frequency.

Simple grammatical analysis made the report's accusation of knowing and willful actions a relatively easy smoking gun to refute. The letter required Hardcoat to: (1) report its frequency of future inspections and (2) send them a copy of the amended inspection schedule. However unclear the meaning of (2) might be, Hardcoat apparently assumed this to mean a copy of Alto Sewer's report on their initial inspection. The letter did *not* request a copy of Alto Sewer's videotape of the sewer line. Instead, it said Hardcoat should have the sewer inspector "provide **you** with a video tape and brief written summary of their findings." Since it did not ask or require Hardcoat to send that videotape to HCES, Hardcoat didn't send it.

Still, the investigator made a big deal of Hardcoat knowingly and willfully not doing so and the indictment treated this as smoking gun evidence.

One of the tasks of linguistic analysis of large amounts of discourse, both spoken and written, is to keep track of who said what to whom. As simple as this may sound, doing so requires considerable care, for it's easy for prosecution's schema of guilt to lead them to overlook or misinterpret their own evidence. And that is what happened here. The Hardcoat executives did not fraudulently withhold information; they simply followed what they could easily understand to be the written instructions given them by HCES.

Fraudulently Misstating the Extent of the Problem

The indictment charged:

> Miklasevics lied when he told HCES that the problem was a blockage, not a break in the lines.

This also was refuted by comparing this charge with the evidence from the investigator's own notes that she preserved in her EPA Activity Reports about meetings that she chose not to preserve on tape and therefore could not be verified. We cannot know exactly what happened in those meetings, but when the investigator's own notes are made available, they became the only useful information about what that investigator apparently believed to have taken place.

Miklasevics's alleged "fraudulent lie" was that he reported to investigator Maurice on September 4, 2003, that Alto Sewer told him that there was a "blockage" in the sewer line, whereas the report of Alto Sewer indicated that there were at least two "breaks" in it. A prosecution for willfully and knowingly making false statements might have been justified here except for the verifiable tape recordings of others showing that Miklasevics was never shown this report and therefore couldn't have seen or heard the exact terms used in Alto's initial inspection of the line. City inspector Brad Dvorak specifically stated that when Alto submitted its application to the city for a permit to inspect the site, it provided this information *only* to the contractor that was hired to make the repairs, Atco Utilities.

Further contradiction to the indictment can be found in investigator Tanya Maurice's tape-recorded interview with Atco Utilities' contractor Timothy Carver. He told her that when he arranged the inspection date with Hardcoat, Heroux informed him that he thought the sewer pipe was "blocked," but he didn't say that it was "broken." Alto's site contractor Andy Carver also told the investigator that when he ran the snake up the line and was not able to push past a certain point, the sewer pipe was "likely to have been broken," not simply "blocked," but he added that he "didn't know this for sure" and more significantly, he didn't communicate this to anyone at Hardcoat. Therefore, since neither Miklasevics nor Heroux were ever told that there was a "break" in the line, they couldn't be expected to know this and therefore would not have been able to tell the HCES investigator that it was "broken."

One major task of linguistic analysis is to match and compare the sequences of language used in a given case. Here the analysis was able to discover a serious flaw in the indictment about Miklasevics's alleged knowingly and willfully fraudulent representation. He couldn't fraudulently lie about the extent of the problem if he wasn't told that there actually was a break in the line.

Fraudulently Failing to Disclose the First Videotape That Showed the Damage to the Sewer Line

The indictment charged:

> Miklasevics sent HCES the second videotape made by Atco Utilities showing the newly replaced sewer line but fraudulently did not disclose the first videotape showing damage.

This charge most likely was based on investigator Maurice's interview with Miklasevics on September 4, 2003:

> MIKLASEVICS: They ran a camera through there and evidently it worked.
>
> INVESTIGATOR MAURICE: They ran another camera through a second time?
>
> MIKLASEVICS: Well, after they took care of the problem. They couldn't quite get through.
>
> INVESTIGATOR MAURICE: They didn't give you a copy of that [first video]?
>
> MIKLASEVICS: No.
>
> INVESTIGATOR MAURICE: So if I wanted to see that copy I'd have to talk with them [the Alto sewer inspection company]?

If Miklasevics was willfully, knowingly, and fraudulently trying to hide the fact that a first videotape existed, it would be counterproductive and illogical for him to have brought up that very subject by saying "they ran *another* camera through there" followed by "they couldn't quite get through," both of which were obvious references to that first videotape made by Alto Sewer Service. This was actually his open admission that there was a first videotape. As noted above, HCES's initial letter requesting Hardcoat to hire a sewer inspection didn't ask them to send a videotape after the initial inspection was done. When Miklasevics voluntarily sent HCES the second videotape made by repair company Atco Utilities that wasn't even requested, he was apparently trying to answer the question about what the "results" were and to inform HCES that the lines were now functioning properly and safely. In short, he did not send the first videotape made by Alto Sewer showing damage because HCES did not request or require it.

Again, careful comparison of statements made over time showed that this charge was based on the prosecution's schema of guilt rather than on the strong contextual clues provided by its own evidence. Miklasevics was not fraudulently failing to disclose the sewer line damage shown on the first videotape.

Fraudulently Reporting the Condition of the Sewer Lines

The indictment charged:

Heroux fraudulently told HCES, "no problems" had been discovered in the lines.

This alleged smoking gun is another classic example of how prosecutors' schemas of guilt can mislead them to decontextualize their accusations from the discourse context in which the alleged fraudulent statements occurred. The actual relevant content of this short telephone conversation between investigator Maurice and Heroux on September 9, 2003, is as follows:

> INVESTIGATOR: I just wanted to contact you because, uh, George sent me that tape of the sewer line inspection.
> HEROUX: Yeah.

INVESTIGATOR: But I haven't had a chance to look at it. I was just hoping you could tell me what the story is, what were the results?

HEROUX: All good.

INVESTIGATOR: All good?

HEROUX: All good, yeah.

INVESTIGATOR: Really?

HEROUX: Yeah.

INVESTIGATOR: No problems at all?

HEROUX: Nope.

INVESTIGATOR: Okay, so you didn't have any problems?

HEROUX: No.

INVESTIGATOR: Okay.

HEROUX: All went well.

This is one of those trains passing in the night conversations in which the participants were talking about two very different topics. As noted above, the investigator asked about the "results" of the inspection done by Atco Utilities after it completed the repairs, probably fishing for Heroux to tell her that Hardcoat learned about breaks in the sewer line that produced contamination of the environment. But she didn't ask that question. Instead, she asked for Heroux's "story" about the inspection. Heroux answered her question by referring to her grammatical sentence subject (the inspection) and replying that it (the inspection) "went well."

How can we know that Heroux was referring to the inspection that took place *after* the repairs were completed rather than the first inspection? Because the investigator introduced the topic by saying that George had sent her the videotape and the only videotape he had sent her was the one done by Atco Utilities after it made the repairs. Heroux was talking about Atco's work, which "went well" and was satisfactory in that he had no "problems" with the repair work because the sewer line had been made whole. He did not say, as the indictment accused him, that no problems had been discovered in either the first inspection by Alto Sewer or the second and final inspection by the repair company, Atco Utilities. It would be equally illogical to believe that Heroux had spent close to $4,000 to replace sewer lines that originally had no problems. It would be even more illogical for him to admit to HCES that he had wasted that amount of money for nothing.

As noted in the above discussion of the ambiguous word *result,* Heroux used the common dictionary definition of "outcome" when talking about the results with investigator Maurice. These results were clearly indicated in the final videotape that Miklasevics had voluntarily sent to the investigator. Heroux apparently had no problems with the repair work and he stayed on that topic during the above exchange with investigator Maurice.

Wrenching words from context can be very dangerous, especially for the government as it looks for smoking gun evidence that it could not find here. The language evidence makes it clear that Heroux did not fraudulently report the condition of the sewer lines.

Fraudulently Reporting That There Was a Blockage Rather Than a Break in the Sewer Lines

The indictment charged:

> Heroux fraudulently told HCES that there was a blockage, not a break in their lines.

As mentioned above, a search through all of the spoken and written evidence yielded nothing that would even suggest, much less affirm, that Heroux was ever told that there was a "break" in the sewer lines. The investigator's notes about her interview with Miklasevics on September 15, 2003, said:

> Miklasevics stated that Heroux told him that Alto Sewer could not get the camera past a certain point in the sewer line during the inspection, and that Hardcoat needed to get the sewer pipe repaired.

Nothing was said about a break in the lines here. Even the investigator's own notes of her interview with Heroux on September 17, 2003, supported Miklasevics's statement:

> Heroux also indicated that he was not aware that the sewer pipe was broken at the time it was replaced. Heroux stated that Alto Sewer conducted the sewer line inspection and discovered a "blockage" in the sewer line. Heroux stated that the Alto representative did not tell Heroux what that cause of the blockage was, and that the "snake" did not work to clear the blockage. Agent showed Heroux a copy of the permit application from the city reflecting that there was a break in the line and not a blockage. Heroux stated that the contractor applied for the permit and that he did not know the sewer pipe was broken. He denied seeing the permit application.

Investigator Maurice appeared to be determined to find evidence supporting her schema that Miklasevics and Heroux willfully had lied about knowing that the sewer line was broken and not merely blocked. To do this she first interviewed Timothy Carver who snaked the line for Alto Sewer the first time on September 11, 2003. Her notes of that un-taped meeting report that when Carver snaked the line, he couldn't get the camera beyond the first 106 feet of the sewer. This supported Heroux's report that the line was blocked, not broken. Maurice, apparently not satisfied, re-interviewed Carver again four days later and her notes of this un-taped meeting show that Carver told her that he "may have told Heroux that the sewer was backing up," but he "could not remember" the specific nature of the problem.

Apparently still not satisfied, investigator Maurice interviewed Carver a third time on September 23, 2003. Apparently his memory purportedly had improved and he now reported that he told Heroux about the break in the line, but that when Heroux called him about the needed repairs, he "thought" Heroux referred to the pipe being blocked, not broken. Carver added that when a camera can't be pushed beyond a certain point "it is likely to be broken and not blocked." Although this appeared to be close to what the investigator's schema was trying so hard to support, it took her three separate interviews with Carver to get him to say that he "thought" Heroux knew that the line "may have been" broken, not blocked. But even Carver's report was far from clear about this, as evidenced by his use of "may" and "likely," to say nothing of possible reasonable doubts about his suddenly improved memory, all of which were unverifiable because investigator Maurice did not tape-record her three interviews with him. Because of this we cannot know how her questions were posed to Carver or whether she possibly influenced or even coerced Carver to give her the answers she seemed to want to hear.

Perhaps recognizing that Carver's recovered memory would not be convincing enough to prove Heroux had lied, on September 30, 2003, investigator Maurice interviewed Brad Dvorak, the city inspector in charge of inspecting the sewer repairs. Her own notes of this un-taped meeting show that Dvorak was equally unhelpful to her about that accusation:

Dvorak stated that Atco Utilities made application for the permit. Dvorak stated that the city does not provide a copy of the permit application or the permit to the business where repairs are being made, but instead provides this information to the contractor.

Finally, Maurice interviewed Hardcoat's secretary/receptionist on December 3, 2003. The investigator's own notes of this un-taped interview say:

> She stated that she has not overheard any conversations about the sewer pipe, except that Heroux had told her of a "blockage" in the pipe. She also stated that Hardcoat never received a copy of the work order prepared by Atco Utilities that referenced a "break" in the sewer pipe.

This too was not helpful to the prosecution's accusation that Heroux had knowingly, willfully, and fraudulently reported that the sewer line was blocked rather than broken. This charge in the indictment ignored all of its own strong contextual evidence to the contrary and was based entirely on Carver's vague impression and improved memory during the third time the investigator interviewed him. This could not be considered very convincing smoking gun evidence that Heroux fraudulently reported blockage rather than a break in the sewer lines.

Fraudulently Conspiring to Withhold Information

The indictment charged:

> Miklasevics fraudulently told HCES that Alto had never given him a videotape of the first inspection and he never sent that videotape to HCES. Heroux and Miklasevics

together fraudulently conspired to keep damaging information from HCES.

Here the government claimed that by not sending the first
Alto Sewer Services videotape to HCES, Miklasevics and Heroux
together knowingly conspired to commit fraud. But the prosecution had no evidence that Miklasevics ever received that first videotape from Alto Sewer Services. This was discussed above under the
conversational strategy category of the meaning of "you." The focus
of this alleged smoking gun now turned to conspiracy, a charge
which, if proven, increases the severity of the penalty.

The surest way to prove a conspiracy is to capture on tape a
conversation between the conspirators. Since there was no such
evidence in this case, the investigation had to be based on the intelligence gathering that included a few recorded interviews and the
investigator's notes made of her own unrecorded interviews. From
these the prosecutor was forced to perform an intelligence analysis
that had to rely on this evidence alone.

As noted above, it was obviously difficult for the prosecutor to
base conspiracy charges on inferences that Heroux and Miklasevics
had conspired to withhold the information provided by the first
video tape of the sewer line made by Alto Sewer, primarily because
the government's own evidence did not support this claim. It was
equally difficult to charge conspiracy about the defendants lying
about knowing there was a break in the sewer line. Such evidence
might be expected to come from the many neutral witnesses interviewed by the investigator. But again the prosecution's evidence
contradicted this claim and therefore it could not adequately demonstrate conspiracy.

Investigator Maurice's attempts to elicit from the defendants
that they knew that the sewer line had contaminated the environment went nowhere because Heroux and Miklasevics provided no

evidence that they knew this. Maurice's own notes of her interview with Heroux on September 17, 2003, demonstrated this:

> Heroux stated that the soil would have contained residue or would have been discolored if the soil had actually been contaminated, and Heroux stated that he did not see any evidence of residue or discoloration. He had not notified the Minnesota duty officer of a release because he was not aware that a release had occurred.

It is possible that Heroux didn't see any discoloration or residue because there was none. But he was not the only one to report that there was no such evidence. The notes made in investigator Maurice's investigative report of her September 15, 2003, interview with Andy Carver of Atco Utilities, who snaked and repaired the sewer lines, said:

> Carver stated that he did not observe any unusual odors or staining of the soil around the sewer pipe.

Her interview notes from a meeting with city inspector Brad Dvorak on September 30, 2003, supported Carver's observation:

> Dvorak stated that he does not remember observing soil staining or odors that may have occurred as a result of the broken sewer pipe.

In her follow-up interview with Andy Carver, the inspector's notes say:

> Carver stated that he did not observe any soil staining or notice any unusual odors during the time he was at Hardcoat.

Even Bruce Bethiaume, field supervisor of the utilities division of the city could not support this charge, as Maurice's notes of her October 1, 2003, interview with him made clear:

> Bethiaume stated that he does not remember observing soil staining or odors emanating from the area where the sewer pipe had been replaced.

In none of the above statements taken from the Investigative Activity Reports are we provided the investigator's questions that yielded these responses about lack of soil staining or unusual odors, but the similarity of the respondents' words suggests that the investigator must have asked them questions using those same or similar words.

It can be expected that if the professional workers and inspectors who worked closely at the site did not notice or otherwise know about any soil contamination, it was also likely that Heroux and Miklasevics also didn't notice or know about it. That there is no evidence that the defendants knew or observed this makes the government's conspiracy charge of their hiding that knowledge quite a huge inferential leap.

Most of the adverbial modifiers that define fraudulent language were repeated in the charges of the indictment. The above analysis of the government's own evidence makes it clear that Heroux and Miklasevics did not fraudulently withhold or misstate information or conspire to do so.

INTERVIEWING STRATEGIES AND COMPETENCE

Effective interviewing technique begins with an obvious requirement that is often overlooked: questioners must be clear, explicit, direct, and unambiguous in the way they ask their questions. The best interview evidence is obtained when the targets make their inculpatory statements clear and explicit. The worst evidence is when inferences have to be made from the targets' statements. Investigator Tanya Maurice failed in these requirements in the following ways:

- She failed to ask specific questions.

She consistently failed to ask Heroux and Miklasevics the questions about which she was most interested—whether or not they knew about any environmental damage resulting from Hardcoat's sewer line. Instead, she took an indirect approach, probing whether or not Heroux and Miklasevics knew that their sewer line pipes were broken and not just blocked. Her reasoning must have been that if they knew the pipes were broken, perhaps this could reveal their knowledge that Hardcoat had been contaminating the environment.

- She failed to avoid relying on inferences.

As a result of the indirectness of her questions, the responses she got from the targets forced her (and the prosecutor as well) to infer the defendants' possible but factually unsupported knowledge of the existence of environmental damage.

- She failed to take advantage of the conversational opportunities to ask the questions in which she was most interested.

As noted above, she missed several opportunities to introduce her primary topic concerning environmental damage.

- She and the prosecutor failed to compare the responses and statements of Heroux and Miklasevics with those of other witnesses as they were reported in the government's own Investigative Activity Reports.

One of the most basic scientific methods is that of comparison, which she and the prosecutor failed to make here.

- She failed to define or seek evidence of the target's understanding of her own ambiguous expressions.

As noted above, Maurice relied heavily on ambiguous terms such as "results," "problems," "fixed/took care of," and "you."

CONCLUSION OF THE CASE

I provided all of the above analysis to the defense attorney, who used it very effectively without requiring my trial testimony. Miklasevics was acquitted of all charges and Heroux was acquitted on all counts but one, for which his company paid a $25,000 fine for not keeping adequate records of batch discharge. He served no time in prison and was not even placed on probation.

[4]

CORRUPT FOREIGN BUSINESS PRACTICES (FRAUD)

The larger the investigation, the more complex the indictments can become. An ongoing FBI investigation in 2009 resulted in the Department of Justice's largest-ever sting operation growing out of violations of the Foreign Corrupt Practices Act of 1977, a law that was enacted to crack down on fraudulent corporate bribery and money laundering in all its forms. This Act, as amended in 1998, prohibits payments to any person

> while knowing that all or a portion of such money or thing of value will be offered, given, promised, directly or indirectly to any foreign official for purposes of—
>
> (A)   (i) influencing any act or decision of such foreign official in his official capacity,
>
>   (ii) inducing such foreign official to do or omit to do any act in violation of the lawful duty of such foreign official, or
>
>   (iii) securing any improper advantage; or inducing such foreign official to use his influence with a foreign government or instrumentality thereof to affect or influence any act or decision of such government or instrumentality.

Although this Act does not specify "fraud" in its name, the defining characteristics of fraudulent language, such as "influencing," "inducing," and "improper advantage," are abundantly present in cases involving corrupt foreign business practices.

BACKGROUND OF THE CASE

On January 18, 2010, the FBI arrested twenty-one executives and employees of US military and law enforcement products companies for engaging in fraudulent schemes to bribe foreign government officials so that they could obtain or retain business and then launder the money so that they would not be detected. The FBI carried out this ambitious sting operation at the 2010 Shooting, Hunting, Outdoor Trade Show and Conference held at the Sands Expo & Convention Center in Las Vegas, where it was known that all twenty-one company executives would be attending. The resulting indictments charged that the defendants agreed to pay a 20 percent commission to a sales agent (actually an undercover FBI agent) in order to win a portion of a $15 million contract for outfitting Gabon's military guard. The defendants were led to believe that one of the undercover agents was Gabon's minister of defense.

The indictment was complex, involving charges of fraudulent money laundering (18 U.S.C. § 1956 h), conspiracy to violate the Foreign Corrupt Practices Act (15 U.S.C. § 78), and aiding and abetting (18 U.S.C. § 2).

Soon after the indictment the defense attorneys for one of the indicted business executives, Yochanan (Yochi) R. Cohen, requested my associate Robert Leonard and me to analyze the dozens of undercover tape-recorded telephone conversations, emails, and four meetings in which Cohen participated, including parts of the Las Vegas meeting in which Cohen was briefly recorded. Tape-recorded conversations were the basis for indicting all the defendants, including Cohen. As the following excerpts from the recorded conversations will indicate, Cohen is not a native speaker of English, which is reflected in the way he understood what the agents said to him in his own somewhat awkward use of the English language.

As stressed in other chapters of this book, the linguistic analysis of large amounts of continuous discourse over long periods of time begins by identifying the speech event or speech events in which the conversations took place. The speech event sets the table for the schemas of the participants and their agendas are revealed by the topics they introduce and the responses they make to the topics introduced by other participants. Their speech acts and conversational strategies provide additional snapshots of the language in evidence. What the prosecution calls the damaging smoking gun passages can be illuminated and contextualized when the snapshots of these speech events, schemas, agendas, speech acts, and conversational strategies are assembled into a panoramic picture of the language evidence.

SPEECH EVENT

The linguistic analysis demonstrated that the taped evidence constituted an extended business negotiation speech event that continued throughout all of Cohen's conversations with two undercover cooperating witnesses who already had been caught in previous sting operations and, for sentencing considerations, were now cooperating with the government to catch others in the same crime. Cohen's company produced body armor used by military and law enforcement agencies and his accustomed role was to sell it to authorized representatives of prospective buyers. It was also common in this business for manufacturers of arms and equipment to work with intermediaries or business agents who represent the potential buyers, for which service they were paid commissions or finder's fees. As far as Cohen appeared to understand, the simplified structure of this business transaction speech event took the normal and predictable four sequential stages.

The Business Transaction Speech Event

Stage 1: Buyer expresses needs
Stage 2: Seller describes his product that matches this need
Stage 3: Buyer and seller negotiate price and conditions
Stage 4: Sale is either completed or aborted

The undercover agents viewed this speech event as an opportunity to insert illegality into it while assuming that Cohen and the other arms manufacturers at the conference would bite at the opportunity to engage in illegal violations of the Foreign Corrupt Practices Act. A snapshot view of the speech event shows that for Cohen this was a normal business transaction speech event, but for the agents this was to be a bribery speech event in which stages 1 and 2 were accomplished while they tried to produce illegal bribery twists into stages 3 and 4. As the language evidence shows, they never reached the stage 4 completion with Cohen.

SCHEMAS

Schemas of the participants grow naturally out of the speech event in which they find themselves. As revealed by his language, Cohen's schema throughout the conversations remained constant. His language indicated that he believed that he was continuously participating in a conventional business transaction speech event. His role in this speech event was that of a salesman trying to convince buyers to purchase his goods, to negotiate the price and conditions, and to reach an agreement that would complete the sale. In contrast, the agent's schema could only be that his inducements could transform the ostensible business transaction speech event into a quid pro quo bribery speech event in which Cohen would offer kickbacks to both him and to the Gabon defense minister so that Cohen could succeed in getting the attractive sales contract.

Since these two very different perceptions of this speech event were going on simultaneously, it was up to the agent to get Cohen to figure out that a bribery speech event was in progress and to act accordingly. If Cohen gave the appearance of willingness to do anything illegal, the agent's task would be easy, but to reach that point Cohen would need to provide language evidence that he understood that he actually was in a bribery speech event. Because Cohen's schema of the event caused him to have difficulty reaching that understanding, the agent resorted to employing a number of strategies to try to change Cohen's schema.

It is unquestioned that the schema of undercover agents is that their targets are predisposed to commit an illegal act and the agent's only task is to elicit language evidence that will implicate their targets in a crime. As revealed by their language, the schema of the two undercover agents was that if Cohen and the other company executives at that meeting were given attractive financial incentives, they would succumb to the opportunity to commit crimes of bribery and money laundering in violation of the Foreign Corrupt Practices Act.

The primary undercover cooperating witness in this investigation represented himself as a middleman broker who was trying to help Cohen's company secure the 15 million dollar contract for arms and body armor that would be purchased by Gabon's minister of defense. This fictitious "minister" was also a cooperating witness in the sting operation. Representatives of the nation of Gabon were not told anything about this operation.

AGENDAS

Participants' schemas, triggered by the nature of the speech event they are in, can be identified and verified by the ensuing conversations in which topics are raised and responses are given to those topics. These provide snapshot views of the participants' clearest tangible clues about their knowing and willful predispositions and intentions.

Cohen's own agenda, as revealed by his language, yielded little or nothing upon which the agent could build his case. Cohen's most frequent topics related to his salesmanship style of describing and bragging about the high quality of his body armor products, his recitations about the required legal processes, and some lengthy descriptions about his own honest business philosophy. Related to the latter topic, Cohen also described a few past business incidents in which he had refused to do business with buyers who did not demonstrate their integrity.

When targets do not implicate themselves with their own agendas, undercover agents commonly introduce different topics that are intended to elicit responses that may elicit their targets' willingness to commit an illegal act. My past analyses of hundreds of undercover cases shows that this technique is common in the work of undercover agents. Agenda analysis is important because examining the entire body of language demonstrates which topics the target introduced (or did not introduce) and recycled in comparison with which ones the agent brought up. This enables a comparison of the important differences. If targets themselves introduce topics of illegality, a very strong case can be made against them. And if their responses to the agents' topics about illegality indicate their willingness to violate the law, the case against them can be equally strong. Because all of the topics Cohen introduced were legally benign, the agent was forced to try to steer the conversations in directions that would give Cohen the opportunity to express his responses to the agent's topics in ways that might inculpate him.

Many law enforcement manuals describe the most efficient ways for the police to interview suspects and obtain admissions of guilt, but there are relatively few publicly available guides or manuals that show undercover agents how to capture evidence of a suspect's guilt. However, because the guiding principles found in police manuals for interviewing suspects in custody are similar to conversational interviewing during undercover operations, agents and cooperating witnesses engaged in this work might be expected to follow the common four-step procedure suggested for police interviews of suspects (Gudjonsson 1993; Shuy 2005, 2013, 2014):

1. Let the targets talk long enough to inculpate themselves. If this does not succeed, go to the next step.
2. Drop hints about potential illegality in the hope that the targets will recognize the true intent and align themselves with it. If this does not succeed, go to the next step.
3. Encourage the targets to retell past events in which they or others may have committed illegal acts. If this does not succeed, go to the next step.
4. Make clear and unambiguous the illegal nature of the enterprise.

Throughout this book, I refer to this four-step sequence as the fishing expedition that is considered effective for capturing guilt in undercover operations, even though in fact neither police interviewers nor undercover agents tend to follow this sequence very closely. As in many other sting operations, the agents in this case skipped the first step entirely, despite the fact that language evidence of this type can provide the most convincing proof of guilt. Clear self-reported illegality cannot result in challenges by the defense. Because law enforcement officers and undercover cooperating witnesses are often too impatient to wait for suspects to implicate themselves, I have found that they tend to begin with steps 2 and 3—hinting at illegality and encouraging the retelling of past events.

As in most undercover operations, these agent's fishing topics were central for determining Cohen's guilt or innocence. The major topics they introduced in this investigation related to their efforts to get Cohen to admit that: (1) he knowingly had made illegal deals in the past; (2) he was willing to pay the agents a bribe to get the contract instead of giving them a legal commission; (3) he was willing to skip the requirement to first obtain an export license; and (4) he would be willing to pay a kickback to the foreign minister of Gabon.

Analysis of these fishing topics illustrates how difficult it can be to search through all of the many conversations to isolate the threaded continuity of a single critical discourse topic that occurs several times in the midst of many other discourse topics, and then to pair those critical topics with the target's responses in order to determine whether or not the agents' fishing efforts were successful. Of special importance here is that throughout these conversations, Cohen frequently recycled the topic of his need to follow the law, which emphasized his own schema and apparent intentions. It's possible that the prosecution could question Cohen's sincerity if he had made only one isolated statement about desiring to follow the law, but his consistently repeated assertions of the need to be legal were more difficult to discount. Topic recycling such as that is an important part of discourse analysis.

The following excerpts describe the agent's four undercover fishing topic strategies along with Cohen's responses.

Undercover Strategy 1 Topic: Agent Encourages the Retelling of Illegal Deals in the Past

The agent began with the step 3 strategy of retelling past events that hint at possible illegality. Knowing that Cohen and his company had done business in other foreign countries in the past, the agent fished for any evidence that his target had violated the law in his former sales of body armor in Peru, in the Middle East, and in Mexico. His hints are emphasized below:

SEPTEMBER 16, 2008

AGENT: So there's **a lot of happy generals** in Peru I think.

COHEN: I don't care about that.

AGENT: In Peru I'm dealing with Carlos too. I mean they're really doing a good job down there. They're **taking care of this guy and that guy to make sure everything is okay.** How do you deal with money like that?

COHEN: Everything comes to us.

AGENT: And you **commission back** to them?

COHEN: I told them, "listen, I don't care that you make ten times. I just make my money, I don't care about you." I said, "you set me a price." I took my cash flow because the companies I work with financially are not stable. They needed the money and I had to pay them, so I paid everybody off.

Here Cohen either missed or ignored the implication of illegality suggested by the agent's hint that Cohen had made the generals happy by bribing them to get the Peruvian contract for body armor. Cohen said he didn't care what the generals did. The government was poised to leap on Cohen's "I paid everybody off," but the defense was quite prepared to show that this referred grammatically to his financially strapped subcontractors ("the companies I work with"). But the agent was undaunted and later in the same conversation he continued to try to get Cohen to talk about illegality in the Peru deal:

SEPTEMBER 16, 2008

AGENT: Speaking of commission, did you get your Peru deal finished finally with GSS?

COHEN: I charged them $800,000 for a lot of (inaudible) and they came to me and started talking. I sensed something was wrong there. I said to them. "Listen guys, I don't care how much you sell it. I'm not giving you credit. Forget about it. If I am dealing directly with the government, it is fine. Letter of credit, I will give you a commission. I don't care how much you make." And then they give me a letter of credit for 1.5 million and they want me to pay everything.

AGENT: And between us girls, I think they told me that the end user payoff was something like $200,000 on that deal.

COHEN: I believe there was some kind of monkey business because they gave him a letter of credit for much more that he charged. However I think that they take advantage of us believing that this is the price that they need to get.

Here Cohen indicated that he suspected the Peruvians wanted him to use some of the money to pay off the police. He called this "monkey business" and, despite the agent's wink-wink "between us girls" hint, Cohen said he refused to deal with extra money. Another failed fishing effort.

In the same conversation the agent then turned his attention to past deals in the Middle East:

AGENT: So you're okay, because if we work in the Middle East or if we ever do something in Asia, it's the same thing. You know that they're paying the guys.

COHEN: I don't care. I do not control everything. As long as I don't do that.

AGENT: Right. Let the agents do it.

COHEN: What the agent does, I don't care. As long as for me it's a straight business, no cash involved with my side.

AGENT: Right. What they do with their commissions—

COHEN: What they do in their side is their problem. I don't care. I don't want to do that. As long as nobody will come and say, "hold on a second, that's not allowed." I don't want to mess with it. I am terrified to do it.

Cohen here made it very clear that he would have nothing to do with "paying the guys." If the broker wanted to do so with his own commission money that Cohen paid him, there was nothing Cohen could do about that.

Finally in the same conversation the agent employed the retell strategy again, this time about alleged kickbacks in Cohen's past sales of body armor in Mexico, telling Cohen that middlemen brokers named Andreas and Carlos had paid off the police. Cohen indicated that he didn't believe the agent's accusation because the brokers were only bragging:

COHEN: And in my opinion they take advantage in saying that because with Mexico we dealing directly with the government. Nobody asked if they want to take care of them, but they are not aggressive and say, "I need $200,000 for this deal to my pocket." I believe the brokers are enjoying the legends about them having to pay that amount of money.

AGENT: Or maybe it's more than they are really paying.

COHEN: I think Andreas and Carlos aren't like that. Really they don't pay $200,000, because I spoke with their agent Haim and he spoke with their agents and he got pennies for that.

This step 3 retell strategy yielded nothing inculpatory from Cohen, who told the agent only that he suspected some "monkey business" was going on but that it didn't involve him. Another failed fishing effort.

Undercover Strategy 2 Topic: Agent Fishes to Associate a Commission with a Kickback

The most critical issue in this case was whether Cohen knowingly and willfully agreed to pay a perfectly legal commission to the agent who brokered the deal or instead gave bribes to the agent and the Gabon minister in order to obtain the contract. Although the indictment claimed that Cohen was willing to offer the agent a quid pro quo bribe to get the contract, analysis of the tape-recorded evidence shows that Cohen's only consideration was to pay the agent a proper commission. The agent began this fishing effort by hinting that it takes a "connection" to get a contract in countries like Turkey:

JANUARY 14, 2009

AGENT: So the agent in Turkey, I have worked with him for ten years at Armor. He is very well connected with gendarmerie and the police. We've done a lot of business with him.

COHEN: Here is my suggestion. Let's simplify our life, your life. You probably will get the project ahead of time or in time. You come to me the project. I tell you immediately if I work with it or not work with it. But you come to me with this project and this is my target price.

AGENT: Okay, I can't. I appreciate that, Yochi, but I can't always do it that way.

COHEN: I know there is always, you know, there is exception, but companies come to me saying, "I want you to give me the best price, best price." You know, I can make it two dollars and a half, but then—let me see if I can make it cheapest.

Cohen's response here indicates that he didn't catch the agent's hint about a needed bribe, instead interpreting the hint to mean his not giving buyers the most attractive price. Undaunted, the agent pursued the Turkey bribe topic again in this same conversation, but with more specificity:

AGENT: And they get paid, just so you know. The gendarmerie and the police in Turkey. They pay with a letter of credit to you and then you commission back to the agent. So there is no problem now.

COHEN: Pay you?

AGENT: Well, you'll reserve a finder's fee for my group, okay?

COHEN: Only a finder's fee?

AGENT: Well, a commission, however you want to call it.

COHEN: That commission, you tell me what you feel comfortable in and we can give it to them and I will do.

Although this topic awkwardly shifted in progress from the agent's past Turkey deal to Cohen's prospective current deal with Gabon, the agent implied that just as his own way of doing business in

Turkey required a kickback to the police, Cohen's possible current contract with Gabon would require the same kind of bribe. However, the agent's use of "commission" triggered Cohen's request that the agent inform him about how much commission he will charge, a rather clear indication that even if Cohen had understood the agent's hint that he had to pay a kickback to the police in Turkey (which understanding was questionable), he gave no evidence of seeing a connection between the agent's deal in Turkey with this current one for Gabon. This fishing effort failed, at least partly because the agent used the word "commission" in relation to the current Gabon deal. From this point onward Cohen further identified his relationship with the agent as a commission:

> MARCH 16, 2009
> AGENT: Do you have a problem building in a 5% commission for me?
> COHEN: No, I don't have a problem with that.

About two months later Cohen also told the agent:

> MAY 22, 2009
> COHEN: You can be our commission agent on this. We need to put you in the contract with Gabon because we need to put the name of everybody that is involved. If there is internal another person involved in Gabon, we need to have his company name and everything like that.

Here Cohen specifically indicated that he was following the legal requirements, contrary to what the agent was so unclearly suggesting. The agent's fishing effort to get Cohen to understand "commission" as a kickback failed.

Undercover Strategy 3 Topic: Agent Fishes to Get Cohen to Avoid an Export License

In the telephone calls that preceded his meetings with Cohen, the agent began with step 2 hinting topics by conveying that Cohen would not need the legally required export license before he shipped the armor. If the agent could get Cohen to admit that he was willing to bypass this legal requirement, it could be a good first step toward his eventual arrest for the even greater crime of bribery. However, Cohen clearly rejected this hint and expressed his desire to be legal by suggesting that the agent seek out a lawyer to make sure that he handled this legally and properly:

MARCH 5, 2009

AGENT: Because of quantity, I don't need pre-approval. I just have to file a report.

COHEN: I don't know that, but I know that everything we export requires an export license.

JUNE 25, 2009

AGENT: Do you want to wait until I give you a copy of your export license?

COHEN: Yes, First we need to get the license. Do you know a law firm in Washington D.C. that specializes in export licenses? We need to show that to someone and therefore would like to have some kind of opinion to help with that.

About three months later, when the export license had still not arrived, Cohen enquired about the contract and repeated his need to receive that license first:

SEPTEMBER 8, 2009

COHEN: Is the Gabon deal okay? Are we getting the order soon?

AGENT: He is coming over with all the contracts.

COHEN: And we need to do the export license.

SEPTEMBER 17, 2009

AGENT: I need to know the delivery time.

COHEN: Let's put it 60 days after we get the export license. I say for you it is all about the process, as long as the process is correct.

Cohen's language during this fishing effort indicated that he would not agree to bypass the important legal step of first obtaining the required export license. The agent's fishing effort also failed on this topic.

Undercover Agent Strategy 4 Topic: Agent Tries to Make a Clear and Unambiguous Representation of Illegality

As noted above, the step 4 undercover strategy is for the agent to be clear and unambiguous to the target about the illegal nature of the enterprise. By now the first undercover agent apparently had given up on using the hinting strategy in his effort to get Cohen to retell anything criminal about his past work in other countries, so the second undercover cooperating witness now took over. Near the end of this meeting, after failing to implicate Cohen in anything illegal about his contract in Peru, this cooperating witness finally used the stage 4 strategy of being clear and unambiguous about the illegal nature of the enterprise.

MAY 22, 2009

AGENT 2: That's Peru, but this is Gabon. The reason I have to ask for 20% commission is because 10% has to go to Alain, to the minister. And then there's 10% for me.

COHEN: Do you mind if I give Richard [Agent 1] a little
   something?

AGENT 2: I would rather not.

COHEN: Because if this is the case, it's really only 10% and you
   get some of that—

AGENT 2: It is not necessary, but thank you.

COHEN: Here is my philosophy. I work in the long term. I don't
   want everybody to grab me and I don't want to grab them.
   I don't know what's happening, you know, everything—

AGENT 2 (INTERRUPTING): So we have one exception.

COHEN: —and I will not say it anymore.

This is one of the many passages in which analysis of Cohen's
responses was very important. When Agent 2 made it clear for the
first time that 10 percent had to go to the Gabon minister, explicitly indicating a kickback, he finally apparently realized that they
needed to make the requirement of a bribe clearly and unambiguously. Cohen's response, however, references only the commission
that he has already agreed to give to Agent 1 and it did not reference
the additional 10 percent for the Gabon minister, Alain. Cohen said
his concern was to make sure that Agent 1, the man Cohen had
agreed to pay a commission for brokering the sale of body armor to
Gabon, would receive the 10 percent commission that Cohen promised him. When Cohen said it's really "only 10%," this was a clear
indication that in this transaction he would not pay more than that
to any other persons, and that if Agent 2 wanted, he could get "some
of that" 10 percent commission. If Agent 2 wanted the Gabon minister, Alain, to be paid an additional 10 percent, it would have to be
taken out of the 10 percent commission Cohen was paying Agent 1,
which means that this amount would be absolutely nothing. Cohen
emphatically capped this exchange by saying that he won't be
"grabbed" by anyone and he doesn't know what's happening outside

the context of his own involvement. When Agent 2 objected, saying that this is "an exception," Cohen put his foot down and firmly responded that he will not say this again. Agent 2's fishing effort to be clear and unambiguous about the illegal nature of the deal also failed to capture Cohen in a criminal act.

Agent 2 made another effort to be clear and unambiguous in that same conversation as he spoke about Cohen's first item to be produced and shipped:

MAY 22, 2009

AGENT 2: The purpose of the first article isn't so much to test the units. It's more. I mean that is the stated purpose, but the under the table purpose is more so that Alain, the minister of defense, sees that he is actually testing me basically that I can produce his commission from each of the 18 line items. So if he sees that he's getting his piece of the action, then he can go ahead to get the bigger piece of the action. There is a freight forwarder in Virginia. It is called Cargo Transport. They are very big so—

COHEN (INTERRUPTING): They will do the transport?

AGENT 2: Right. So what we need, Yochi, in the Gabonese Embassy in DC then have a dollar account. So we need the Proforma Dulles, Virginia, to the government of Gabon, Ministry of Defense.

COHEN: You will send me the information and we will do this.

The prosecution was primed to make much of the fact that Agent 2 said "under the table purpose" and "his piece of the action," which were clear representations of illegality. The following sections on conversational strategies and smoking guns deal with this issue. For now, however, notice how the agent used the hit-and-run strategy of quickly changing his own topic to the method of shipment before Cohen had a chance to respond to his expressions of illegality.

SPEECH ACTS

As in most fraud cases, the most salient speech acts are agreeing, denying, promising, requesting, admitting, and offering, all of which must be accomplished clearly and felicitously in order to be understood and effective. As can be seen in the selections of their conversations noted above, Cohen did not admit, promise, offer, request, or agree to anything illegal and he strongly worded his denials of the agents' suggestions to do something illegal. This snapshot of his speech acts supported the panoramic picture of his innocence.

CONVERSATIONAL STRATEGIES

Effective communication requires clarity and specificity, but both the agents and Cohen himself were well aware that his shortcomings in English could make this difficult. Cohen demonstrated his difficulty in understanding the often vague and ambiguous language of the agents, especially their hints of illegality. This made him vulnerable to the agents' conversational strategies, especially in the way they used the ambiguity strategy in their hints of illegality. In themselves, hints and indirectness are inherently and sometimes even intentionally ambiguous. As noted above, the agents' use of vague and grammatically stripped expressions such as "end users," "happy generals in Peru," "paying the guys," and others were subject to more than a single illegal interpretation. Cohen's language made it clear that he didn't even get the drift of the agents' ambiguous hints about giving them "an exception." His response indicated that to him the "exception" they suggested was to give the buyer a cheaper price than normal. And Cohen offered no evidence that he even understood the agent's ambiguous hints that the "gendarmerie" in Turkey getting paid for transactions done by other arms manufacturers had anything to do with him. When the agents then talked ambiguously about "taking care of this guy and that guy," Cohen's response indicated that he understood this to mean either paying a legitimate commission to brokers and not to anyone else or to unscrupulous people that had nothing to do with him.

The agents also used the hit-and-run conversational strategy, which can make meaning problematic for even native English speakers to untangle. When Agent 2 tried to be clear and unambiguous by saying "under the table" and "piece of the action," he blocked any response to this by using the hit-and-run strategy of changing his own subject before Cohen could respond to it. The agent's newly created subject was the means of transportation, which was of importance to Cohen because he needed to know where to ship his body armor once it was finished. When undercover agents use the hit-and-run strategy, they depend on the recency principle to divert their targets from responding negatively to their suggestions. By focusing on what matters to the target (methods of shipping in this case), they lull them into ignoring the illegality of their original but suddenly dropped topic. This strategy can work especially well with targets whose English ability is not native.

Even when the agents used step 4 efforts to be clear and unambiguous, they left the door wide open for misunderstanding. Both Cohen and the agents often used pronouns and prepositions ambiguously, especially "you," "they," "it," and "he," leading to comprehension problems on both sides. Adding to Cohen's difficulty was his constant preoccupation with promoting his own company's business, which often sidetracked him into bragging about what his company does and could do. His schema was to encourage and promote his company's business and, as the agents discovered, it was very hard to divert him from this.

SMOKING GUNS

What the prosecution considered the major smoking guns have already been identified above. These all needed to be contextualized by (1) the speech event Cohen thought he was in; (2) his resulting schema about what was going on; (3) his agenda revealed by the topics he introduced and his responses to the agents' topics; and (4) his speech acts that did not include agreement with the agents. None of these could support the prosecution's belief that he was knowingly and willingly ready to commit a crime.

Even when the cooperating witnesses employed the conversational strategies of ambiguity and hit-and-run they did not succeed in eliciting anything that would inculpate Cohen. For example, their conversational strategies did not get Cohen to avoid obtaining the legally required export license. Despite many efforts to discourage him from doing this, Cohen persisted in following the legal procedures.

Cohen flatly denied paying bribes for his contract with Peru, even after the agent mentioned the vague and ambiguous "end user payoff." He missed or didn't understand the agent's wink-wink expression "between us girls," as somehow relating to him, replying that if there was any "monkey business," it was done by someone else. When he was told that in Asia "they're paying the guys," Cohen said he didn't care what they do there "as long as I don't do that ... As long as for me it's a straight business, no cash involved with my side." When Agent 2 began to be clear and unambiguous about the illegality of what he suggested by telling Cohen, "10% has to go to Alain, to the minister ... and there's 10% for me," Cohen responded in no uncertain terms that there would be only a 10 percent commission and even more strongly that he didn't want to have to tell him that again.

Undaunted, Agent 2 kept trying, next using the expressions, "under the table purpose" and "piece of the action," but before Cohen could even react, the agent quickly employed the hit-and-run strategy that set the exchange off in a different direction.

Yes, there were smoking gun expressions here, but careful analysis shows that they were all made by the undercover operatives and not by Cohen, who rejected them whenever he managed to understand them. The alleged smoking guns were all defeated by the language evidence gathered by the government's own agents.

CONCLUSION OF THE CASE

One might wonder why Cohen did not catch on to the early hints of illegality that the undercover agent provided. One answer is often found in the participants' schemas, the knowledge that people bring with them as they encounter new information. The agents brought with them their schema that Cohen was a dishonest arms dealer who, with proper inducement, would certainly succumb to their offer. This schema was undaunted by Cohen's many efforts to demonstrate his integrity. His continuing schema was that he was in a conventional business transaction speech event and that the agents' efforts were about something or somebody else, but not about him. Unless listeners have good reasons to suspect that the people with whom they associate are dishonest, their tendency is to assume that everything is aboveboard. As Grice (1975) pointed out, conversation is made possible and managed by the cooperative principle.

Cohen was a businessman whose contributions to the conversations displayed his awareness of the rules and laws and he produced no language evidence of wanting to violate them. His constant schema was that this was just another opportunity to sell his products during a business transaction speech event. The undercover agents' schema was the same as those in virtually all such operations—that Cohen was a criminal-minded manufacturer who could be convinced to knowingly and willfully violate the law. These two different schemas collided throughout their conversations.

The primary method of assessing Cohen's schema was to discover his agenda by identifying the topics he introduced and the responses he gave to the topics of the undercover agents. As the above analysis demonstrated, Cohen's topics were consistently legal. Even the agents themselves must have realized that their hinting and retelling past scenarios strategies were getting them nowhere, because they finally tried the strategy of being clear and unambiguous about the illegal nature of their plans. Although the agents used smoking gun expressions as they did this, Cohen successfully defused them and didn't adopt them as his own.

Reprising the adverbial modifiers that characterize fraudulent language noted in chapter 1, the government's own evidence clearly was unable to demonstrate that Cohen unconscientiously abused his power, intentionally or willfully concealed or misrepresented information, knowingly deceived, acted surreptitiously, or spoke without belief in what he said. The same could not be said about the agents.

When the snapshot views of Cohen's perception of the speech event, his schema, his speech acts, his conversational agenda, and the agents' conversational strategies were assembled together, they provided a panoramic picture of the language evidence, showing that the government's case against Cohen could take a severe beating. Armed with this linguistic analysis of the government's evidence, Cohen's lawyers were prepared to defend their client at trial.

The Court decided that with so many defendants, it would be more efficient to have three trials with some of the defendants in each. It appeared that the prosecutors selected what they considered their strongest cases to go first, the next strongest second, leaving Cohen and a few other defendants scheduled for the third trial.

The first two trials lasted six months, both ending with hung juries for seven of the defendants and acquittals for three others. At that point the government made a motion to dismiss the indictments of the rest of the defendants, including the still-untried Cohen.

The government's motion to dismiss gingerly explained that the first two trials produced no convictions and resulted in "implications" for the final trial while draining "substantial government resources." It concluded, "The government respectfully submits that continued prosecution of this case is not warranted under the circumstances."

[5]

TRADE SECRETS FRAUD
AND ECONOMIC ESPIONAGE

Most people think of "espionage" in terms of famous spies such as Harriet Tubman in the Civil War, Mata Hara in World War II, Julius and Ethel Rosenberg during the Cold War, or the more recent prosecution and conviction of spies Jonathan Pollard (1985), Aldrich Ames (1993), Wen Ho Lee (1999), and Robert Hanssen (2001). And, of course, there is also the fictional James Bond to let us know what a real spy does for a living. *Merriam Webster's Collegiate Dictionary* defines *espionage* as the practice of spying or using spies to obtain information about the plans and activities especially of a foreign government. *Black's Law Dictionary* says the same but also adds industrial espionage and intellectual property, meaning one company spying on another to steal trade secrets or other proprietary information.

In American legal history, the crime of stealing or misappropriating the critical information of one entity by another is similar to matters of both espionage relating to national security and to unfair competition in commerce. But concerns about espionage of state secrets appeared on the scene first.

About at the time the United States was entering World War I, Congress passed the Espionage Act of 1917, which prohibited any attempt to interfere with military operations or support US enemies during wartime. Its obvious purpose was to prevent thefts made by foreign governments and agents. Since that time the Act has been amended many times, and there is still some controversy about its constitutionality in relationship to the meaning of the First Amendment right to freedom of speech. In 1996, Congress passed the Economic Espionage Act (18 U.S.C. § 1831-91), which continued this concern about national security but also added the protection of critical US corporate information from theft and economic espionage by criminalizing the theft of trade secrets (18 USC § 1832):

(a) Whoever, with intent to convert a trade secret, that is related to or included in a product that is produced for or placed in interstate or foreign commerce, to the economic benefit of anyone other than the owner thereof, and intending or knowing that the offense will injure any owner of that trade secret, knowingly—

    (1) steals, or without authorization appropriates, takes, carries away, or conceals, or by fraud, artifice, or deception obtains such information;

    (2) without authorization copies, duplicates, sketches, draws, photographs, downloads, uploads, alters, destroys, photocopies, replicates, transmits, delivers, sends, mails, communicates, or conveys such information;

    (3) receives, buys, or possesses such information, knowing the same to have been stolen or appropriated, obtained, or converted without authorization;

    (4) attempts to commit any offense described in paragraphs (1) through (3); or

(5) conspires with one or more other persons to commit any offense described in paragraphs (1) through (3), and one or more of such persons do any act to effect the object of the conspiracy, shall, except as provided in subsection (b), be fined under this title or imprisoned not more than 10 years, or both.

(b) Any organization that commits any offense described in subsection (a) shall be fined not more than $5,000,000.

Although preventing the theft of vital national information is very important, some have estimated that about 90% of the cases brought by the government relate to the theft or misappropriation of commercial trade secrets.

Even before the Economic Espionage Act, the Uniform Trade Secrets Act (UTSA) of 1979 was enacted to provide protection to the intellectual property of industries within the states because theft of trade secrets is harmful to businesses that would otherwise be able to compete fairly. Patent protection of intellectual property, like espionage relating to national security, operates at the federal level while trade secret theft or misappropriation is now addressed at the state level.

Another protection of proprietary commercial information comes through trademarks (the Lanham Act) and patents (the Patent Act) that are protected under federal statutes, both of which specify that the marks and patents be publicly disclosed so that others can make use of the products. In contrast, state laws protect the owners of trade secrets and prevent others from using them as long as the trade secrets have *not* been disclosed publicly. Major factors considered are the value of the information to competitors, the expense involved in developing the information, the extent to which the information is known by other businesses, and the extent to which the owner of the information tried to keep it secret. UTSA defines a "trade secret" as follows:

> **"Trade secret"** means information, including a formula, pattern,
>
> A. compilation, program, device, method, technique, or process, that:
>   (i) derives independent economic value, actual or potential, from not being generally known to, and not being readily ascertainable by proper means by, other persons who can obtain economic value from its disclosure or use, and
>   (ii) is the subject of efforts that are reasonable under the circumstances to maintain its secrecy.

Holders of trade secret information are required to have taken reasonable precaution that would prevent disclosure of the information and to be able to prove that another party wrongly acquired it. Misappropriation of trade secrets, considered a form of enabling unfair competition, is most commonly done by poaching employees from companies that hold such trade secrets or by misappropriating confidential information through various forms of industrial espionage.

This chapter describes how linguistic analysis was used in a case that the government brought against targets allegedly attempting to steal proprietary trade secrets.

BACKGROUND OF THE CASE

In July 1997, an eleven-count indictment charged three defendants with attempting to steal trade secrets from the pharmaceutical company, Bristol-Myers-Squibb, specifying the processes, methods, and formulas for manufacturing an anti-cancer drug known as Taxol, a product derived from the bark of the Pacific yew tree (*United States v. Kai-Lo Hsu, Jessica Chou, and Chester Ho*, Criminal No. 97-323).

The indictment included six counts of wire fraud, three counts of violating foreign and interstate travel to facilitate commercial bribery, one count of conspiracy, one count of attempted theft of trade secrets, and one count of aiding and abetting. At that time Bristol-Myers Squib scientists were collaborating with another company, Phyton Catalytic, about how to synthesize endophytic fungi in the bark of a yew tree, calling the result Pacilitaxel, a formulation that created an amitotic inhibitor used in cancer chemotherapy.

The indictment of Hsu, Chou, and Ho ended two years of investigating a Taiwanese company known as the Development Center for Biotechnology (DCB). A single undercover FBI agent who used the pseudonym, John Mano, carried out the entire investigation. In May 1995 the agent began his investigation by publicly advertising his services as a technology information specialist who could provide helpful services on a commission basis to companies such as DCB. A month later DCB's international business coordinator, Jessica Chou, wrote to Mano and expressed her interest in having him become their "partner in Asia." Another month later Mano responded, but by then Chou had left DCB and had taken a new position as manager of business development at the Yuen Foong Paper Company (YFP), where her task was to expand the operations from paper products into biotechnology. At that point Mano's target became the paper company, YFP.

After Mano requested information about the biotechnology for which Chou had expressed interest, Chou asked him which companies might have an interest in cooperating with YFP in joint-venture investments and marketing. She added that she had already received an inquiry from someone wanting to distribute Taxol as raw material for pharmaceuticals. Mano then emailed Chou several times saying that he would like to know the types of technologies Chou would like to obtain, but she didn't respond until six months later when she finally told him that she was interested in obtaining licensure for promising technologies that produce Taxol, adding that she would like Mano to contact the American company, Phyton Catalytic, Inc. about its possible willingness to collaborate with them in their research on plant cell culturing. In terms of predisposition to commit a crime, there was nothing here for the FBI to go on because Chou made it clear that her only plan was to cooperate lawfully with an American company by means of licensure, joint venture collaboration, or distribution rights. Mano then tried to discourage Chou about these possible relationships, saying that it was impossible for YFP to be able to enter into any licensing agreements.

Throughout the month of January 1996, Mano wrote several letters and emails to Chou but received no responses at all from her. Finally, Mano requested a meeting with Chou's immediate superior, Kai-Lo Hsu, the next time he happened to be in the United States. In February 1996, this meeting took place, during which Hsu provided information about YPF while Mano continued to discourage Hsu from pursuing a licensing agreement relating to existing Taxol technology. When it apparently became clear to Mano that nothing was being accomplished at this meeting, he suggested that they meet again at some later date. Still no predisposition to commit a crime was evident.

In spite of Mano's persistent requests, neither Hsu nor Chou responded to his letters and emails further until March 1996, when in an email Mano offered to obtain Taxol technology from an unidentified person. Hsu did not respond, but in May 1996 Chou wrote to Mano:

We shall refrain from any action that will cause my company to violate any intellectual property laws or other jurisdiction laws in the United States of America and other countries. John, when we agree with a particular transaction, please notice its intellectual property protection status and its strategy in the future which may be useful for us to avoid predictable infringements.

One might think that an FBI investigator would take this response as a clear signal that Chou and Hsu were not predisposed to commit a crime and were a bit suspicious about the direction the agent was going. This was so clear, in fact, that Chou unambiguously stated that they would not do anything illegal to further the goals of their company. But Mano did not give up easily. After some vague correspondence from him in June, Chou wrote back again, making it clear that she and YFP had no experience or ability to proceed unless Mano would clarify his own "procedures, participation, and commitment." During the next few months Mano continued to write letters and emails to Chou but did not answer her earlier requests for clarity about their possible relationship. Since Chou did not respond to him, Mano then wrote to Hsu, saying that his "contact" was putting considerable pressure on him and was considering other buyers. Again, this strategy failed to work, because Hsu did not even answer. It was time for the agent to try still another approach.

In January 1997, Mano emailed Hsu saying that because he had not heard from him, he would be sending him a bill for his services in the amount of $6,400. Even this threat did not stir Hsu to action, so Mano wrote to Chou again, this time telling her the same thing he told Hsu about the dire possibility of his having to deal with another investor instead of her company, adding, "you must provide something to show that you are committed." Note, however, that he did not make clear what such a commitment might be, apparently still fishing for something self-inculpatory from Chou.

Mano's constant entreaties continued through the spring of 1997, at which time the agent appeared to begin to overcome the resistance of Hsu and Chou. Part of Mano's strategy then was to keep lowering the price for his alleged information about the technology that he said he could provide. The price started at $800,000, then dropped to $750,000, next to $600,000 and finally to $200,000. This apparently didn't work either, for even then Chou continued to express her reluctance to proceed. She wrote to Mano on April 25, 1997, describing Hsu's feelings about the project: "I felt he is not interested in the project because of the news and the scale, unless we provide him some explanation. I am sorry for this result. Please advise if you want to continue the project."

Still they reached no agreement. A week later, Mano telephoned Hsu and told him, "All I need, Kai-Lo, is an answer. I just need to know if we're going to have a deal." Hsu replied in his normal indirect style, "If your contact already have another customer and he does not working with two customers same time, we understand." This may have been Hsu's best effort to say "no" politely. Chou made their withdrawal even clearer in a follow-up email saying, "In consideration of the time consumption and derived investment, I am sorry to inform you that I decided to withdraw myself from the project. In other words, if you desire, you shall pursue another contacts the project." This can only be considered Chou's clear statement about terminating their still unclear possible business relationship.

Chou's continuous rejections didn't deter Mano, who then pressed for a meeting in Philadelphia. Hsu was finally overcome by Mano's repeated and increasing overtures over the two-year period in which they were unable to determine how his company could work in the area of Taxol technology. So he agreed to meet with Mano and a scientist that Mano said he would bring along with him. That scientist actually was employed by Bristol-Myers Squibb (BMS). Mano had convinced the scientist to agree to work under-cover with him when they were to meet with Hsu. Chou, who had clearly separated herself from this matter, asked Mano to advise the BMS scientist that this was just "a general meeting," also adding "but we don't want to see a bunch of information."

Agent Mano apparently was not pleased to hear this, for his goal in the proposed meeting could be only to capture an illegal exchange of trade secrets on tape. So he then went over Chou's head directly to Hsu, explaining that the accompanying scientist would bring "some documents" to their meeting, but characteristi-cally he did not explain what these documents were. The meeting took place on June 14, 1997, at the Four Seasons hotel, while Hsu was in the United States on other business. Hsu decided to invite a technologist unaffiliated with YFP, Dr. Chester Ho, a professor of biochemistry who spoke English fluently, to accompany him in order to evaluate the representation of the information that would be presented by Mano's BMS scientist. By the end of this meeting, no agreements were reached, but Hsu and Ho were arrested.

It was important for the FBI to capture Kai-Lo Hsu while he was inside the country because Taiwan does not have an extra-dition treaty with the United States. Jessica Chou could not be arrested because she did not attend the meeting and was not on United States' soil. Chester Ho was arrested at the meeting and considered by the government to be part of the conspiracy.

I described the chronology above to provide readers with a sense of the general continuity of this two-year investigation. Summary versions of some of the important language evidence can be found in it. The total evidence consisted of seventy-nine emails and let-ters, most of which were unanswered by the targets, ten phone calls, thirty-nine faxes, and two face-to-face tape-recorded meetings.

It should also be clear that the government had not previously established any reason to suspect that anyone at the Yuen Foong Paper Company had acted illegally in the past or had a predisposition to do so in the future. Apparently this investigation was a trolling operation that targeted the officers of various companies in the hope that they might yield to a tempting opportunity offered by the FBI agent. According to Phillip Heymann, then US Assistant Attorney General, it is common practice for government agents to provide what is considered an "opportunity" to commit a crime, apparently regardless of whether the targets had any known intention or predisposition to do so (1984, Report of the Subcommittee on Civil and Constitutional Rights, 37).

SPEECH EVENT

The entire communications between the agent and Chou and Hsu can be considered a single business transaction speech event that has the following sequential stages and structure.

Business Transaction Speech Event

---

1. Presentation of the problem by the buyer

2. Offer of relevant services by the seller

3. Discussion and negotiation of how to resolve the buyer's problem

4. Agreement or disagreement about terms of any deals to be made

5. Completion (an explicit agreement or disagreement to any deal or deals)

Unless stages three and four are reached in a business transaction speech event, the deal cannot be considered to have been successful. The stage 4 agreement to engage in an illegal act is called an inchoate crime, because such agreement is in itself considered serious enough to merit punishment. In most inchoate crimes, such as soliciting murder (Shuy 2014), indictments do not require the physical act such as a murder to have taken place. The agreement to commit it (or to have someone else commit it) is sufficient evidence. The language evidence in the current case demonstrates that the defendants did not get beyond the stage 2 discussion about how to resolve their problem. In fact, even the problem was never fully defined to mutual satisfaction, much less clarified or agreed upon.

As noted in the chronology above, it was the agent who initiated the two-year series of exchanges when he wrote to Chou offering to share his business contacts. For Chou, the speech event was a potential business arrangement with the agent, as she outlined in her email to him on August 8, 1995 (emphasis added):

> CHOU: I suggest the start point could be to identify American biotechnology companies who actually intend to **collaborate** with Taiwanese company for **selling or promoting** their products or services to Taiwan as well as Hong Kong, Mainland China, and other Southeast Asia countries. The American companies could **use YFP market channels to access China markets**. Methods of cooperation may include **joint venture investment, marketing, and distribution.** From the Taiwanese side, many companies are looking forward to diversify their business into the field of biotechnology and up-grade their technology by acquiring high technology via **technology transfer or cooperation.** I can, acting as a consultant for domestic companies, contact suitable counterparts to make the business. It is likely

desirable that we may establish a working relationship of matching Taiwanese companies with American companies to fulfill their benefits. Recently, I have received an inquiry for distributing TAXOL as a raw material for pharmaceutical preparations.

This is a clear snapshot of the intention, predisposition, and state of mind of Chou personally and on behalf of her company during stage 1 of this business negotiation speech event. The agent's contributions during their many exchanges indicated that he continuously supported this understanding of the speech event that Chou described and apparently believed she was in. The agent's very different goal, however, was to try to make this otherwise legal business transaction speech event take an illegal twist, which task was probably made more difficult by the Taiwanese targets' cultural differences and their limited English ability.

SCHEMAS

Chou's schema grew naturally out of her perception of the speech event noted above. At first her schema was that Mano might be helpful to the development of her company, YFP, but as time passed her view of this changed radically to skepticism and doubt.

In spite of Chou's caution and because he came into the discussion very late, Hsu's schema was that there was a slight possibility that there be something in this possible relationship with Mano, but this was more as an afterthought after Chou decided to opt out of any relationship with the agent. Hsu's lack of enthusiasm was evidenced when he agreed to meet with Mano only because he was in the United States on other business, but even then he was aware enough of potential problems to ask a more proficient English-speaking scientist to come with him to help him figure out what was happening.

As Dr. Ho's questions in the meeting with Mano and the BMS scientist made evident, he had only one schema—that of finding out whether or not the technology described briefly by the BMS scientist was sound enough for YFP to enter into a technology transfer arrangement of some kind. That schema disintegrated, however, once it became clear that the scientist was there to sell trade secrets to YFP.

In contrast, the ongoing schema of Mano, as with virtually all undercover agents, was that the targets are predisposed to be corrupt and eventually would corroborate their guilt by knowingly and willfully agreeing to purchase the trade secrets offered by the BMS scientist.

The ensuing conversational encounters were a product of the conflict between these very different schemas, both of which endured throughout their exchanges until the final minutes of the meeting when Hsu and Dr. Ho were arrested. Supporting proof of these different schemas is found in their differing agendas, as revealed by the topics they introduced and their responses to the topics introduced by the other party.

AGENDAS

Chou clearly defined her agenda by her topic introductions on August 8, 1995, in the email to Mano cited above. She did not stray from this agenda throughout the two years of her correspondence

with Mano. Since in his responses to Chou's topics Mano continued to either ignore or be vague about how he could assist YFP's
efforts to collaborate, promote, or enter into a joint venture involving investment, marketing, and distribution, one can only deduce
that his agenda was very different from Chou's. As is often the case,
evidence of an agenda also can be found in what is not said. This
is hardly surprising, for the only agenda of undercover agents is to
capture illegal behavior on tape.

Before her August 8, 1995, exchange with Mano, Chou had
replied to him very infrequently, but when she did reply, her language made it clear that she tried very hard to repeat and clarify
her agenda while at the same time urging that they needed more
and clearer information before moving to any possible next stage in
their business relationship (emphasis added):

MAY 7, 1995
CHAO: I am writing to find specific products and technologies
 which you and your customers are interested in **marketing**
 to Taiwan.

JUNE 7, 1995
CHOU: Our services include **joint venture** opportunities,
 technology transfer opportunities.

NOVEMBER 4, 1995
CHOU: There are two to four Taiwanese companies interested
 in **licensing** promising techniques to make taxol.

NOVEMBER 23, 1995
CHOU: As I knew, BMS has exclusively licensed the Phyton's
 tissue culture techniques to make palitaxel. Can Phyton
 still be available to accept **contract researches** on projects developing tissues having high taxol content? I am

thinking possible opportunities for further proceeding as follows:

1. Providing fresh tissues
2. Technology **Consultancy** on Tissue Culture Scale up Technology
3. **Technology Transfer**
4. **Contract** Research
5. Others

To this Mano replied that technology transfer and licensing would be "difficult," saying, "If a licensing arrangement were possible for these technologies, the price would be in the millions of dollars." He concluded: "Thereafter, I will work on obtaining the specific technology." It is very clear that Chou had not asked him for "specific technology." He introduced this topic out of the blue with no evidence of encouragement from her. The agent then went on to suggest "confidentiality" in their communications until they could have a face-to-face meeting.

This exchange was followed by a long period in which Chou did not answer the several follow-up emails Mano continued to send to her. Finally, on January 4, 1996, she responded to Mano's expression, "obtaining the specific technology," in a way that suggested that her schema of their potential relationship did not allow her to understand his hint of illegality about it. Her response indicated that she interpreted the agent to mean some kind of "international cooperation business":

JANUARY 4, 1996

CHOU: Concerning to transfer proprietary technologies from Phyton for my clients, I would like to know what technologies or services Phyton can or is willing to offer for us. Could you contact your friends at Phyton to see what they are doing in their **international cooperation business?**

This time it was the agent who was slow to respond, so Chou wrote to him once more, repeating her continuing interest in collaboration with other companies:

JANUARY 20, 1996

CHOU: Concerning the Phyton contact, we are pretty open for any possible **collaborative project** in fields of tissue culture technology.

Still receiving no response, three months later Chou tried again:

APRIL 11, 1996

CHOU: How is your project in finding proper technologies and **partners** for my company? Do you remember in my last August letter about **distributing** bulk chemical for pharmaceutical companies who are interested in producing vials of taxol injection? Are you still interested?

Probably because Chou's agenda was contrary to his own, agent Mano ignored Chou's above three messages in his response on the following day. He wrote only about his plans for obtaining the technology, at the same time adding the needs for confidentiality and payment for such technology. With no response from Chou, three days later Mano gave her the bad news that Phyton already had a collaboration agreement with a company called Indena, while continuing to whittle away at Chou's agenda and trying to replace it with his own agenda of obtaining the technology for her.

By the end of April, Chou suggested an alternative arrangement with Mano, this one for her company to become a supplier for Phyton's products that Mano's business contacts might want to sell in the United States:

APRIL 30, 1996

CHOU: Since I have sources who are manufacturing Product #1 with purification greater than 98%, I would like to know if you are interested to **resell** Product #1 to your contacts in the USA.

It is not totally clear why Chou referred to taxol as Product #1 in this email, but it was not hard to figure out that since she had first talked about taxol and then later about paclitaxel, she might refer to these two products Product 1 and Product 2. The prosecution, however, believed she was using a coded language typical of criminals. Up to this point Mano had shot down all of Chou's alternative ways to collaborate with him. The agent's problem was that Chou's suggestions for doing business together were all perfectly legal. So, perhaps encouraged by her purported coded expression, once again Mano ignored the content of Chou's most recent legal suggestion and pushed even harder for a face-to-face meeting:

MAY 3, 1996

MANO: This transaction will be strictly person-to-person. In regard to the Chinese raw material question, I will provide the technical answers to these questions in exchange for good faith from your company that you are a serious buyer.

Mano's promise to provide a "technical answer" to Chou's question about the possibility of reselling products must have sounded odd to her (as it would probably sound odd to even a native speaker of English). His expression, "strictly person to person" was probably equally vague to her for it could convey a conventional face-to-face meeting as much as something illegal. But she was not a native speaker of English. What Chou failed to understand was Mano's unstated meaning: "I won't help you with your legitimate issues unless you agree to my illegitimate ones."

Mano's continuing undercover strategy was to deflect Chou's latest agenda item away from legally reselling products into something illegal. As described elsewhere (Shuy 2005), undercover agents often use the conversational strategies of ambiguously hinting about illegality in their exchanges, hoping their targets will bite. But when their ambiguous hints fail to yield a target's willingness to implicate themselves, many agents then try to couch their hints more clearly and strongly. But only when their targets fail to understand even their clearer hints do agents try to become clear and unambiguous about the illegality of the enterprise. Naturally, the agent's hinting strategy is more difficult to grasp for targets that are not a native speakers of English. The extent to which Chou understood Mano's meaning when he said he would provide "the technical answers to these questions" may not be clear, but in her next email to him she tried once again to be transparent about where her own interests reside:

MAY 4: 1996
CHOU: Just want you to know that I am not seeking for a formulation to make same product that are being sold to market, but interested in a formulation to make so-called 2nd generation product.

To this, Mano acknowledged that Chou was interested only in second-generation advancements but, in his usual fashion, he went on to ignore what he had just acknowledged and again returned to his contradictory topic asking, "What specific technology do you require?"

Another period of silence followed. Two months later Chou sent an internal memo to her superior at YFP, Kai-Lo Hsu. The relevant excerpts of this memo follow (emphasis added):

July 2, 1996, Memo from Chou to Hsu (written in English)

There are only two sources of Paclitaxel allowed by FDA:

(1) Extraction from yew tree bark BMS exclusive marketing right being expired in the end of Year 1997 and
(2) Product semi-synthesized from extraction of needles of yew back (BMS patent protection until Year 2011).

Mano has authorization from the technical supplier for **collaboration**, the tissue culture Bioreactor considered for the **technology transfer** is applicable to other fields. Paclitaxel pharmaceutical material produced from tissue culture may be provided to GENERIC DRUG companies without existing contract suppliers.

This internal memo reveals much about Chou's ongoing and unchanging agenda. Since up to this point, Hsu had not been very involved in Chou's relationship with agent Mano, Chou now explained the importance of the derivative Paclitaxel to him for the first time, adding something that did not appear in any of the evidence that she and Mano had discussed—that the patents held by Bristol-Myers Squibb soon would be expiring. She pointed out to Hsu that with the expiring patents in mind, YFP might be in a favorable position to collaborate in supplying technology transfer to manufacturers of generic drugs. Chou had still not agreed to do anything illegal, but the agent's communications made her sense that something may be amiss and this apparently was making her become uncomfortable. Therefore, in her YFP internal memo she also wrote:

JULY 17, 1996

I must protect myself well from potential difficulties arised from the licensing. The normal procedures of selling technologies will include:

Clear documentation for **technology transfer** with no legal complication whatsoever. It almost needs to come up with a proposal for **licensing.** As you may see, one can keep asking a lot of questions about the technology since we are working in the dark. If we forget something, we may end up with crippled technology. No one can accept this type of deal. If he wants to sell, let us do it formally and normally.

This memo offers still more evidence of Chou's state of mind at this point in her discussions with agent Mano. She now appeared to be nearly giving up on the idea of licensing, but she still held open the possibility of technology transfer, as long as it was purchased "formally and normally." The government apparently believed that her use of "technology transfer" meant purchasing trade secrets, but such an interpretation was not supported by her use of that term in the contexts in which she used it to refer to a legal transfer of technology.

In September 1996, Chou recycled her older idea that YFP could *sell* a product to a buyer that Mano had in mind, as opposed to accepting Mano's suggestion that YFP buy technology:

SEPTEMBER 8, 1996

CHOU: Concerning your offer of Product #1 of 60% concentration for buyers, are your contacts interested in this offer?

Apparently discouraged about his correspondence with Chou, later that year Mano stopped writing to her but increased the number of his emails to Hsu, and in one of them Hsu responded:

NOVEMBER 5, 1996

HSU: Our R&D group is worrying about their language barrier may hinder their effectiveness in the **technology transfer phase**.

Mano's response on that same day made no mention of Hsu's use of "technology transfer phase." If there was ever a good time for the agent to have been clear and unambiguous about what he meant by the expression (probably "illegal purchase of technology") as opposed to Hsu's understanding of the common business term, this would have been a very good time for him to have done so. But he didn't. Instead, Mano again chose to let his interpretation remain ambiguous.

This exchange was followed by more silence until March 1997, when Mano had finally convinced Chou that they needed to have a meeting. Chou returned to the topic of licensing once more in another YFP internal memo in which she used "license" seven times, three of which are in this excerpt:

March 13, 1997, excerpt of Chou's memo to YFP company head

The **licensor** is a bench scientist in company B and has access to company P's technical data and procedures and know-how. It is adaptable to other aspects of identification, development and commercialization of valuable compounds of plan origin. Hsu, you, and I shall be working closely and confidentially to match **licensor and licensee**.

Chou's internal memos continued to refer to the possibility that YFP could obtain a license to work with paclitaxel, including one memo on March 17 that referred to licensing thirteen times. Her March 21 memo to Hsu continued to discuss licensing six times and her April 23 memo to Hsu said that this would be "win-win to both the licensor and the buyer." But by the following day, Chou's email to Mano was less optimistic:

APRIL 23, 1997, EMAIL TO MANO

CHOU: I am worry we will not really attain the contact's supports during the **technology transfer** process and after sales and my kind of arrangement for you may lead to nowhere. It may happen that we gain nothing after he is paid. How can we legally protected? Once a **licensor** is matched for my contact, such a **licensor's** desire, John, I would like you to know that we are looking for a **licensor** who is really interested.

Chou's plea for Mano to explain how she could be "legally protected" went unanswered, as usual, for that was contrary to Mano's goal. Nevertheless, Chou prepared a Feasibility Study for Technology Transfer for YFP on April 24, 1997, in which *technology transfer* is mentioned thirteen times and *licensing* twelve times. The prosecution relied heavily on one paragraph of this study, in which Chou mentioned trade secrets:

APRIL 24, 1997, IN FEASIBILITY STUDY

CHOU: Since involves probably trade secrets of BMS it shall be predetermined to protect execution of the substantial production, including clear and written documentation exchanges for the technology transfer. We intend to formally inquire the possibility of technology cooperation, licensing, or joint venture directly with Phyton.

In light of all Chou's previous insistence to Mano that they do this work legally (she referred to licensing six times in this feasibility study), her use of "trade secrets" here was puzzling. The defense attorney called on a native Chinese linguist, Dr. Weiping Wu, to explain and report Chou's possible meaning in this context. At that time Dr. Wu held a PhD in linguistics and was working at the Center for Applied Linguistics in Washington DC, where he was involved in developing language testing materials in Mandarin and Cantonese. Shortly after this he was invited to become head of the Yale in China program at the Chinese University of Hong Kong, which position he has held to this day. In this case he called on his expertise in assessing and testing meaning across cultures and languages to explain that Chou's expression, "since involves probably trade secrets" could be understood to mean "since there could be an accusation of a trade secrecy violation." Chou's English was fairly good, but not good enough to capture subtleties like this.

On May 2, 1997, Hsu emailed Mano that he would be in the United States on other business and could work a meeting with him into his schedule while he was in Philadelphia with an associate, Ms. Wang. But before the meeting took place, Hsu made clear his purpose for it:

MAY 2, 1997

HSU: The purpose of the meeting is to evaluate the usefulness of the technology to the buyer's organization. However, I do not think Ms. Wang will be able to make the final decision of the purchase in the meeting.

Chou echoed Hsu's purpose for the meeting in a telephone call to Mano ten days later, and Mano appeared to agree with her completely:

MAY 12, 1997

CHOU: He [Hsu] only want to uh see to be how's the feasibility. Just a general meeting. But you have to let him know it's just a general meeting. We don't have a meeting to see his the bunch of information. Exchange of concerns.

AGENT: I understand that—a general meeting.

Hsu's indication that there would be no final purchase at this meeting is consistent with his earlier statements to Mano that the purpose of the meeting was to evaluate the potential usefulness of any technology they might receive, as both Chou and Hsu had consistently put it, in the form of a cooperative agreement, licensure, or as a distributor. But the speech act of agreeing to any type of relationship was not to be placed on the table. Mano continued to insist that his own BMS scientist would describe the technology in detail at the meeting, to which Hsu continued to explain that this was not what he wanted to know:

MAY 22, 1997, EMAIL FROM HSU TO AGENT MANO

HSU: The owner expressed that the final decision has to be made by the buyer himself. Since no money is likely to be exchanged, I will suggest you contacts do not reveal the whole documentation and only show enough to prove the worthfulness of the technology.

As usual, Mano ignored Hsu's statement, emailing back and asking him what the buyers are interested in so that they may bring the appropriate documents to prove its value. The agent continued his strategy of agreeing verbally with the wishes of his targets, but, as will be seen, doing so was a camouflage for what he apparently planned to do at that meeting. He vaguely repeated this agreement to Hsu as they talked before the meeting began:

JUNE 14, 1997

MANO: We're not going to talk about a transaction.

HSU: Right. They just want to know—

MANO (FINISHING HSU'S SENTENCE FOR HIM): —to evaluate the transaction.

On June 14, 1997, the meeting that agent Mano had been trying to create for many months finally took place at a Philadelphia hotel. It was attended by agent Mano, Hsu, Ms. Wang (a lab scientist at YFP), and Dr. Chester Ho, a technology expert consultant who was Ms. Wang's friend. Hsu asked Dr. Ho to accompany them to help determine the scientific accuracy of whatever would be discussed. Ms. Chou was unable to travel to America to join the group. Since at the end of this meeting Hsu and Ho were arrested, it is important to determine whether or not they reached any illegal agreement with Mano and whether they understood that an illegal agreement was even on the table.

As revealed by the topics introduced, Hsu's agenda was to learn by way of his consultant, Dr. Ho, whether the science underlying any possible proposed affiliation was sound and potentially worth it for YFP to enter into any type of relationship. The two years of off-and-on discussion had ended with Hsu still hopeful for some kind of joint venture, licensing, or, as he put it, "technology transfer," a term that the prosecution subsequently tried to use against him.

Agent Mano tried to make it clear to Hsu that none of these suggested relationships were possible, but Hsu's poor English ability did not seem to let him understand this. Even more problematic,

Mano's vague hints that this was actually an illegal process apparently went right past Hsu, for his responses gave no indication that he caught the hints. Before the meeting took place, Chou's last email to Mano made it clear that YFP was not interested in pursuing this relationship further. Despite this, Hsu remained willing to meet with Mano to find out exactly what if anything could be salvaged. This is why he asked Dr. Ho to accompany him to determine whether the science underlying the project was sound.

Dr. Chester Ho's agenda was to understand the general principles of the technology, in order to determine whether or not it would be worthwhile for YFP to be involved in any possible joint ventures. Ho had not met Hsu beforehand and he did not represent himself as knowledgeable about business matters. He spoke Taiwanese natively but he also spoke English with almost native speaker skills.

Ms. Wang, a biologist who spoke no English at all, was asked to be there to help Hsu understand what the BMS scientist was saying, although she had to get Dr. Ho to first explain it to her in Taiwanese.

Mano's agenda remained the same throughout the two years of discussion with Chou and Hsu. As with virtually all undercover agents, it was solely to capture crime on tape. Mano continued to offer confusing and sometimes conflicting statements to Hsu and Ho, at one point denying his own previous comment relating to what Ho and Wang knew:

> MANO: Do they understand the nature of the transaction?
> HSU: So you're talking about a transaction?
> MANO: No. I know you mentioned that we're not going to talk about the transaction.
> HSU: No, they don't even know the background.
> MANO: They just want to evaluate the technology.

HSU: Evaluate the technology. I have never worked with them. And they don't have any backgrounds or resources even making up the technology. I think he (Dr. Ho) has a mixed chemical/biochemical kind of background. He knows about Taxol, but never has he had any real hands-on experience. Just talking.

The BMS scientist then described how BMS developed the technology and sold ownership of that technology to Phyton to commercialize it. Phyton was now waiting for the FDA approval for commercial use. Mano and the BMS scientist repeatedly offered to show Hsu and Ho the documents they brought along with them, even though as the meeting started Hsu had made it clear that they did not want to see any documents and Mano had agreed to this. Hsu quickly redirected the conversation back to talking rather than reviewing documents. The BMS scientist obliged as he explained to Dr. Ho the scientific process that the BMS scientists had followed, using the words "confidentiality" several times. When this part of the conversation neared its close, Mano asked if they were getting the right answers for their questions. Hsu responded:

HSU: We do have quite a bit of concern now. We discussed that. There is only one single purpose on our mind. That is we want to do this thing to go and in a safe fashion. We don't want to hurt anyone. There are still some technical things probably that we still have to go back and talk about. Is there is any other ways of doing business here; could it be other ways?

MANO: Do you mean like technology transfer?

HO: Right. I'm just saying is there a way here that we can all collectively think about that?

MANO: There are two chances for a start-up company to get this technology; it's either to develop it themselves or to obtain a license for it.

BMS SCIENTIST: About technology transfer, that's done with a cadre of hundreds of people representing their particular technical expertise, teaching the other company their techniques and methods. This is not, it can't be done.

HO: Mr. Mano, that's actually the point that Kai-Lo was raising. Then you started raising, you said "let's talk about technology." That's interesting. You're going to block other people from using it?

BMS SCIENTIST: That is correct.

MANO: But if a competent company obtains this technology, they will become a competitor of Bristol-Myers. If it has the guidance.

HO: Let's say we don't have to be their competitors. Give them 20% of their equity. We're talking about 150 kilos of Taxol we can sell (in the Asian market) but Bristol-Myers can't. We're part of Bristol-Myers. So I guess forming a sort of joint venture, if at all possible with Bristol-Myers, is not such a bad idea.

MANO: Bristol-Myers has nothing to gain by that situation.

HO: Yes they would. They can buy the yew (from us). Then why would they need to spend ten million dollars for those guys at Phyton? If you view it as a subsidiary, or a joint venture, a company away from the company, I don't know why Bristol-Myers would be so—

MANO (INTERRUPTING): Look, this gentleman is not here to represent the company. He is here representing himself. So he's not in a position to go back and negotiate anything, other than how much he's going to get paid to steal this technology for whoever wants to buy it.

HO: (long pause) As a hypothetical question, my answer would be that it's very, very unlikely that our company would be interested.

MANO: I think if it was possible two years ago, we would have already gone down that road, if it was possible. I think you now understand the situation.

HO: Okay, now I know.

A snapshot view of the competing agendas showed that Chou and Hsu clearly had in mind a relationship first with Mano and later Bristol-Myers that would involve them in licensing, technology transfer, marketing, or some form of joint venture. In sharp contrast, the single agenda of Mano was that YFP would purchase trade secrets stolen from Bristol-Myers. The language evidence made it even clearer that with Dr. Ho's help, Hsu rejected Mano's offer for them to steal Bristol-Myers's trade secrets.

SPEECH ACTS

In cases involving the theft or potential theft of trade secrets, the required speech acts are offering, promising, requesting, agreeing, admitting, denying, and advising. Although some speech acts can be expressed indirectly, in order to achieve mutual understanding they still must be uttered felicitously and unambiguously. In this potential business transaction speech event, Mano functioned as the intermediary of a potential seller while Chou and Hsu functioned as the potential buyers. Mano's primary role was to offer goods and services that Chou and Hsu could be expected to promise, agree, or deny to purchase. Dr. Ho's role was to offer technical advice to Hsu at the meeting in which Mano and the BMS scientist represented the technology underlying the relationship YFP might establish.

Space does not permit including all of the speech acts used in these many exchanges over a two-year period, but they are represented here in summary form.

Offering

Mano's job was to broker the sale of a product or service to YFP. Chou and Hsu consistently said that the service they were interested in was to purchase a licensing arrangement, to be commercially involved in marketing BMS products in Asia, or to engage in joint venture or technology transfer between BMS and their company. Mano apparently tried to make it clear that such offers were not possible, but since he was not clear enough about what he did have to offer, Chou and Hsu kept repeating their willingness to agree that their offer related to licensing, a joint venture, marketing, or technology transfer. Chou finally gave up and stopped communicating with Mano, but the agent managed to convince Hsu to meet him the next time Hsu was in the United States and Hsu agreed. Finally, when Dr. Ho joined Hsu at the June 14, 1997, meeting, his near-native English ability enabled him to finally understand what Mano had been so indirectly offering. As noted above, agent Mano for the first time made his own offer clear and unambiguous:

JUNE 14, 1997, MEETING
MANO: He's [the BMS scientist] not in a position to go back and negotiate anything other than how much he's going to be paid to **steal** this technology for whoever wants to buy it.

To Mano's offer, Dr. Ho spoke on behalf of Hsu, rejecting it:

HO: As a hypothetical question, my answer would be that it's very, very unlikely that our company would be interested.

The targets' language indicated that they had not understood Mano's cryptic proposal offers until the above exchange in which the BMS scientist had helped make it clear for the first time. Even the BMS scientist understood that Ho's "very unlikely" meant the offer was rejected, but apparently the prosecutor did not.

Promising

Chou promised Mano that she would communicate the agent's cryptic information to her superior at YFP, and she apparently tried to do so. She never promised to steal trade secrets, however, and when she began to suspect something amiss, she said as much on April 24, some two months before the Philadelphia meeting, in the passage cited above. Hsu promised nothing except to meet with Mano, and even then he promised only to learn something about the technology the agent claimed to make available to them. Oddly in this business transaction speech event, Mano promised little or nothing himself.

Requesting

Chou and Hsu constantly requested general information from agent Mano, but received back nothing specific enough for them to act upon. Mano ignored virtually every request, most likely because an answer would not further his agenda of capturing the Taiwanese in illegality. Toward the end of their two years of exchanges, Mano requested a face-to-face meeting, and finally got Hsu's agreement to do so. During this case-culminating meeting, Dr. Ho asked many questions of the BMS scientist about the technical issues involved in the BMS's processes, because that was why Hsu invited him to the meeting. When Mano finally interrupted Ho and told him that the BMS scientist represented only himself rather than his company and that the deal actually was to steal the technology from BMS, Ho stopped requesting information and said on behalf of Hsu, "okay, now I know," and "it is very, very unlikely that our company would be interested."

Agreeing

Most important in this case was that Chou or Hsu never agreed to Mano's cryptic hints that the deal involved stealing trade secrets. Based on the language they used, it is equally clear that they gave no evidence that they understood his hints of illegality at all. As noted above, they were seeking a more benign business relationship with Mano that related to licensing, collaboration with other companies, marketing, or what they called "technology transfer," an expression that apparently held a different meanings for Hsu than it did for Mano, as will be discussed later under the section about smoking guns.

Denying

Mano didn't deny many of Hsu's and Chou's requests as much as he simply ignored them. Eventually he did deny that both licensing and collaboration were possible, but his denials apparently didn't register with Chou and Hsu because they kept on requesting the same things anyway. Chou began to suspect that something was wrong and then denied that her company would do any business with Mano, at which point he stopped dealing with her, instead turning his attention to Hsu, who had even less knowledge about technology issues than Chou. For that reason, Mano probably considered him an easier mark. As noted above, Dr. Ho clearly denied that FYP could go further with Mano, at which point their discussion ended.

Advising

Dr. Ho's only role in this case was to advise Hsu about the technical skills and effectiveness provided by the BMS scientist at the Philadelphia meeting. From the BMS scientist's answers to Ho's probing questions, Ho agreed that this scientist's lab procedures indicated that he was very competent.

Like the preceding snapshots of the speech event, schemas, and agendas, this snapshot of the speech acts did not support the prosecution's stance in this case.

CONVERSATIONAL STRATEGIES

In an earlier book, I described a number of conversational strategies commonly used in undercover operations (Shuy 2005). Such strategies are used to move the agent's goal along more smoothly and to advance the agent's agenda on tape. Conversational strategies fall loosely into the category of rhetorical persuasion, but some of them can persuade in an unfair manner. Mano's four major conversational strategies were (1) the use of ambiguity; (2) withholding important information that could reveal illegality to the target; (3) camouflaging illegality to make it look legal; and (4) blocking the targets from having the information needed to protect themselves from trouble.

Agent Mano used the ambiguity strategy continuously with Chou throughout their emails. Normally, an ambiguous comment causes a listener either to request clarification or try to infer what the speaker meant. It sounds very simple and logical to request clarification when we don't understand something, but this speech act is not always that simple or easy to accomplish, especially cross-culturally. When faced with Mano's ambiguous statements,

Chou's technique was to not request clarification, but rather to simply repeat her request for information after she didn't understand Mano's vague or ambiguous statements. Her responses demonstrate that she seldom accurately inferred what Mano's hints apparently meant. Nevertheless, she finally figured out that Mano was up to no good and extracted herself from the discussion. Hsu was more susceptible to Mano's inferences, but his language indicated that he inferred them as good intentions, which is one reason he brought Dr. Ho with him, not only to help him with the technology presentation but also to benefit from Ho's much better English skills.

Perhaps more important, by not answering Chou's many questions, Mano at the same time employed the conversational strategy of withholding important information that would help Chou determine what their proposed relationship actually would be. He also interrupted Hsu's response that appeared to be negative before he managed to finish his sentence. Mano's other effective conversational strategy was to camouflage the illegality of what he was hinting about until their final meeting, at which time he made it clear that this was trade secrets theft.

Snapshots of the undercover agents' conversational strategies do not establish a target's innocence, but they can offer important information to juries about the unfair techniques used during the investigation.

SMOKING GUNS

The government's indictment pointed to the smoking gun evidence it planned to use at trial in which Hsu, Chou, and Ho were charged with eleven counts of wire fraud, conspiracy, foreign and interstate travel to facilitate commercial bribery, conspiracy to steal trade secrets, attempted theft of trade secrets, and aiding and abetting. The prosecution focused on the following smoking gun expressions.

Technology Transfer

Perhaps the most important smoking gun cited by the government in this case actually was not a smoking gun at all. Chou and Hsu spoke regularly about being interested in *technology transfer* and even Dr. Ho suggested it in the final meeting. The agent and the prosecution team apparently considered this term to mean an illegal transfer of technology. In contrast, the defendants used this technical term, also called *transfer of technology (TOT)* and *technology commercialization,* in its common and conventional way—the process of transferring skills, knowledge, technology, methods of manufacturing used by governments, universities and businesses to ensure that scientific and technological developments are made available to a wider range of users in order to develop into new applications and uses. Technology transfer can be accomplished through licensing agreements, joint ventures, and partnerships, especially when the host organization does not have the needed resources or skills to develop the product or its distribution further. Many companies and universities have offices of technology transfer.

As noted in the passages cited above, Chou, Hsu, and Ho used the terms, *technology transfer, licensing,* and *joint venture* throughout their communications with agent Mano. It was not until their final meeting in Philadelphia that the defendants had the opportunity to reject the proposed deal after he the agent finally revealed his true meaning about their relationship and said that the deal was to *steal* the technology. This is an example of the prosecution inferring the meaning of technology transfer that is simply not supported by the way the business world uses it.

We'll Get Another Way

On February 27, 1996, the agent explained to Hsu that joint ventures and licensing were very expensive and contrary to the interest of Bristol-Myers, after which Hsu said, "We'll get another way." The prosecution apparently inferred that when Hsu said this, he meant he wanted to steal the trade secrets. This decontextualized inference was not supported by anything Hsu, Chou, or Ho said before, during, or after this statement. At their Philadelphia meeting, when the agent finally was clear and explicit that he was talking about stealing trade secrets, Hsu and Ho rejected the idea outright. The prosecution's inference here is a classic example of how the overall context of language defines the individual words that are used. Apparently the prosecutor's schema of guilt prevented him from considering the many other possibilities that Hsu could have meant when he said "another way," including benign ones.

Confidentiality

Although there are some semantic similarities between *confidentiality* and *secrecy*, the latter is more associated with overall illegality and covertness while *confidentiality* is used more with situations of intimacy and privacy. Many business discussions require protective confidentiality rather than covert secrecy. Until the very end of his two years of correspondence with Chou and Hsu, the agent had never mentioned stealing "secrets." Up to that point Mano used only "confidentiality," and very generously at that. The word *secret* might have tipped Hsu off that this could be illegal, but *confidentiality* camouflaged Mano's intention and made it sound benign.

This distinction did not seem to bother the government, however, for the indictment claimed that between February 27 and March 12, 1997, the agent "told Chou and Hsu that a corrupt scientist at BMS was willing to sell them their secret Taxol technology."

The language evidence collected during that period simply does not support this charge. The BMS scientist was never previously described to the defendants as "corrupt" and nowhere did either the agent or the scientist say that he was willing to "sell them their *secret* technology."

The prosecution further claimed that on April 23, 1997, Chou "acknowledged that payment would constitute theft of secrets." Nothing like this can be found in the government's own evidence. In her email Chou's language indicated very clearly that she wanted to protect herself from any possible criminal behavior. There she repeated what she had said earlier—that she wanted to conduct a transaction that was perfectly legal and above board. Again, the prosecution inferred meaning for which there is simply no evidence.

The prosecution also said that on May 1, 1997, some six weeks before the meeting in Philadelphia, Hsu "acknowledged that purchase of secrets from BMS is illegal and promised to keep this confidential," adding that Dr. Ho also "understood the nature of the transaction." It is difficult to imagine how the government could have come to those conclusions if they had careful examined their own language evidence, where these statements simply did not occur. Again, the government tried to make a case on totally inaccurate representations of the actual words used.

The indictment of Dr. Ho was also based on the prosecution's inferences about the smoking gun expressions uttered during that final meeting. As they began to talk, agent Mano asked Hsu if Dr. Ho understood the nature of the transaction and the need for "confidentiality." Hsu replied that he had already explained "this" to Ho. The question here was exactly what Hsu had explained to his consultant. If Hsu had not himself understood that they were involved in illegality, there was no way he could have communicated this to Dr. Ho. And it is equally unlikely that Dr. Ho, who before this meeting did not even know Hsu and who had no previous relationship with YFP, would have been willing to engage in the meeting had he known all the time that it was for stealing trade secrets.

CONCLUSION OF THE CASE

Linguistic analysis of the evidence in this case made it clear that (1) the government relied heavily on its own inferences derived from the exchanges between agent Mano and the defendants; (2) that the prosecution mischaracterized what was said in its own tape-recorded evidence; and (3) that the prosecution misperceived why Hsu and Chou were not clearer in telling did Mano "no" more strongly. The report made by my colleague, Dr. Wu, he explained the indirectness in the cultural patterns of Asians during the speech act of refusing.

The Government's Reliance on Inferences

The agent's undercover strategy of hinting and alluding might have worked a bit better in cases involving targets that had native English-speaking abilities. The language evidence demonstrates clearly, however, that his hinting didn't succeed in this case. But Mano's intelligence gathering was no more flawed about this than was the prosecutor's intelligence analysis.

One way to deal with a prosecution based on inferences is to assemble the snapshot analyses of the speech event, schemas, agendas, speech acts, and conversational strategies used by the agent into a panoramic view of the government's own evidence. First, the analysis demonstrated that the language used by the agent and the defendants provided evidence that they talked as though they were in different speech events. The defendants' language conveyed that they were participating in a business transaction speech event while agent tried to make their exchanges appear to be an illegal theft of trade secrets speech event. Unless participants realize which speech event they are in, there is bound to be lack of mutual understanding. This lack of mutual understanding caused both the defendants and the agent to have conflicting schemas about what they were discussing. Their language made this difference evident throughout their exchanges up to the final meeting, when finally there was a merging of schemas that caused the defendants to reject the agent's proposal. At that point the agent stopped providing inferential evidence and once it was clear to the defendants what was happening, the prosecution's case fell apart.

Parallel to their schemas were their different agendas, as revealed by the topics they introduced and their responses to the topics introduced by the other participants. Chou and Hsu introduced topics that related only to their legal involvement through licensure, a joint venture, contract research, technological consulting, technology transfer, or possible distribution of BMS's research and products. But the agent rejected these ideas and left Hsu unclear about what he had in mind for that final meeting to yield. Hsu invited Dr. Ho to accompany him to help him understand technological issues for which Hsu had no background or knowledge. During that meeting the agent and Hsu introduced contradictory topics. Hsu insisted that they not see any documents, but instead to talk only about technological issues. No matter. Mano brought the documents anyway, although Hsu and Ho managed to avoid receiving and reviewing them. Again, the agent's case based on inferences of guilt was gutted.

A criminal case like this requires the occurrence of the felicitous speech acts of offering, requesting, promising, accepting, and denying/rejecting. Mano made his offer unclear and ambiguous until the final meeting, when the defendants rejected it. Chou and Hsu made a multitude of requests for information that Mano ignored. They did not agree to the agent's offer once he finally made it clear. Dr. Ho's only role was to advise Hsu about what he began to understand about the technology that BMS used. Examination of the speech acts used in this case might have been sufficient for the government's intelligence analyst to see that inferences would not win the case for the prosecution.

The conversational strategies of agent Mano demonstrated that he must have realized that his many hints were not advancing his agenda. When agents feel the need to be ambiguous, to withhold information that the targets would need in order to understand, and to camouflage illegality by making it appear to be legal, it is a sure sign that they know their hints have not been succeeding. Simply pointing this out to the jury or judge can produce a crucial advantage to the defense.

All that remained were the alleged smoking guns that prosecutors usually rely on to make their cases. As noted above, the three major smoking guns cited by the prosecution were based on their inferences about the meanings of *technology transfer*, their responses to the agent's use of *confidentiality*, and Hsu's statement, "We'll get it another way." These were all discussed above and demonstrated to have failed as smoking gun evidence.

The Government's Mischaracterization of Its Own Evidence

Comparison and contrast is one of the basic principles of the scientific method. It was surprisingly easy to compare and contrast what the indictment asserted with what was actually on the tape recordings.

This comparison speaks for itself and clearly demonstrates how the prosecution mischaracterized its own evidence.

Indictment	Language Evidence
Chou asked for information about technology	Chou explored the possibility of joint venture, licensing, and technology transfer
Agent represented that the BMS scientist would be willing to sell trade secrets	BMS scientist explained various lab procedures in general and represented nothing of the kind
On May 1, 1997, the agent told Hsu that this was illegal	Illegality was not suggested until the last meeting on June 14 at which time defendants rejected the idea
Hsu communicated with agent to meet in Philadelphia	Agent insisted on meeting because Hsu would then be in the United States on other business
Hsu attempted to bribe BMS scientist	Hsu tried to purchase distribution rights from BMS
Chou negotiated purchase price of stolen technology	Chou negotiated purchase price of distribution rights
Hsu and Ho did not reveal their true identities to scientist during the meeting	The agent suggested they use only first names during the meeting
Hsu and Ho reviewed confidential documents	Hsu insisted that he did not want to see the documents; only talk. They did not review documents the agent brought with him
Agent represented that a corrupt BMS scientist was willing to sell trade secrets	Agent represented that a BMS would describe the lab processes
Defendants promised to keep secret their effort to bribe the corrupt BMS scientist	They agreed to agent's request to keep their discussions about technology transfer confidential

Hsu and Chou Never Said "No" to the Agent

My Chinese linguist colleague in this case, Dr. Weiping Wu, was prepared to explain the cultural differences between American and Taiwanese politeness interactions, which included the Taiwanese speaker's reluctance to say "no" because they regard direct negative answers as impoliteness and a failure to save face for the other person. He pointed out that it is far more polite to offer alternatives, put off making a negative decision, or change the subject altogether in order to avoid saying "no." This is precisely what Chou and Hsu did. Dr. Wu also pointed out that the Chinese desire to be polite, together with Hsu's and Chou's lack of competence in English, led them to respond to Mano in ways that didn't make clear what they had in mind. Hsu, for example, tended to reply to questions positively even before he understood exactly what was being asked of him. For example, when Mano asked Hsu if he understood the transaction, Hsu said "exactly, exactly." Then he caught himself and asked, "And, uh, we're talking about the transaction?" Note that he agreed saying "exactly" before he requested clarification about what Mano was talking about. In sharp contrast, when Mano finally made it clear to Dr. Ho that the transaction was about "stealing" trade secrets, he and Hsu backed off quickly and clearly.

CONCLUSION OF THE CASE

As noted earlier, the agent's undercover strategy of hinting and alluding might have worked better in cases that involved targets that had native English-speaking abilities. The language evidence demonstrates clearly, however, that hinting and alluding didn't succeed in this case. But again, Mano's intelligence gathering was no more flawed than the prosecutor's intelligence analysis. They both inferred things that their own evidence could not support.

The indictment revealed the government's focus on what it believed to be the defendants' knowing and willing "scheme and artifice to defraud by depriving Bristol-Myers its right to the honest and faithful services of its employee by offering to pay bribes to an employee to obtain secret proprietary information owned by and licensed to Bristol-Myers, that is, Taxol technology, without permission of Bristol-Myers." It would prove difficult for the prosecutor to overcome the fact that his intelligence analysis of the evidence was flawed by being based primarily on inferences, on mischaracterizations of what Hsu and Chou actually said, and on a misperception about why Hsu and Chou did not say "no" more clearly.

Inferences may be useful unless the evidence proves them wrong. Misstatements and mischaracterization of what was actually said in the recorded evidence is inexcusable at best. It remains unclear why the prosecution was willing to infer guilt from evidence that did not support it but at the same time was unwilling to infer Hsu's and Chou's legal intentions when they did not express a flat out "no."

Reprising the adverbial modifiers that characterize fraudulent language noted in chapter 1, there is no language evidence showing that the defendants used their power unconscientiously. If anything, this could be ascribed to agent Mano who, unlike the defendants, was the one who withheld information, misrepresented, acted surreptitiously, knowingly deceived, and spoke without belief in what he said. Finally, after closely examining the snapshots provided by the speech event, schemas, agendas, speech acts, and conversational agendas, the defense attorneys were able to assemble them to find explanations to the prosecution's alleged smoking guns.

Although Ms. Chou was included in the indictment, she was not prosecuted because she chose to remain in Taiwan, a country that has no reciprocal extradition agreement with the United States.

Not surprisingly, the defense attorney was successful in getting the prosecutor to drop all of the charges against Dr. Ho before trial, leaving Hsu as the only defendant present.

The trial never took place because on March 31, 1999, Kai-Lo Hsu's attorney negotiated a plea of guilty to only one count of conspiracy to commit trade secret theft, for which Hsu was given what his lawyer called a slap-on-the-wrist fine of $10,000 with no probation attached, after which Hsu left the United States never to return again. The prosecutor dropped all of the other ten charges in the indictment and Hsu was given no jail sentence.

[6]

MONEY LAUNDERING (FRAUD)

Money laundering refers to various processes used to knowingly, willfully, and fraudulently hide the sources of money acquired and used illegally, as in money related to the purchase and sale of prohibited drugs, in carrying out terrorist activities, or simply to avoid paying taxes.

The crime of money laundering is considered to have three stages. First, cash is placed into financial institutions or converted into negotiable instruments in ways that avoid being detected. The cash is routed through fronts such as cashier's checks, money orders, traveler's checks, jewelry businesses, or check cashing companies. Or it can even be smuggled into the country. Then the ownership of the money is layered by fraudulently concealing it to avoid an auditing trail, usually by transferring the money in and out of offshore bank accounts by electronic wire transfers of funds. The high volume of daily wire transfers and stock trading makes it difficult for the government to monitor and distinguish legal from illegal transfers. Finally, the cash is integrated into the legitimate financial system, giving the appearance of legality.

Money launderers often set up anonymous shell or holding companies in countries where the depositor's right to confidentiality is freely granted and where huge cash deposits are not questioned.

These companies then move the money around in ways that can help them avoid paying US taxes. Some wealthy individuals use offshore banks simply to avoid taxes although the extent to which this is legitimate or ethical is debated. But unless it can be proved that their money was derived illegally or that they are violating existing tax laws, the process often appears to be beyond the reach of law enforcement.

In 1970 the US Congress passed the Bank Secrecy Act that required banks to report any financial transactions of $10,000 or more. This Act was followed by the Money Laundering Control Act of 1986, which made money laundering a federal crime. The US Patriot Act of 2001 then expanded the reporting requirements of banks and other types of financial institutions.

Prosecutors have to prove that the concealment of money is for criminal purposes rather than legal goals. The federal statute concerning the criminal fraud of money laundering, 18 U.S.C 1956A3, reads in part as follows:

(3) Whoever with the intent—
    (A) to promote the carrying on of specified unlawful activity;
    (B) to conceal or disguise the nature, location, source, ownership or control of property believed to be the proceeds of specified unlawful activity; or
    (C) to avoid a transaction reporting requirement under State or Federal law, conducts or attempts to conduct a financial transaction involving property represented by a law enforcement officer to be the proceeds of specified unlawful activity, or property used to conduct or facilitate specified unlawful activity . . .

Although the word, "fraud," does not appear in the name or words of this law, acts of knowingly and willfully avoiding detection, concealing, disguising, and avoiding legal procedures make fraudulent language central. The money laundering statute contains the operative words used in definitions of *fraud*, outlined in chapter 1, including *promote, conceal, disguise, avoid*, and *unlawful activity*. Since laundering money is a physical action that is usually accompanied by talk or writing, the ways that suspects' use spoken and written language to accomplish their illegal promotion, concealment, disguising, and avoidance noted in the statute are subject to linguistic analysis.

Because those who launder money are usually careful to not leave traces in writing, many of the government's investigations of money laundering involve spoken language captured and recorded during undercover sting operations that are based on suspicion that certain suspects have laundered money in the past and will do so again when given the opportunity. Alternatively, the government also may simply troll among financial advisers and bankers whose work might be considered ripe for money laundering but who to that point have not been accused of such crimes.

Money laundering comes in many sizes, ranging from capturing car dealers who fail to report cash payments of over $10,000 for selling cars during undercover sting operations, to multi-million dollar transactions made by international financing specialists whose job is to help clients hide their money in overseas banks. Sometimes the laundered money acquired from illegal drug transactions helps drug dealers hide their sales of cocaine and at other times it results in different types of cash exchanges.

The case of *United States v. Karl Burkhardt* (96-00313-A) appeared to have originated in the mind of the government informant. Similar to the case of Hu, Chou, and Ho (chapter 5), this operation can be categorized as trolling for crime, because any evidence of Burkhardt's alleged predisposition was reported by the informant, not by any evidence that the government discovered when they tape-recorded Burkhardt's language. The fact that the government had no evidence of Burkhardt's previous bad acts meant that the investigator had to make a strong and convincing effort to capture any illegal intentions revealed by Burkhardt while his conversations were being tape-recorded.

The following description of the linguistic analysis did not lead to a positive result for Burkhardt because he eventually pleaded guilty to most of the charges the government made against him. Nevertheless I've decided to present this description as an example of how such analysis could be used in such cases. I provided it to Burkhardt's lawyers, but either my analysis was unconvincing or there was other important evidence in the case not made available to me. It is impossible for linguistic consultants to become aware of all of the issues in cases in which their single task is to analyze only the language evidence provided to them. At any rate, the tape-recorded evidence was all I was given to analyze in Burkhardt's case.

BACKGROUND

Karl Burkhardt was born in Switzerland and owned homes in both Zurich and Florida. He was a lawyer who simultaneously acquired great wealth as a specialist in international financing and investment counseling. When in the mid-1990s the US Drug Enforcement Agency began to intensify its search for money laundering involving cocaine sales in Virginia, one of the DEA agents called on the services of an informant named Manuel who had helped him in other cases and conveniently lived in that area.

In January 1996, Manuel notified the agent that he had met a man named Fernando who told him that he knew of a local company that supplies cocaine and that he also knew of a Swiss banker named Karl Burkhardt who could arrange money laundering services for that operation. During an unrecorded meeting the agent then talked with Fernando, who claimed that Burkhardt would be willing to set up an offshore corporation and a Swiss bank account. The following day, Fernando telephoned the agent saying Burkhardt had told him that he was agreeable to doing such a deal for him. Note that to this point these phone calls and meetings were not verifiable since they were not tape-recorded.

On February 5 informants Manuel and Fernando flew to Florida to meet with Burkhardt at this home. The DEA agent, who eventually assumed the role of a drug dealer, was not present and since this meeting also was not recorded, the predicate for the investigation was still based entirely on the report of Fernando, who claimed that during this meeting Burkhardt told him he was willing to launder the money for him through Swiss bank accounts, that he had done other money laundering transactions in the past, and that he was willing to meet with the drug dealer (who was actually the DEA agent). Again no tape recording was made of this meeting.

Up to that point, the only language evidence against Burkhardt consisted of unverifiable information reported by Fernando. Since this likely was not enough to produce probable cause for the target's arrest, on February 22 the agent met with Burkhardt, Fernando, and Manuel at Burkhardt's home in Florida. This introductory meeting also was not tape-recorded, but in his probable cause complaint the agent asserted that Burkhardt told him that he was a Swiss banker and lawyer who specialized in banking services, in forming offshore corporations, and in investment counseling. Allegedly Burkhardt added that it is difficult to trace transfers to and from corporate accounts and that he prefers to open offshore accounts in Liechtenstein, where assets could be shielded through the use of a corporation rather than in the name of the true owners of the funds. The agent also reported that at this meeting Burkhardt offered to open an offshore corporation in a Swiss bank for him, where he could direct the money anywhere he wanted.

This information purportedly given by Burkhardt represented the current standard procedures for transactions with some overseas banks. According to the agent's own report, they discussed nothing illegal. But what was troublesome for Burkhardt was that the agent's report indicated that prior to this meeting, Fernando said he had explained to Burkhardt that the person he would be working with was a drug dealer and that Burkhardt had agreed to "launder" $200,000 as a test of the system that later would contain larger banking transactions. The accuracy of the agent's interpretation of what Fernando reported to him when all three of them met couldn't be verified because surprisingly the agent again didn't tape-record that meeting.

Again, no tape recording was made on March 19 when the agent met with Fernando in Virginia and gave him $200,000 in cash for the forthcoming transaction. The agent's written report of that meeting said that Fernando told him that Burkhardt was not willing to incur the expense of flying to Zurich to "pay off" people for the paltry transaction of a mere $200,000. Fernando told the agent that he and the informant, Manuel, would drive to Burkhardt's house in Florida to deliver the $200,000 as a test transaction. Subsequently, they did this while under careful DEA visual surveillance.

In still another unrecorded call on March 21 the agent telephoned Burkhardt, who purportedly told him the $200,000 had been delivered to him but that any future transactions would have to be in larger amounts.

From the end of January through March 21, the DEA agent communicated by telephone or in person with Fernando many times, but he tape-recorded only three of these calls along with two calls that he made to Burkhardt. The first recorded call to Burkhardt was on March 21, when Burkhardt informed the agent only that he had received the $200,000 along with the deposit information and that any future transactions should be in larger amounts.

The four face-to-face meetings between the agent and Burkhardt took place on April 4, April 16, June 6, and August 14. The language of these meetings is discussed in the following sections.

The subsequent indictment charged that Burkhardt knowingly and willfully conspired to provide laundering services by taking cash in small bills from a purported drug dealer, laundering the cash, and depositing the laundered funds into an account designated by the drug dealer with the specific intent to promote the drug dealer's unlawful activities and to conceal and disguise the nature, location, source, ownership, and control of the cash given him by that purported drug dealer.

The reported overt acts in the indictment said that Burkhardt had:

- told the agent he could launder large amounts of money using foreign bank accounts (based on the agent's report of the January 30 unrecorded phone call)
- told the informant that he had laundered money in the past and was willing to launder money for a drug dealer in the DC area (based on the agent's report of the February 5 unrecorded phone call)
- met with the DEA agent posing as a drug dealer and told him he would deposit his proceeds from drug trafficking into foreign bank accounts (based on the agent's report of the February 22 unrecorded meeting)

- told the DEA agent that he would use an associate to assist in future money laundering transactions (based on the April 4 tape-recorded meeting)
- met with the DEA agent and received $2 million in purported drug proceeds from that agent, after which Burkhardt was arrested (based on the August 14 tape-recorded meeting)

The indictment also listed a number of banking transactions that took place during this entire period showing that large amounts of money indeed had been sent, received, and processed.

It cannot be denied that Burkhardt's international banking and investment consulting services was a business that was ripe for an investigation of this type. Using overseas banks that promised confidentiality and made transfers of funds easily possible was a risky business for him to be in and it is therefore not surprising that the government would troll for illegality in such activities. The agent's legitimate and important task was to discover and record evidence of any illegal procedures that Burkhardt's services entailed. Because it was not possible to verify the charges stemming from the agent's reports of conversations with Burkhardt that were not preserved on tape, the defense was left with only the tape-recorded evidence by which the accuracy of these charges could be determined.

THE TAPE-RECORDED EVIDENCE

Against the backdrop of the agent's investigative reports and the indictment, the tape recordings provided the only verifiable language evidence. As for Burkhardt's alleged predisposition to commit a crime, both the agent's informants Manuel and Fernando were the ones who represented Burkhardt's possible willingness to launder money that led up to the agent's first meeting with Burkhardt. As noted above, since the representations of these less-than-reputable informants likely were not considered to be reliable, verifiable or convincing evidence, the agent needed to capture Burkhardt's illegality in his own words. The tape recordings of the four meetings of the agent with Burkhardt obviously were intended to provide that verifiable evidence.

That the DEA agent used his former informants is not surprising, for such contacts often can serve the prosecution's purposes effectively. But however useful such informants may be, law enforcement also is well aware that such informants cannot always be trusted to be truthful and accurate. Since the predicate for investigating Burkhardt was supplied by the informant's unrecorded and therefore unverifiable claims, it became absolutely necessary for the agent to meet Burkhardt in person and record any purported illegality on tape.

One of the major requirements of undercover sting operations is that the illegal nature of the enterprise must be clearly presented by the agent and clearly understood by the target. This requirement was made available by the then Assistant Attorney General Philip Heymann in his testimony before the US House of Representative's Committee on the Judiciary (FBI Safeguards, 1984). When this is not clear, the government has to resort to inferring that the target's contributions to the conversations were inculpatory. There is virtually always a problem when the agent has to infer the target's meaning, because inferences cannot be considered conclusive, verifiable evidence.

When agents try to elicit information from informants, the task requires considerable sensitivity and skill. The best evidence comes from the target's self-incrimination. When this happens, the agent can avoid the criticisms of putting words in their targets' mouths. As I've noted in other publications (Shuy 2005, 2013, 2014) effective undercover agents often follow the very indirect strategy of first letting their targets talk until they say something incrimina-tory. When the targets are careful to avoid exposing their guilt, the agents switch to a slightly more direct strategy of offering vague or ambiguous hints in the hope that the targets will understand them and then go on to inculpate themselves. A related strategy is for agents to mention similar illegal acts done by others in the hope that the targets will join in and self-incriminate. When targets catch on to the vague and ambiguous hints or the mentions of similar bad acts to the extent that they incriminate themselves, a good case against them can be made. In many criminal cases I've worked on I have found that only as a last resort do agents employ the totally direct strategy of making the illegal nature of the enterprise clearly and unambiguously clear.

SPEECH EVENT

As noted in the other cases described in this book, speech events provide the first snapshot for determining the significance of the participants' language (Shuy 2013, 2014). Based on the conversa-tional evidence, there is every reason for Burkhardt to have believed that he was doing what he normally does in a business transac-tion speech event—selling his banking services to a customer. In contrast, the agent's language demonstrated that for him this speech event focused on money laundering of narcotics. Since the major goal and task of any undercover agent is to capture a crime in progress, there can be no question that the agent believed that Burkhardt would agree to commit a crime at some time during this speech event.

The agent's problem was how to elicit and record such incrimi-nating words during what would otherwise be a normal business transaction speech event. He could have let Burkhardt talk freely until he revealed his own illegal predisposition and intention, but since this target talked mostly about his normal banking procedures, the agent had to use the strategy of dropping hints or uttering ambiguous statements that might move the inculpation process along. Of course, the agent could have told Burkhardt clearly and unambiguously that his money came from drug deals, which would make his illegal goal clear and unambiguous. The fact that he didn't do this could suggest that Burkhardt may not have been knowingly or willingly predisposed to do anything illegal or have that intention.

The linguistic analysis identifies and applies the major components of language discourse found in the many telephone calls and meetings that serve as snapshot evidence in the case. The first component is the speech event itself (Hymes 1972; Gumperz 1982; Shuy 2013, 2014). Based on Burkhardt's language, it was his perspective that he and the agent were involved in a business sales speech event. The agent shared Burkhardt's perspective of a business sales speech event but had the added task of converting it from legal to illegal by representing his resources as drug related. The business sales speech event, like all speech events, has a structure that prescribes the appropriate language that can be expected to be used (Gumperz 1982, 9). Burkhardt was the seller who had a product (banking services) to provide, for which he would receive a percentage of the money that he processed and serviced for the buyer. An unsuccessful business transaction speech event can fail at stages 2, 3, 4, or 5 below. When successful, it contains the following five sequential, predictable stages that prescribe the language outline that is appropriate to be used at each stage.

In this case the tape-recorded evidence indicates that stages 1 and 2 were fairly straightforward and led to a mutual agreement about the service and conditions of the prospective transaction. The agent quibbled a bit about the stage 3 price (Burkhardt's

Business Transaction Speech Event

Buyer	Seller
1. Presents need	Describes service
2. Negotiates conditions	Negotiates conditions
3. Negotiates price	Negotiates price
4. Agrees on price	Agrees on price
5. Agrees to buy	Agrees to sell

20 percent commission), but they eventually agreed to that amount in stage 4 and to the entire transaction in stage 5. At that point this speech event was completed. The agent then transferred $200,000 in cash to Burkhardt, who set up an account for the agent at a bank in Lichtenstein.

The legal issue here arose not as much from this speech event itself as from the agent's source of the money that Burkhardt was servicing. Thus, there were two overall themes here, the first being the banking speech event and the second being the agent's attempt at representing that the money came from illegal drug sources. The agent's apparent task was to camouflage a normal business transaction speech event by making it appear to be illegal without at the same time discouraging Burkhardt from staying away from what could appear to be a legal deal. The resulting legal question was whether Burkhardt understood or failed to understand the agent's strategy.

The recorded language in this case indicates that at no time did Burkhardt explicitly reveal a predisposition, schema, or intention to launder drug money. As will be demonstrated, the agent had to work very hard during his efforts to create the impression that Burkhardt understood that the money he was helping the agent deposit was derived from the agent's cocaine sales. Analysis of the schemas, agendas, speech acts, and conversational strategies used by the participants provided individual snapshots that contributed to a panoramic picture of how the participants' language demonstrated their understanding of what was going on.

SCHEMAS

There can be little doubt that the agent's schema was that he would be able to capture Burkhardt in illegality by getting him eventually to say something incriminating. I have found that it is only natural for most undercover agents to think that their targets are very likely criminals. The four face-to-face tape-recorded meetings between the agent and Burkhardt on April 4, April 16, June 6, and August 14 provided verifiable language evidence that during these conversations the agent's schema remained unchanged. I compared the agent's investigative reports of these four meetings with the spoken language upon which these reports were made that provided further evidence revealing the agent's schema.

During their first meeting on April 4, the agent's investigative report of that meeting said that they discussed "future money laundering" of the agent's "cocaine proceeds" during which Burkhardt described the methods he used to "conceal and disguise" the transfer of accounts and assets so that nothing could be traced. In spite of the lack of any recorded language evidence that related specifically to money laundering, the agent had to infer that Burkhardt had told him about his banking procedures as though they were criminal activities.

During their April 16 meeting, the agent's investigation report said that Burkhardt gave him documents indicating that he had established a corporation in Liechtenstein for the agent and provided the name of the trustee, an investment lawyer, who would administer the account. This much was verifiable, but the agent also wrote in this report that Burkhardt purportedly also told him how to "conceal" the ownership of the property using various corporate entities. The tapes did not confirm this. The agent's report indicated that he then gave Burkhardt $200,000 in cash claiming that he identified the money as "the proceeds of drug transactions," which words were also not found on the tape. This investigative report also listed a number of deposits of under $10,000, each made to several different banks.

During their June 6 tape-recorded meeting the discussion was almost entirely about the methods by which the investments could remain "confidential," a word with several equally benign meanings, especially in the banking business.

During their final tape-recorded meeting on August 14, the agent gave Burkhardt two million dollars in US currency and quickly departed as Burkhardt was being arrested. The subsequent indictment charged Burkhardt with two counts of conspiracy to launder money (18 U.S.C. § 1956(h), seven counts of money laundering (18 U.S.C. § 1956 (a) (B), 1956 § (a) (3) (B), and 1956 (a) (2) (B) (i) and (ii). It read in part:

> . . . the knowing, intentional, and unlawful transportation, transmission, and transfer and attempted transportation, transmission, and transfer of monetary instruments and funds from and through a place outside the United States and to a place in the United States from and through a place outside the United States, with the intent to promote the carrying on of a specified unlawful activity, in violation of Title 18, United

States Code, Section 1956(a) (A) ... knowing that ... [it] was designed in whole or in part to conceal and disguise the nature, location, source, ownership, and control of the proceeds of unlawful activity and to avoid transaction reporting requirements.

As will be discussed later in the section on smoking guns, the agent revealed his schema in this snapshot by the words he used to report the events. More important, this snapshot showed that the agent's choice of words differed significantly from those that appeared on the very tape recordings that he made.

One might wonder how such schemas can persevere when the language evidence does not support them. When I conducted a training program for DEA agents a few years ago, I discovered an important schema held by many undercover agents. They begin their investigations with a schema of guilt even when they are loathe to be clear and unambiguous about the alleged criminal enterprise out of fear that doing so will scare their targets away. When I pointed out to them that it's at least possible that some targets might say "no" because they didn't want to become engaged in an illegal act, the agents simply laughed. Their schema apparently was that anyone who is in a conversation in which drugs are discussed must be guilty or they wouldn't be in that situation in the first place. Some of the problems with an agent's schema of guilt are discussed at length in specific bribery and murder cases in my earlier books (Shuy 2013, 2014). They are equally relevant to Burkhardt's case.

AGENDAS

Like virtually all conversations, the recorded exchanges between the agent and Burkhardt contained several large, overall themes that commonly included intervening topics such as small talk, plans to meet, and other things that were not germane for the prosecution. In most money laundering investigations, the central themes in which many topics were introduced are (1) the agents' representations that his investment came from illegal sources such as narcotics and (2) the targets' representations of the banking or other procedures they will use. No matter how straightforward and honest the targets' banking procedures might be, if they relate to money derived from drug-related activities, the banker can be implicated in a money laundering crime. Therefore, the individual topics that are introduced and recycled within these overall themes became the focus of analysis, along with the targets' responses to the topics introduced by the agent. The issues are whether or not the topics were presented clearly and unambiguously and whether or not there was language evidence indicating that the targets understood or could have understood them.

Although speakers' agendas in conversations are heavily influenced by both the speech event and their schemas, the participants' more readily recognizable agendas are what frame the clearest snapshot reflections of their intentions. A person's agenda can be defined as the language that gives strong clues about what is on that person's mind (Shuy 2013, 52–56). Nobody can probe into speakers' minds to determine their actual inner intentions, but what they say and how they say it can offer some very important clues. In fact, their language is probably the very best clue, if not only clue, to a person's predisposition and intentionality.

Examination of the topics that speakers introduce and recycle provides one of the clearest indications of their agendas. Listeners' responses to the topics introduced by the other participants is another strong indication of what is on their minds. We can learn something when they embrace the topic, reject it, change the subject, give a non-evaluative feedback marker such as "uh-huh," or say nothing at all.

In Burkhardt's case it was important not only to discover who introduced certain critical topics but also which critical topics were introduced to some listeners but were *not* introduced to other listeners at all. It is also necessary to demonstrate who gave indications that they heard and understood the substantive topics and who did not, which is often made evident by their responses to such topics. As can be seen in the other cases described in this book, sometimes what is not said often can be as important as what is said.

In this case it is critical to note that a snapshot view of all of the substantive topics Burkhardt introduced were about his business, the complex processes of offshore banking, the confidentiality of business transactions, and other benign matters. Even if his consulting business is considered questionably ethical, it was not at that time considered illegal. As will be noted, it was Burkhardt's responses to the agent's feeble efforts to represent that his money was derived from drug transactions that frame the major evidence against him in this case.

To this point I have noted the major elements that constitute the internal structure of conversations, but there also is one more unit that needs to be recognized—themes. Agendas have themes in which relevant and related topics reside. Some topics can be on one theme while other topics can relate to other different themes. The themes of a conversation normally begin with and grow out of the previously agreed upon and understood speech event and corresponding schemas of the participants. Participants reveal their conversational agendas, the clearest evidence available about what is on their minds, in the topics they introduce and recycle, and in their responses to the topics of the other speakers. Within these topics and responses, the speech acts that speakers use can provide additional snapshot evidence of their intentionality and predisposition.

Conversational strategies demonstrate how speakers try to manipulate the conversation to suit their own position, providing still another snapshot of the language evidence.

As noted above, two substantive themes are apparent in this case. The first theme related directly to the speech event that both Burkhardt and the agent shared: they both knew or talked as though they knew that they were participating in a business sales speech event. The second theme was held and promoted by the agent alone—his attempts to represent that the money he wanted Burkhardt to bank for him was derived from illegal drug sales. If he could get Burkhardt to understand this and provide his own language evidence indicating that he knew this, the agent could give this evidence to the prosecutor to bring a criminal indictment against the target.

As in all effective communication, these two recurring themes occurring over a six-month period required both parties not only to present their ideas clearly and unambiguously but also to understand what the other participant was saying. Following Grice's cooperative principle (1975), conversational participants are expected to say that which is necessary, to say that which is true, to be relevant, and to be clear and unambiguous. Doing otherwise can lead to serious miscommunication. With this principle in mind, we turn to the themes.

Theme 1: Burkhardt's Representation of the Business Transaction

Other than small talk about irrelevant things, all of the substantive topics that Burkhardt introduced were about the banking business in general, his own specialties, in particular, and the specific procedures that would be followed in his proposed transaction with the agent. These topics provided a favorable negative picture for an indictment. This, of course, is not the end of the matter. A second question is how Burkhardt responded to the agent's topics. This is discussed in theme 2.

Theme 2: The Agent's Representation that Drugs Were Involved

This theme was critical, because Burkhardt's indictment for money laundering was directly related to the fact that the money came from a cocaine dealer. The question was whether he did or could knowingly understand the agent's efforts to present the crime clearly and unambiguously.

After the agent met with Burkhardt in a brief unrecorded meeting on February 22, in his own investigative report he admitted that he didn't mention or even hint that he was using drug money to make this banking transaction. We can confirm this because in the agent's later March 20 tape-recorded meeting with Fernando (when Burkhardt was not present) the agent made it very clear to Fernando that he was a drug dealer and that same conversation he admitted that he didn't even mention this crucial fact to Burkhardt and had no intention to do so:

> AGENT: We would never openly discuss that fact that I was dealing with cocaine. I mean I never would have mentioned that. So he just knows that you are getting the money. He doesn't know where you are getting it from.

The agent made very clear to Fernando some other important aspects of money laundering. He told Fernando that they would be dealing in small bills, that Colombia was the source of the money, and that he didn't want the drugs to go through an airport where police dogs can sniff it out. While the agent was still alone with Fernando he said clearly and explicitly, "I was dealing with cocaine," "they are selling some of the coke," "the Columbians we are dealing with," and "if the money goes through an airport, a dog will hit on the money."

In contrast, during the agent's three early brief recorded telephone conversations with Burkhardt on March 21, 26, and 28 he made no mention of the origin of the money. They talked only about making meeting arrangements and the agent assured Burkhardt that he had assembled the money he wanted to bank. Burkhart offered general information about how the investment banking business works, but the agent had made no effort to inform Burkhardt about his drug-related business in any of these calls.

True to his March 20 promise to Fernando, the agent met with Burkhardt for the second time on April 4 and did not bring up these topics but instead mentioned vaguely "the business that I'm in," and "the stuff that I purchase." The prosecution apparently inferred that these expressions constituted smoking gun evidence and that Burkhardt should have understood these words as evidence of illegality. The defense, in contrast, was poised to present the common understandings of these words found in everyday dictionary definitions of "business" and "stuff," especially when seen in the conversational context of Burkhardt's understanding that this was a business transaction speech event in which his schema and his agenda were revealed by his topics and responses.

April 4 Meeting

The first business meeting between the agent and Burkhardt took place at the Ritz Carlton hotel in Washington, DC, on April 4, 1996. As noted above, when the agent first met with Fernando in Florida, he strongly denied that he mentioned drugs to

Burkhardt and in his March phone calls to Burkhardt he never even approached that topic. If the agent had been trying to follow the suggested undercover procedure of first letting the target talk freely and thereby implicate himself, by April 4, he abandoned that approach and began to offer vague hints of illegality. For example, during a lengthy topic about the difficulties of travel these days, Burkhardt mentioned that he had read about a recent airplane crash in Croatia, to which the agent responded by describing a different recent airplane crash in Colombia, a possible but very weak hint that Colombian drugs were involved in their transaction, even though this hint apparently went right by Burkhardt who returned immediately to their ongoing topic of air travel problems.

Next, while Burkhardt was discussing the safety advantages that Swiss banks provide people who want to keep their transactions confidential, the agent tried to turn the topic into safety from being caught, hinting "I'm aware of the safety factor with the business I'm in." Then, employing the hit-and-run conversational strategy, he quickly changed the subject to the size of bills involved in such transactions before Burkhardt got the chance to respond to his hint. Burkhart either missed the hint or ignored it as he responded by continuing with his ongoing topic about how the banking operation works:

BURKHARDT: The company would belong to you. You would get all the documentation, I could bring it here or you could take it there and pick it up and leave the shares in the company in a safe, somewhere where only you know where it is, or wherever you want to. We would make payments to this account. You would have the power to sign on it, or somebody else that you're trusting. I wouldn't know it, so whenever you need a certain amount, you just tell the people to transfer it wherever you want it.

Offering assurance in case the agent might think Burkhardt could steal his money somehow during the transaction, Burkhardt continued, denying that this transaction would be illegal and adding a warning:

> BURKHARDT: Now that's the only thing I can do, otherwise you can go there and ask how much money is in the bank. I could fake the slip you know, but I mean, we are not in that business. We are in just, you know, we are bankers basically. I don't know your business, but there are a lot of people worldwide that have a lot connections to this bank. If the bank follows the exact rules, they want to know where the money comes from.

The agent then offered another vague hint similar to his earlier "the business I'm in," and "stuff," but again Burkhardt apparently didn't interpret his expression, "the situation I'm in," as anything illegal. Instead he related the agent's "the situation I'm in" to the situation concerning his own knowledge about how the banks work:

> AGENT: Well, you know, the situation that I'm in, why it's difficult for me because I've got to be, I don't want anybody, you know.
> BURKHARDT: The situation is that our know-how is that we have, you know, I couldn't walk into each bank, you know, there are few banks where they don't ask questions. This is what we offer. It's simple but it's difficult.

Next, again far from telling Burkhardt that his money comes from drug trafficking, the agent told him that he was involved in several pieces of real estate: "I don't want to put them in my name." To this, Burkhardt warned:

BURKHARDT: You would also have to talk to a tax expert here. These corporations very often give loans and you can deduct the interest, these tax gadgets. I don't know exactly, but it's done, you know. If the land is a big value, you know.

By telling Burkhardt that his money was involved in the business of real estate investments, the agent camouflaged his own effort to try to make Burkhardt think his money related to drugs.

The prosecution considered a single instance later in this conversation when the agent said the word "cocaine," as a critical smoking gun. The problem with this interpretation was that the word was extracted from the topic context in which it occurred, as follows. The two men had been talking about how many transactions they might do and the denominations of the bills. The agent suggested that they start with a small transaction of $200,000 to see how it went before doing more. It would, as the agent put it, "build up some trust." He then suggested that this be followed with a transaction of two million dollars. Burkhardt asked if the cash would be in small bills and the agent then responded:

AGENT: Well, the problem with the small bills is the fact that, I mean, you got those people out there who are selling cocaine, okay, and they get small bills back. And it's difficult for me to change those from small bills into big bills, one of the reasons why your service is so valuable to me.
BURKHARDT: But I mean, if you are—

AGENT: [interrupting] I can, I can work on that, I mean, if you
need larger bills. I'll see what I can do.

BURKHARDT: You know, if it would be two million, it would be
too much volume.

AGENT: Right. If it was small bills, I know.

Here the agent came as close as he ever did to associating his
money with drug proceeds. The question is whether or not Burkhardt
was now informed that when the agent said "you got those people out
there who are selling cocaine," he meant that his money was indeed
derived from cocaine sales. The agent chose to tiptoe around this by
using the second person pronoun, "you got," instead of the first person pronouns "I got" or "we got." The meaning of "you" in such sentences also is potentially ambiguous, for it can also mean "there are
people out there who are selling cocaine." As for the topic of small
bills, this can refer to either the agent's own cash or cash that might
have passed through the hands of other people who might possibly
be dealing in drugs.

Burkhardt's response to the agent is also important here. He
began it with "but," a discourse marker often indicating that the
speaker is not in full agreement with what had just said. Burkhart's
following "if you are" was immediately interrupted by the agent,
who modified the topic about the size of the bills, saying that he
can supply larger bills if necessary. Interrupting a target when he
appears to be disagreeing or seeking clarification is a common strategy used by undercover agents (Shuy 2005), especially when a target appears to be on the verge of disagreeing. Once the agent agreed
to supply cash in larger bills, Burkhardt appeared to be satisfied
because that would solve his problem of the volume for transporting so much cash to the overseas bank.

Other related aspects of this theme included the agent's efforts
to try to make covert and secretive Burkhardt's topics concerning

the safety of the process of transporting the money to the overseas bank and the confidentiality of the transaction once the money was deposited there. When the agent hinted about the "safety" of their transaction, Burkhardt's response made it clear that he understood this to mean safety in transporting the money rather than being safe from being caught in an illegal act. He illustrated this as he then told the agent that if he has someone driving the cash from Washington, DC, all the way to his office in Florida, it's not exactly safe, because the driver might get robbed along the way. Burkhardt's definition of "safety" was apparently not what the agent wanted to hear, so he tried to clarify by adding once more, saying, "with the business that I'm in." He abandoned that hint immediately, however, finishing the sentence by adopting Burkhardt's interpretation of "safety" saying: "of the safety factor here I'm not sure I feel comfortable with somebody driving all over the place with this stuff." Early in this conversation, it had begun to be common for this agent to dip his toe gently into hints of illegality, then pull it out quickly to the safe shore of apparent legality.

As the conversation continued, the agent got a bit bolder while Burkhardt discussed the confidentiality of the banking transaction. As he was doing this, the agent tried to associate the topic of security with the unspoken topic of his fear of being exposed as a drug dealer, although he still only hinted at this vaguely, once again using the expression, "the situation I'm in." Burkhardt dismissed this hint, telling him that confidentiality in such transactions is very important and he didn't know or want to know what that "situation" is and nobody has told him what it is:

> BURKHARDT: So somebody arrives there, goes to the lawyer, which is the board member, and gives him the money in cash. He goes to the bank and pays it in cash. No way to

find out where the money comes from. The deposit can be made without identification. I mean they just pay it into the account. This is a very technical matter. The only thing is we have the right relations at the bank that they never ask questions. But if you would walk into the bank with two million of cash, I mean, it will be immediately reported.

AGENT: Right, there'd be big problems.

BURKHARDT: Our know-how is that we have an organization that nobody is asking questions, that's all. I mean it's simple, but that is why I am asking for my commission.

AGENT: What about somebody outside the bank that might try to look at something like that?

BURKHARDT: No way to look at it, but as I said, I don't know your business but there are a lot of people worldwide that have a lot of connections to this bank. If the bank follows the exact rules, they want to know where the money comes from. This is a step that we have to overcome.

AGENT: Well, this is the situation that I'm in and why it's difficult for me because I've got to be, I don't want anybody, you know.

BURKHARDT: Yeah, I didn't really want to know. I didn't ever ask Fernando. I never asked. I didn't really want to know. Our know-how is what we have. There are a few banks where they don't ask questions. This is what we can offer.

Next, after Burkhardt stopped trying to explain the confidentiality of this banking procedure, the agent recycled the topic of "security" once again, still apparently trying to relate to the possibility of being found out for doing something illegal: "That's why it helps to talk with you because I don't know how secure that is." In his response, Burkhardt's once again interpreted this as the issue of safety in transporting the cash:

> BURKHARDT: Yeah, I know. The thing I'm more worried is here. Let's say if you have ten employees that know there's cash given to this guy, he's driving the car and stopped on the highway and shot, this is more a worry. Once it's over there, you're fine.

The agent then quickly changed the subject to the amount of money they would be dealing with, finally deciding on $200,000 as a test run to find out how the system works. Burkhardt responded that for larger amounts he would "organize a special plane" to transport the money overseas, but if it would be smaller amounts, such as $200,000, it would be safe, just in case the agent might think Burkhardt would "run with it" himself.

After an hour and a half, their meeting ended with the agent saying, "I'm glad to hear your views on this thing because they are totally different than what I was thinking beforehand," to which Burkhardt replied, "There is no secret behind it. Everybody who has this kind of relationship could do it."

April 16 Phone Call

Their next telephone conversation took place when the agent called Burkhardt on April 16, complaining that Burkhardt had not only taken out his previously agreed-upon commission for setting up the new corporation in Zurich but also had deducted $5,000 for the cost of incorporation and $5,000 for the annual lawyer's fees and taxes. By the end of this twenty-minute call, the agent agreed with Burkhardt's accounting and all was well between them. The agent made no effort to represent illegality in this call.

June 6 Meeting

During the third meeting when the agent and Burkhardt were together on June 6 at the Ritz Carlton Hotel in Washington, DC, they had a thirty-minute recorded conversation during which Burkhardt delivered the ownership papers and stock certificates to the agent for the new fiduciary company he had just set up, legalized by the authorities in Liechtenstein. Burkhardt then described the material and the process the agent would need to follow when he used his new account. When the agent recycled his earlier topic of dealing with large pieces of real estate, Burkhardt advised him to create several offshore corporations to avoid taxes. Then they discussed their next meeting, at which time the agent promised that he'd be bringing him up to two million dollars in cash in mixed denominations. The fact that the agent mentioned mixed denomination might have been another hint, but once again he made no mention of the source of the money.

All of Burkhart's topics were about their next transaction and his offers of financial investment advice, once again saying, "we advise clients how to invest their money. This is our real job." When he added, "you will have all of the risks of losing, of course," the agent may have thought this an opportunity to suggest that their risk was that of being caught in illegality, but Burkhardt warded that idea off immediately as he explained that the risk he was talking about was that if there was no activity in the account for six months, the bank would close it. They ended the meeting by deciding when the agent would bring the two million dollars to Burkhardt to take to Europe for him.

August 14 Meeting

At their final meeting, the agent delivered a suitcase full of cash to Burkhardt at the Ritz Carlton Hotel in Washington, DC. The agent continued to employ the vague language about his work up to that point:

> AGENT: I mean, it's really worked out well. I've got no complaints at all because, I mean, you are able to, you know, take the small stuff and change it, and it really helps, helps me with what I'm doing.

Two points are particularly important about this utterance. The first is that even at this final stage in their conversations, the agent still appeared to be unwilling to say explicitly something like, "you understand, of course, that I get my small bills from drug dealers." His "change it" may have meant "launder it," but Burkhardt apparently missed that hint as well. The agent had not been clear and unambiguous about this from their beginning exchanges and even now he was not clear and unambiguous that this transaction involved laundering his dirty money.

When undercover agents use the conversational strategy of camouflaging the illegality of the enterprise with their targets, it usually occurs in the early stages of their conversations. Even then this practice is highly questionable, but when they continue to camouflage illegality in final stages as the transaction is being completed, it is particularly problematic for the prosecution, because at that stage camouflage and indirectness would not appear to be necessary if the target's recorded language showed that he had already taken the bait and demonstrated he was knowingly and willingly engaging in an illegal act.

The second noteworthy point is the agent's use of the pause fillers, "I mean" and "you know" and his repetition of the word, "helps," all of which came immediately before the expressions that he was apparently trying to be most careful to choose—"small stuff" and "what I'm doing." The agent used these expressions throughout their calls and meetings in a way that can be called a partially disguised code. In another book (Shuy 2013) I described the questionable tape-recorded evidence in the case of US Federal Judge Alcee Hastings, who was impeached and stripped of his appointment as a federal judge by the United States Congress even after having been acquitted of bribery at trial. The evidence was a tape-recorded conversation between Hastings and his friend in which both parties used what I determined to be a hastily constructed, partially disguised code that only insiders could understand.

The difference between the Hastings tape and the tapes of Burkhardt with this agent is that their language indicates that only the agent understood the code he was using and it was not a mutually understood partial code. Throughout their conversations Burkhardt provided no language recognition that the agent's earlier phrases, "the business I'm in," "stuff," "the situation I'm in," "safety," "security," and "mixed denominations," were associated with drug money. Because hastily constructed partial codes are usually tentative and uncertain, the speakers often tip off where the word is coded with statements like "I mean," and "you know," in a wink-wink, non-nod, effort to seek confirmation that the other party understands that it is code. They also require confirmation by the listener that he understood the speaker's code word. If partially disguised coded language is expected to work at all, it must be understood by both parties. Similar to the agent's other attempts to suggest illegality without being clear and unambiguous, the last one, "with what I'm doing," yielded no evidence of Burkhardt's mutual understanding of it. He responded only by asking the agent when he might expect to do his next transaction.

The agent continued to drop vague hints of illegality during the rest of their meeting, but Burkhardt continued to provide language evidence that he was not on the same page. Referring to the fact that Burkhardt was personally flying the two million to Switzerland, the agent's weak effort to associate it with illegality was, "That part of your service is invaluable," to which Burkhardt said nothing at all. And when the agent said that he wanted to withdraw $500,000 of the two million out of the account fairly quickly and deposit in his Riggs Bank in Washington, DC, Burkhardt agreed that this could be done. Apparently not satisfied with this response, the agent then said, "I didn't want to raise any eyebrows or anything so, I mean, I don't want to move it too quickly." Burkhardt's only reply was that doing so could take a month. The agent then repeated, "we don't, you know, want to arouse any suspicions or anything," to which Burkhardt assured him only that the Riggs Bank was used to processing large amounts of money.

Since "raise any eyebrows" and "arouse any suspicions" didn't trigger the response that the agent was apparently looking for, he next tried the word, "problems," saying: "just let me know if there's any problems at all over on your end." Burkhardt apparently assumed that he meant problems in depositing the money when he responded: "I would withdraw it and close the account, but the nice thing over there is that they would pre-warn you." This left unclear what the bank would pre-warn about. But since their ongoing topic was any possible problems of withdrawing large amounts of money very quickly after depositing it, Burkhardt responded, "it could come out of your end," which can only mean that the pre-warning from Riggs Bank was that early withdrawal of money from the account couldn't be done.

Burkhardt then added that he didn't know whether US banking laws would require Riggs Bank to report a transfer of $500,000. The agent supported Burkhardt's understanding that they were discussing this topic by saying, " I don't foresee any problems here. If there's a problem, my only concern is over there on your side." Based on the way the agent said this, Burkhart could have understood it to mean that the agent has no problems on his end (purportedly including the source of the money) but that his only concern is with the banking procedures that Burkhardt was providing. If the agent's goal was to associate the banking process with his illegal drug money, this statement actually worked against such an understanding. In contrast, the government took this as a smoking gun that meant the bank would pre-warn about the illegality of the transaction.

At that point the agent asked more broadly about the dangers inherent in this banking process. Here we can observe Burkhardt's perspective on the legality of his banking advice and procedures:

BURKHARDT: Someone in the US administration would have to make a request to the administration, the Secretary of State over there, and ask for legal assistance. They would have to prove it first. I mean they can only prove it if they have the reality. It would go to the local judge, who would tell my man, 'I have a request here.' My man would call me immediately. England or other countries think the thing is in the legislation that if you don't pay taxes, it's a crime. Over there it's not considered a crime so most of the people are going there and bringing the money because they don't want to pay taxes. So it's not a thing they would say. The man over there has no idea. He can only say what he knows.

AGENT: I think you told me before you've never had a problem before over there with anything.

BURKHARDT: No, but from my experience the problems always come from the clients because sometimes they brag and of course somebody is listening.

Virtually all of the conversations of the agent with Burkhardt could be considered fishing efforts. Their meeting then ended with small talk. Shortly after it was over, Burkhardt was arrested in the lobby of the Ritz Carlton Hotel and charged with laundering the proceeds of drug dealers.

It can't be denied that when taken as a whole, the many tape recordings in this case might allow someone to infer that all of the participants, including Burkhardt, were talking about laundering drug money. For this reason it was critical to carry out an analysis of the topics that occurred within the two major themes of narcotics and banking procedures that took place during this six-month investigation.

The underlying theme of the prosecution was that the agent's money was derived from illegal drug transactions. The underlying theme of the defense was that Burkhardt was following the normal and acceptable banking practices of that time, however questionable and perhaps even unethical it might be for him to engage in such practices. Since ethics and questionable practices were not the legal issue here, the case against Burkhardt depended entirely on whether or not the agent represented his drug dealing clearly and unambiguously enough for Burkhardt to have understood it and knowingly and willingly carried out the transaction. This issue will be discussed further under the heading of smoking guns.

SPEECH ACTS

Critical in most criminal cases are the speech acts that represent the target's felicitous offers, agreements, disagreements, and promises

(Shuy 2013, 2014). As the language evidence in these conversations demonstrates, Burkhardt offered to set up the banking process and he promised to carry out the work he agreed to do for the agent. The conflict between the prosecution and defense concerned whether or not Burkhardt agreed to, acknowledged, or gave indication of understanding the agent's vaguely worded hints that his money came from drug sales.

Curiously, the agent had clearly told Fernando, the man who initially contacted Burkhardt, that his money came from drug transactions, but when he talked with Burkhardt himself, he didn't mention this. To Burkhardt he ambiguously sidestepped and referred to it as "the business I'm in." When they were talking about the denominations of the cash the agent would bring, he ambiguously mentioned, "people are out there selling cocaine," as though it would be obvious to Burkhardt that this meant that his own money came from drugs.

Throughout the conversations, Burkhardt's major speech acts were reporting the banking procedures they would follow, asking questions about the denominations of the cash, advising that the bank will ask where the money comes from, reporting that the bank offers confidentiality, advising the agent to consult with a tax expert about his real estate deals, and warning him that the bank will report large transactions of money. He also warned the agent that when he has his own associates transport the cash, he should be concerned about them stealing it or being robbed.

If one were to provide an analysis of nothing but the speech acts used by Burkhardt to the agent, the result would provide a snapshot that does not show Burkhardt referring to any explicit indications of money laundering. Likewise, the snapshot would show that the speech acts used by the agent to Burkhardt never explicitly reported his illegal intentions.

CONVERSATIONAL STRATEGIES

When people try to convince each other about various things, they are often tempted to cut corners a bit by using conversational strategies such as interrupting, being ambiguous, quickly changing the subject before the listener can respond (the hit-and-run strategy), and isolating the other person from important information they need to know in order to fully understand what is going on (Shuy 2005). As shown by the passages cited above, the snapshot of the conversational strategies revealed that the agent relied heavily on the ambiguity strategy in his hints about the origin of his money, which helps explain why Burkhardt appeared to not understand the propositions the agent believed he had made clear.

SMOKING GUNS

Most criminal cases focus heavily (if not entirely) on alleged smoking gun statements made by the target that show that the target knowingly and willfully acknowledged and agreed to the agent's representations of illegality. In this case the prosecution relied heavily on what it inferred to be the language evidence showing that Burkhardt knew and acknowledged the agent's representation that his money derived from drug sales and that he agreed to do the transaction anyway. Examination of the government's smoking guns, already discussed above, provides a final snapshot of the government's case. The agent's smoking gun expressions that purportedly informed Burkhardt about the illegal nature of the enterprise were:

- the business that I'm in
- the stuff that I purchase

- the situation that I'm in
- the airplane crash in Colombia
- the safety factor
- the size of the bills
- you got those people out there who are selling cocaine
- I don't want anybody, you know—
- secure
- It helps me with what I'm doing
- I don't want to raise any eyebrows
- I don't want to arouse any suspicions
- this part of your service is invaluable

These very vanilla smoking gun efforts to represent illegality, placed alongside the snapshots of the speech event, schemas, agendas, speech acts, and conversational strategies, provide a panoramic picture of these conversations.

CONCLUSION OF THE CASE

As might be expected, the prosecution based its case on four things: the testimony of the informants, the agent's investigative reports, the smoking gun passages noted above, and the ambiguous inferences that the agent conveyed to Burkhardt during the tape-recorded calls and meetings.

Even the prosecutors were not willing to base their case on the questionable words of the informants, which is the obvious reason that they found it necessary to tape-record conversations with Burkhardt himself. Nor could the investigative reports of the agent suffice, because some were based on the questionable veracity of the informants and, even more important, they included subjective and creative interpretations of unrecorded conversations that the agent made in his investigative reports. When these interpretations were compared with what turned out to be the actual taped evidence, they lost their impact. And the smoking gun passages could certainly be challenged when viewed in the contextual snapshots of the speech event, schemas, agendas, and speech acts of the participants, as noted above. In the end, the snapshots produced by these analytical procedures produced a panoramic picture that could not support the government's money laundering charges.

Reprising the adverbial modifier's that characterize fraudulent language noted in chapter 1, it would be difficult to claim that Burkhardt used his power unconscientiously, that he intentionally or willfully withheld, concealed, or misrepresented information, that he knowingly deceived the agent, or that he spoke without belief in what he said. However, he did appear to act surreptitiously, whether or not he did so illegally. In contrast, the agent can be said to have accomplished all of these characteristics of fraudulent language. Whether the jury was able to distinguish between Burkhardt's and the agent's use of these things is an open question. The contamination effect is always a possibility.

I provided the above analysis to the defense attorneys, but I don't know how effective they were in using it or even whether they used it at all. Since in many cases the retaining lawyers do not always make all of the non-language evidence available to their linguistics experts, there may have been other evidence I was not shown that may have caused Burkhardt to decide to plead guilty to one of the three counts of the indictment, which he did. I can only speculate that his lawyers realized that his questionably ethical offshore banking business of helping wealthy people avoid paying taxes would not play well with a jury. Or perhaps there was something else involved.

In hindsight it might seem that in this shaky business Burkhardt might have suspected from the start that the agent might be a drug dealer. It probably did his cause no good when at one point he blatantly said that he didn't know where the money came from and didn't want to know. Some businessmen are often so predisposed to pursue the opportunity to make large amounts of money on individual transactions that they blind themselves to any hints of warning signs that occur. Burkhardt's banking advice business gave evidence that his goal was largely about a desire make a lot money as a financial advisor who knew the overseas banking system so well that he could help clients use banking confidentiality to avoid paying US taxes.

[7]

SECURITIES FRAUD

The laws relating to securities fraud are complex, and it is not my intention to describe them in detail. At their core, however, they relate to the use of interstate commerce for the purpose of fraud or deceit. Federal law 15 USC § 77q declares it unlawful for people to offer for sale any securities using any means or instruments of transportation or communication in interstate commerce or the mails:

(1) to employ any device, scheme, or artifice to defraud; or,

(2) to obtain money or property by means of an untrue statement of a material fact; or,

(3) to omit any omission of a material fact necessary to the statement made; or,

(4) to engage in any transaction, practice, or course of business that operates or would operate as a fraud or deceit upon the purchaser.

Here the necessary words used in definitions of *fraud*, discussed in chapter 1, are very evident: *device, scheme, artifice, defraud, untrue statement,* and *deceit.* To the other laws relating to fraud, securities fraud adds the omission of necessary information or, to use Galasinski's phrase (2000, 18) the "information manipulation or omission."

Sometimes fraudulent language is discovered after the fraud has occurred and sometimes it is found as it takes place during sting operations devised to catch it. One of the problems with sting operations is that the targets must be caught using language that proves that they intentionally, willfully, and knowingly participated in a scheme using artifice to falsify evidence and defraud someone else, including the government, in an effort to enrich themselves. In such sting operations, government agents and cooperating witnesses secretly tape-record conversations with their targets. Because language is the resulting evidence, linguists are sometimes called upon to analyze the taped conversations, especially when defense attorneys suspect that the government's evidence was questionable or weak. Such analysis can sometimes reveal that the government's case has weakness, especially when the agents have to resort to using the conversational strategies of camouflaging, ambiguity, and contamination during their conversations, as happened in the securities fraud case of *United States v. Mark Valentine.*

BACKGROUND OF THE CASE

In May 2002, a grand jury brought an indictment in the US District Court of the Southern District of Florida, charging Mark Valentine, chairman of a large Canadian investment company, with one count of wire, mail, and securities fraud conspiracy in violation of 18 U.S.C. § 371, and with two counts of securities fraud in violation of 15 U.S.C. § 78j(b) and 17 C.F.R. § 240.10b-5. Valentine was accused of unlawfully enriching himself by fraudulently causing the price of various stocks to be artificially increased through payoffs and kickbacks to brokers in a sting operation during which cooperating witnesses and an FBI agent posed as businessmen with mutual funds they were trying to invest with Valentine. The government also alleged that Valentine sold his stocks at a higher value than they were actually worth.

The undercover government operatives in this FBI operation were two stockbrokers, Robert Schlien and Dave Jones, who previously had been caught in similar securities fraud stings. After indicting them, the prosecutors persuaded them to agree to be cooperating witnesses in the effort to broaden their net of suspected criminals. As is usual in such cases, the two cooperating witnesses expected to receive consideration at their sentencing hearing in relationship to the value of their undercover efforts.

Because they had been engaged in securities fraud themselves, Schlien and Jones were experts in the mechanics and techniques of doing this and they either knew or knew about other traders and brokers who they believed to be doing the same thing or might be inclined to do so if given the opportunity. Schlien and Jones did not know Valentine, but they did know about a broker named Paul Lemmon, whose reputation the investigators considered somewhat shaky. Because Lemmon had worked with Valentine on a stock transaction in the past, the cooperating witnesses first investigated Lemmon and this investigation then led them to Valentine, who up to that time the government had no reason to suspect.

As usual, the cooperating witness's assignment was to tape-record their conversations with Valentine and get him to say something on tape that would implicate him in an alleged securities fraud. An undercover FBI agent also participated briefly in the tapings, posing as the "money man" for Schlien and Jones. Common to such cases, the experts in this type of fraud were these two co-opted cooperating witnesses while the FBI agent, less skilled in such matters, tended to hover in the background, making minimal contributions to the conversations.

What followed was a slow-moving sting operation. From May 2000 to August 2001, some fifty-four conversations were recorded and submitted as evidence. Valentine participated in thirty-eight of them. The only face-to-face, tape-recorded meeting with him took place on November 23, 2000, and the remaining thirty-seven recordings were telephone calls. Sixteen of these telephone calls were between the cooperating witnesses and the co-defendant in this case, Paul Lemmon.

Somewhat swamped by all of these tapes, Valentine's attorney called on me for linguistic assistance. We discovered that many of the phone calls were of little probative value. Some contained only recorded answering machine messages indicating that the speaker was not available. Some were made to set up the single meeting that was held. Others contained nothing more than a "how are you?" and small talk. In all, only sixteen of the thirty-eight tapes in which Valentine participated, including the meeting tape, were considered salient for analysis.

After reviewing these tapes, it became clear that the major questions to be addressed by the defense were ones in which the speech event, schemas, agendas, speech acts, and conversational strategies played a central role in addressing six questions:

1. Did Valentine provide clear language evidence demonstrating that he considered what he was doing to be perfectly legal?
2. Did Valentine's topic introductions and his responses to the topics of the agents indicate that he ever agreed to participate in what is legally defined as securities fraud?
3. Did Valentine's language indicate that he was alert enough to be able to hear and understand the agents' agenda as revealed by their topics in which they offered hints of illegality?
4. Did the undercover agents represent the illegality of their proposals clearly and unambiguously or did they

camouflage the illegality to make the transaction appear to be legal? Specifically in this case, did the agents represent that the proposed "test trade" (a procedure sometimes used in transactions of large amounts of money) was a guise for providing a kickback to two men working at their fictitious Atlanta office?

5. Did the agents criminalize the tapes with irrelevant words and topics that could give later listeners the impression of the illegality to the entire transaction?

6. Were the alleged smoking gun expressions used by the cooperating witnesses such as "paper trail," "vig," "kick," "polish things," "cuts," "avoid being questioned" and "avoid talking on the phone," recognized and understood by Valentine as clues to the agents' illegal behavior?

To answer the questions about whether Valentine was willing to knowingly and willfully engage in securities fraud, analysis of the conversations provided by snapshots of the speech event, schemas, agendas, speech acts, and conversational strategies together could provide a panoramic picture for addressing what the government believed to be the smoking gun evidence. A major task of linguistic analysis is to demonstrate how the smoking gun evidence can either be supported or rejected by the cumulative panoramic picture that the various linguistic procedures demonstrate.

SPEECH EVENT

As in most undercover operations, the agents' only task is to capture their target's illegality that takes place in a speech event such as a stock sale. Valentine's language indicated throughout that his understanding was that he was involved in a conventional business transaction speech event relating to a stock transaction. In the particular business of stock transactions, the initiator of the transaction can be either the buyer or the seller. That is, the buyer can approach the seller to purchase stock or the seller can approach the buyer and offer the stock for purchase. Once the participants reach an agreement, modern developments in electronic transactions have made it possible to first carry out an optional "test trade" before consummating the proposed entire larger transaction. The purported benign purpose of a test trade is to assure that all the potential bugs and glitches are repaired and removed to prevent the participants from experiencing any future problems in the main transaction. When the government's money is used in a sting operation, the test trade also assures that if the target should decide to flee with the money, the government will not risk losing its entire investment in the operation. In this investigation, the agent requested the test trade and Valentine agreed to it.

The outline of the conventional structural stages of the speech event of a stock sale transaction is as follows.

If the participants do not reach a stage 3 agreement, the speech event ends. If the participants do reach a stage 3 agreement, a stage 4 test trade can take place and if that works properly, a stage 5 sale can be transacted. Although the optional stage 6 discussion of future deals is not relevant to the completion of the main transaction, it is included here as optional because it occurs in some stock sale speech events, as it did in this case.

The buyers here were the undercover agents who agreed to buy the stock while the seller, Valentine, agreed to sell it. All of the required stages of the stock sale speech event were followed during this investigation, but the legal issue was whether or not Valentine knew and understood that the stock sale transaction involved illegal kickbacks, which Schlien and Jones were required to make sure

Stock Sale Speech Event

Buyer	Seller
1. Represents interest in product	Describes product
2. Negotiates details and conditions	Negotiates details and conditions
3. Agrees (or disagrees) to buy	Agrees (or disagrees) to sell
4. (optional) Requests a test trade	(optional) Agrees to a test trade
5. Purchases the remainder	Sells the remainder
6. (optional)Discuss future deals	(optional) Discuss future deals

that Valentine understood. The extent to which they succeeded or failed to accomplish this was revealed by the language they used to Valentine, by the topics Valentine introduced, and by his responses to the agents' topics. Analysis of this is a natural language task for linguists.

Throughout the transaction, the agents' language was geared to make Valentine understand that this stock sale speech event was not aboveboard and legal, even though many of the things they said were vague and ambiguous. Nevertheless, the government considered that the conversations contained smoking gun evidence of Valentine's agreement. These are discussed under the sections below on conversational strategies and smoking guns. But first we must consider the rest of the context in which the smoking guns appeared.

SCHEMAS

The speech event leads naturally to the schemas of the participants in the conversations. Since Valentine's language gave every indication that he thought he was participating in a normal stock sale speech event, his schema was geared to similar stock sale transactions in which he normally participated. The agent's schemas followed their own very different goals for this speech event. That is, their primary schema, as revealed by their language, was that when they gave Valentine the opportunity, he would expose his guilt and they would capture it on tape.

AGENDAS

The schemas of the participants were heavily influenced by their understanding of the speech event they believed they were in and evidence of their schemas is demonstrated by their agendas, primarily revealed by the topics they choose to introduce. The following summarizes these.

Topics Introduced by the Agents

Since the agents' major topic was to suggest that Valentine get his stocks "on the books" at their Atlanta firm, it first would be necessary for him to send their office $20,000 for which representatives in their Atlanta office would pick some stocks for Valentine to buy:

November 11

- We need to do what we call a test trade.
- We need to do a small trade to get the deal on the books.

- The stocks are picked by two guys in Atlanta.
- Theoretically there's a Chinese wall between them and Mike.
- To get them to put the deal on the books we need to generate $20,000 in fees back to our side.
- We turn around and get a $20,000 credit back.
- That's basically the toll to get this thing on the books of the fund.

From these expressions Valentine could understand that even though this may not be how a normal test trade worked, it related to some kind of internal procedure that the buyer's company preferred or required. It's usually the buyer who tests the electronic and accounting systems by buying a small amount of stock to test how effectively a forthcoming transaction will work. In this case, however, the agents proposed that before they would buy a huge amount of Valentine's stocks, Valentine first would have to buy a small amount of stock selected by their office in order to get the larger sale they would later purchase from Valentine "on their books." According to the agent's description, his "two guys" in Atlanta would pick the stock that Valentine would buy and Valentine's transaction then would be "on the books of the fund" after which he would then get his $20,000 back as a credit, presumably as part of the money they would pay for the stocks they were then going to buy from him (referring the agent's "on the books of the fund"). If Valentine had been more alert, he might have recognized that something was amiss here, but he also knew that $20,000 was a tiny fraction of the money that would be generated in the main stock transaction and it may not have mattered that much to him. However idiosyncratic this procedure might be, he could easily believe he would get it back once the main sale was completed.

As is common in cases of this type, by far most of the agents' agenda was focused on the product they were buying, the manner in which the sale could be consummated, and various ancillary topics not related to the sale. On the whole, this gave the appearance of a normal stock sale speech event. Their crucial topics, however, focused on the test trade.

Topics Introduced by Valentine

Typically, convincing evidence that targets like Valentine are up to no good comes from two linguistic sources: (1) their self-generated statements indicating a willingness to commit an illegal act; and (2) the way they respond to the agents' hints, suggestions, or representations of illegality.

The following excerpts show that Valentine represented himself as acting in a perfectly legal fashion:

November 2

- (when asked if he has any insiders) No. The company just came out really in April. So I mean the 144 rule kicks in next April.

November 7

- We merged with the company totally above board.
- The total float truly is freely tradable uh, bonafide, there are no insiders.

November 23

- We have the papers, you know, with our account, that we're paying, you know, guys for consulting.

- We've got a pretty good Chinese wall inside our firm so the analysts don't talk to me, you know, on the price targets.
- We trade 10, 12 million shares a day, every day, 'cause it's uh, you know, how we make that our pennies. We don't gouge.
- Our company isn't like a lot of brokers down here. Our reputation in the investment community, it's not uh, a shlocky boiler room operation.

November 27

- I don't want to get negatively tainted just because, you know, I happen to know the guy (Lemmon).

November 30

- Listen, I'll use the fund if the fund is gonna be real.

January 3

- I'd rather go with the highest quality of transaction.

These excerpts provide a snapshot of Valentine's agenda. He introduced no topics suggesting directly or indirectly any possible illegality of this stock sale. If he had done so, this would have produced the best evidence against him. But since he didn't, it fell to the undercover agents to fish for his responses to their own topics in which they hinted and indirectly suggested illegality. These are discussed below in the section on smoking guns.

SPEECH ACTS

Valentine did not admit, agree, promise, offer, request, or agree to do anything illegal in these conversations. A chart of all of his speech acts (too numerous to present here) demonstrated that they consisted entirely of requesting information about the agents' stocks, reporting facts about his own company's business practices and fine reputation, and agreeing to the purchase and test trade preceding it.

The agents' speech acts consisted of requesting information, proposing the test trade, criticizing other stock traders, representing the legality of their own business, and agreeing to purchase Valentine's stock.

These speech acts provided their own snapshots of their conversations that related to the speech event and they pointed to nothing illegal.

CONVERSATIONAL STRATEGIES AND SMOKING GUNS

The agents' conversational strategies are closely linked to the alleged smoking guns in this case and are treated here together. When it is clear that a target is willing to engage in illegal activity, there is no need for the agents to be indirect, offer hints, and camouflage their intentions. But when the target appears to be unlikely to do anything untoward, agents seldom come right out and clearly indicate that the transaction is blatantly illegal, even though the FBI guidelines for undercover operations (1984) make it abundantly clear that an essential ingredient for making a criminal indictment is that their agents must represent the illegal nature of the enterprise clearly and unambiguously.

In this case the agents made abundant use of three conversational strategies: ambiguity, camouflage, and criminalizing, the results of which constituted the major language evidence used by the prosecution against Valentine.

The Ambiguity Strategy

Quite the opposite of making the illegal nature of the transaction clear and unambiguous is illustrated when the agents rely heavily on the conversational strategy of ambiguity (Shuy 2005). Since stock trading involves moving money electronically rather than by physical face-to-face exchanges of cash, it may not have been surprising to Valentine that the agents first suggested what they called a "test trade." The agents requested that a small amount of money ($20,000) would be used to test the electronic system first, before the larger trade would be consummated on the theory that if the test trade went smoothly, the larger trade could be assured to do the same. As noted above, this was an unusual test trade, however, in which the agents claimed that it would be Valentine's purchase of a small amount of the agents' stock that would reveal any bugs and glitches in the electronic system. Their apparent strategy was to suggest the test trade as a vehicle for providing kickbacks to two fictitious men who worked at the agents' fictitious brokerage in Atlanta. The effectiveness of the agents' representation of their strategy was crucial to this case. The following are the exact words of the agents as they tried to associate the test trade with an alleged kickback (key expressions are emphasized).

November 7

- We need to do what we call a test trade.
- We need to do a small trade to *get the deal on the books*.
- The stocks get *picked* by two guys in Atlanta.
- *Theoretically* there's a *Chinese wall* between them and Mike.
  (Mike was the FBI agent acting as their moneyman)
- To get them to *put the deal on the books* we need to generate 20,000 in fees back to our side.

- Typically we get with the seller, do a $20,000 *buy authorized out of Atlanta center.*
- We turn around and get a $20,000 credit back.
- Mike *takes care of things* in person so there is *not trace of anything.*
- That's basically the *toll* to get this thing *on the books* of the fund.
- These guys then *approve* it.
- Mike has a trader out there, based on him *getting the nod from, uh, research.*
- Mike is gonna walk 20 grand of that over to the fund guys.
- Those kids are gonna *take* 10,000 each.
- Now the stock *goes on the books.*
- 48 hours later we do a 3.1, 3.2 million dollar transaction.
- You'll have to do a pretty quick wire transfer so we can *take care of what we've gotta do.*
- Three days later comes the second traunch.
- Three days later comes the third traunch.

November 17

- Mike will go *see these guys* in person in Atlanta.
- He'll *take care of things.*
- He'll *give* them their 20 and then we'll *get this thing on the buy list.*

November 20

- You guys sent us too much money (valentine mistakenly sent 25). We only need the 20 to *take care of* the people in Atlanta.
- We're not gonna do any deal with anybody unless it's impeccable.

- And that's even with *taking care of* the kids in Atlanta, which is small anyway, *that's the due diligence department.*
- 'Cause it helps a lot with the guys in Atlanta, *Chinese wall,* they still have to be *the wall between Mike.* They put the deals on the books. They figure out what they like. And when Mike takes a look at what they like . . . then with this *research report authority.*
- Same test trade. These guys'll *get their end.* They *throw it on the books,* we're clear to go.

November 30

- I mean the 20, we *gave* each of the kids in Atlanta *ten grand each to put it on the books.*

December 8 (discussing a new trade)

- his people all gotta be *taken care of* on the way up on this thing.
- Meanwhile we got with these two kids in Atlanta.
- we're gonna do a test trade but the 20 grand from before *takes care of* them.
- They still need to *put some on the books.*

It's important to note that the agents' initial descriptions of the test trade on November 7 indicated that this is their conventional way of getting a deal on the books so that their later purchases involving large money tranches will work efficiently. They said that they couldn't do anything until they get the okay from the "two guys in Atlanta" who pick the stocks. We also learn that "theoretically" there was a Chinese wall between "the two guys" and Mike, who is the person who activates the transaction once the "two guys" have authorized the purchase. On November 20, they recycled this, saying that the two men "have to be the wall between Mike." On various occasions the jobs of these two men were called "the due diligence department," "research," and the people who "approve" and "authorize."

With the possible exception of their adverb, "theoretically," the camouflage was carefully accomplished. "Theoretically" was apparently a hint that the requirement of the Chinese wall may not be followed, but the power of this hint was offset by the rest of their description of the work of the two guys, which gave the outward appearance of this being legitimate. Even their use of "theoretically" was somewhat contradicted by their later statement that the two men "have to be" a wall. In my past experience in criminal cases I have learned that it is not uncommon in undercover cases for initial hints of illegality to be later repaired to make the initial expression sound more benign. This repair is used commonly when the targets appear to have no inclination to do anything illegal. But whether contradicted or not, the initial hints remained on the tape, ready to be wrenched from their overall context at trial. Obviously, it behooved the defense attorney to call attention to the way the agents later repaired their word "theoretically."

Equally important were the verbs used by the agents to indicate what happens to the money used in the test trade. Mike (the FBI undercover agent posing as the money man) was said to be the person who would "take care of things," "take care of what we gotta do," and "take care of the guys in Atlanta." There was no mention of a "kickback," "bribe," or "quid pro quo" here. If the agents had wanted to be explicit in their representation of the illegality of their proposal, they certainly had many opportunities to do so. They apparently did not want to take the chance that explicit words would have turned Valentine off completely.

Although "take care of things" can certainly have an illegal connotation, it conventionally means attending to or providing for the needs, operation, or treatment of something or someone. This expression is used commonly in benign, perfectly legal, everyday talk. If Valentine had a predisposition to commit an illegal act, such hints might work well. But Valentine's language provided evidence of no such predisposition, suggesting rather that he was likely to have understood only the everyday meaning of "take care of" here—that of doing a test trade to get the transaction on the books so that the agents' company could determine an efficient and safe way to carry out the later, much larger traunches of money.

The prosecution claimed that some of the terms used by the agents in reference to the test trade were evidence of illegality, including "fees," "credit," "toll," "their end," "not a trace of anything," and "10,000 each." "Fees," "credit," and "toll" could support the agents' claim that this was their company's way of testing the system with the test trade. The expressions, "their end" and "not a trace of anything" are equally ambiguous enough to be understood as part of the required procedure in which every trace of it went well as far as the two men in Atlanta were concerned. If the agents had wanted to be explicit here, it would have been easy for them to say "kickback," "bribe," "cut," "take," or some other term that more accurately reflected the speaker's apparent intended meaning. The agents had made it crystal clear to Valentine that the test trade was only a first smaller transaction made to test how the system works, not an additional cost, fee, or toll to him. Referring to this as "a credit" seems to support the understanding that this money would subsequently be credited to their later purchase of Valentine's stock.

Why then, didn't Valentine catch on to the agents' intended illegal effect of these apparent hints in the November and December calls cited above? We can never know for sure, but from the language evidence indicating that Valentine believed he was in a conventional stock sale speech event, from his apparent schema of the interaction, from the topics he introduced, and from his patterns of conversation throughout the tapes, he provided many indications that he was not alert to the possibility that the agents were leading him into an fraudulent transaction.

In many of the telephone calls, Valentine was preoccupied with other matters, often taking several other calls that interrupted his conversations with the agents. His language showed that he was fairly inattentive and off-guard to the agents' co-occurring terms that hinted at illegality. In that sense, he became an easy mark for agents who decided to pick the low-hanging fruit. Nor is it uncommon for some business executives to fail to pay attention to details that they often have underlings to take care of for them. Whatever the reason, Valentine's responses to the agents' use of "fees" and "toll" gave no indication that these words registered with him as representations of illegality. Evidence of this was that in spite of the agent's hints, his language focused on the transaction as though it was normal and aboveboard.

When the agents used the expressions, "these guys get their end," and "we gave each of the kids in Atlanta ten grand each to put it on the books," they appeared to come closer to representing illegality. But did they? The expression, "their end," conveys considerable ambiguity. There are two ends in any transaction, the sending end and the receiving end. In this case, Valentine could reasonably understand "their end" to mean the receiving end of the $20,000 he was to wire to the two guys in Atlanta who would receive it for the purpose of setting the test trade in motion. Such an understanding might not easily lead Valentine to be suspicious of any wrongdoing.

Likewise, there is nothing in the expression "their end" to indicate explicitly that it meant that the two guys in Atlanta pocketed the money themselves, although without doubt that's what the agents had in mind. Once again, the agents could have been more explicit about what "their end" meant, but they apparently decided not to be clear and unambiguous, leaving it up to Valentine to infer their intention. The two guys were a part of the Atlanta company whose roles the agents' at various times described as representing "research," "due diligence," and the ones who "authorized" the sale. Whatever their role was in this unusual test trade, they represented the buyer of this small transaction and to Valentine "their end" could easily mean the buying company's "end."

Potentially troublesome for Valentine was the agents' expression, "I mean the 20, we gave each of the kids in Atlanta ten grand to put it on the books." The agents no doubt intended the verb, "gave," to mean that the "two kids" got the money personally. But "gave" has many meanings, one of which can indicate that it was "turned over" to them. Why "each" would be necessary here was unclear, but perhaps from lack of attention Valentine gave no indication of understanding the agent's apparent intent. The prosecutor could infer that Valentine was so inclined to engage in the fraud that he didn't need to have it explained in clearer terms, but the ambiguity remains nonetheless.

When the agents separated "the 20" into two separate amounts with each of the kids getting ten, they apparently tried to be a clearer about where this test trade money actually was going. So why didn't Valentine catch on to this? One possibility stems from the way the agents at various times previously had described the jobs of the two "kids" as "research," as "due diligence," as "for consulting as fund administrators," and as people requiring "management fees." Again, Valentine may not have been attentive enough to perceive any hidden meaning that would help him figure out that it meant a kickback. If the agents wanted Valentine to know that the two kids would get a kickback for putting the later trade on the books, they could have been clear and direct about this. Instead they used the "ten grand each" expression here, apparently expecting Valentine to disregard what they also had already told him about having to pay them for their "research," carrying out "due diligence," "managing," and "consulting." Causing the target confusion is a common strategy used in some undercover operations (Shuy 2013, 2014). Saying opposite things at the same general time is sometimes perceived to be simply misstating something. If the prosecution were to claim that "each of them" meant that separate kickbacks were required, it would also be necessary to deal with the way the agents' muddied up the issue about what the two kids were being paid to do.

The Camouflaging Strategy

In contrast with representations of illegality, many times throughout the tapes the agents represented that what they were doing was perfectly legal and legitimate, revealing the conversational undercover strategy of camouflaging their effort to express illegality while at the same time making it sound legal:

November 2

- We're protecting the fund so there's not any embarrassing things that occur . . . we look for stability.
- We're imploring Lemmon to give us this situation where there won't be an embarrassment, there won't be some guy carted off to jail.

November 7

- We just need a stable situation.
- I'm concerned from a regulatory hat now.
- From a due diligence standpoint, uh, it's one that we've already gotten a pre-approval on.

November 20

- We already did our due diligence.
- I don't want anything to even look at anyway sideways at all in this thing.

November 23

- It can't become a pump and dump.
- Most of that part is finding a good deal, a legitimate deal.
- We're not gonna do any deal with anybody unless it's impeccable.
- 'Cause it helps a lot with the guys in Atlanta, a Chinese wall, they still have to be the wall between Mike.

November 28

- We found a much better firm that's a legitimate brokerage, international brokerage firm.
- We're trying to bring validity to the deal.

November 30

- If they're gonna do a deal, it's gotta be a clean, 100% deal, like Jag, as we know, is a clean 100% deal. (Jag was one of Valentine's stocks)

December 6

- And the deal is impeccably clean. There's nothing out there.
- There's no skeletons. So it looks good.

In addition to these representations that tried to make the deal look legitimate, there are several sequences in which undercover agents typically used the camouflage strategy. Often they first declared the operation perfectly legal and then later dropped in some hints about its illegality. Or they reversed this sequence by first dropping hints about illegality, and then later repairing them with clear statements of legality. Or they intermingled the two throughout their conversations.

Part of the camouflage strategy is to hint at illegality, but not to express it explicitly. The process of hinting is tricky, because the clarity and relevance of the hint depends on the listener's schema and sense of the context in which the hint is given. Unless hints are mutually understood by targets as clues to illegality, this strategy fails. In some criminal investigations, the target can understand the hints and implicate himself through his responses to them. To complicate their hints of illegality here, the agents sometimes confused the matter by juxtaposing their hints with simultaneous expressions about the legality of their statements. And this is what the agents did with Valentine. Sequentially comparing the previously noted list of the agents' expressions of legality with a list of their hints of illegality displays an interesting sequential mixture of both as follows:

November 2	legality only
November 7	mixed legality with hints of illegality
November 17	hints of illegality only
November 20	mixed legality and hints of illegality
November 23	legality only
November 28	legality only
November 30	mixed legality and hints of illegality
December 6	legality only
December 8	hints of illegality only

This comparison indicates that the agents began by encouraging Valentine to believe that the deal was legitimate and legal. Then, for a while they began hinting that it might not be legal until they returned again to giving hints of illegality, followed by statements of legality, then mixtures of both, then legality again, and ending with hints of illegality.

The agents' apparent need to switch back and forth from hinting at illegality to claiming the deal was legitimate suggests strongly that they had not become confident that Valentine understood their hinting strategy. If he had understood these hints, there would be no need for the agents to repeat the legality of the enterprise, because by then Valentine would have realized that what they were doing was illegal. And what would be the point of their hinting if he already understood this?

It's also important to remember that these cooperating witnesses were tape-recording their conversations only in order to receive a more favorable sentencing from the government. The best evidence they could provide would be to capture clearly on tape Valentine's knowledge that the transaction was illegal and his willingness to go through with it. That they were unsuccessful in this effort is underlined by their need to keep on hinting to the very end of their conversations.

Although hinting evidence such as this is common in some undercover operations, the prosecution always has to try to overcome the target's indications of confusion and ambiguity, hoping that a jury will believe that the target possibly understood that the agents' expressions of legality were used for ironic effect and were not expected to be believed. To reach such a conclusion, however, juries must also have evidence that the target said something that justified the prosecution's inferences. This snapshot view of Valentine's confusion stemming from the agent's use of the camouflage strategy provided the prosecution with nothing useful.

The Strategy of Criminalizing the Tapes

The agents sometimes assumed a version of stereotyped gangster speaking style in their conversations with Valentine, uttering crude expressions and references. They also used the common undercover strategy of hinting that it is dangerous to talk on the telephone and they described their Mafia-like need for eye contact to determine trust. They sounded greedy, used a Mafia term, "vig" (a Yiddish slang term borrowed from the Russian word, "vigorish," a word that conveys the meaning of questionable gambling or interest fees), expressed worry about a "paper trail," and occasionally threw in words like "cuts," "polish things," and "kick." Then, midway in their meeting with Valentine, they mentioned that Lemmon's company, Voyager, was likely to have legal problems. The following illustrate the efforts of the agents to criminalize the tapes (key words emphasized):

October 30

- We hate *talking on the phone.*
- There are things that should not be discussed on a regular *phone.*

November 2

- I grew up in New York and there's a certain amount of *eye contact* and what not and, developing a trusting relationship.
- We're probably gonna have to put 'em (brokerage firms) off to the side for the time being and not have to pay these guys,

so to speak, so why pay 'em if we don't have to? *Just keep it for ourselves.*

- CMeRun (one of the stocks the agents were thinking about buying from Valentine), which is obviously the one where we've got more, uh, *vig* to work with.
- Do you wanna get that paperwork out that you need signed off on by Mike to, uh, *cover the trail* on that?

November 28

- He just wants to make sure that *the path*, how did he put it? He didn't want to tarnish you with the *problems we had with Voyager.*
- Something else is going on right now, something away from you. Something that's between us and Lemmon.
- They (another company that they have in mind that could buy Valentine's stock) don't know anything about the *cuts.* It's just him and the two guys here in Atlanta so, you know, he's got to *polish things* so if it ever *got questioned*, he has the answers.

January 9

- As soon as the money comes back for Nigel's, uh, *kick*, then he'll release the second.

The need for corporate confidentiality and security is not the same as the need for illegal secrecy and deception, but in my past experience with many criminal cases I've found that undercover operators sometimes try to confuse the two. When distrust of the telephone is mentioned on tape, it can create an illusion of covertness or illegality, even though the need to take care in using the telephone is widely understood in an era of corporate electronic spying and espionage. An unsuspecting target's schema about the need for "confidentiality" as opposed to the more covert sounding "secrecy" often doesn't allow the target to grasp the significance of this distinction, especially in fast-moving undercover conversations.

Likewise, targets can easily misinterpret the created persona of the undercover agents. Are they simply crude guys from different cultural backgrounds or are they actually criminals? If the target's schemas and understanding of the speech event provide no particular reason to suspect the agents, they also can let this created illusion slide right by them. Greed is common in the business world anyway, so expressions like "just keep it for ourselves" may not even seem too unusual to them.

In the effort to add an illusion of illegality to the conversation, undercover operatives commonly contaminate the conversation by bringing up instances of other people who have been caught in wrongdoings. Cooperating witnesses like Schlien and Jones, who themselves already had been arrested in stings, are apt to know much more about such matters than unsuspecting targets for whom information like this can be new and unexpected. The agents did this here when they told Valentine about the legal troubles of Lemmon's company, Voyager. Even though they pointed out that this was "something away from you . . . that's between us and Lemmon," the illusory damage was done. The bad stuff had been put on the tape and later listeners such as jurors could have a difficult time sorting out what it really implies.

Sometimes even ambiguous and relatively benign words such as "cuts," "kick," "paper trails," and "polish things," can take on the illusion of illegality to jurors who are unaccustomed to the terms of art and shorthand expressions commonly used by stock dealers. And, of course, not wanting to "get questioned" can seem sneaky, despite the fact that even honest people who fill out their tax returns clearly and accurately want to avoid the nuisance of being questioned about them and for that reason they try to leave a clear "paper trail" in case they happen to get audited.

Reprising the adverbial modifiers that characterize fraudulent language noted in chapter 1, the evidence in this case does not show that Valentine displayed an unconscientious use of power, that he intentionally and willfully withheld, concealed, or misrepresented information, that he knowing deceived, acted surreptitiously, or spoke without belief of the truth of what he said. As in other cases described in this book, the cooperating witnesses and agent were the ones who used fraudulent language with a high potential of confusing the jury about who said it.

In summary, their language indicates that cooperating witnesses and agent did not represent the illegality of their proposal in ways that were clear, unambiguous, and unhidden. In most cases I've analyzed in the past, it is common for the agent's early representations to be no more than vague hints that might flush out a participant's willfully self-generated guilt. As the taping progresses and no clear evidence of guilt is present, the agents then try to become much clearer about their intentions. This did not happen in Valentine's case. The hints yielded no clearly inculpatory responses from him because the agents' hints were not clear and unambiguous enough to him. They camouflaged, used ambiguity, and contaminated the tape from beginning to end. No matter. Valentine was indicted just the same.

CONCLUSION OF THE CASE

I provided the above combined snapshot analyses to Valentine's defense attorneys and they may have used at least some of it in their negotiations with the prosecutor. The case never went to trial, because in March 2004 before the US District Court for the Southern District of Florida, Valentine's lawyers negotiated a plea of guilty to only one of the three counts of securities fraud. He was sentenced to four years of probation with nine months of home detention and other special conditions of supervision.

[8]

ART THEFT FRAUD

The following art theft fraud case illustrates how even high-level professionals like physicians and lawyers can get themselves into serious legal trouble. Although fraud was at the center of this case, the evidence often made it difficult to tell exactly who was doing the trickery, lying, and cheating to whom. Sorting this out required a linguistic analysis of the participants' language evidence. It quickly became clear, however, that some or all of the participants were indeed committing acts of fraud. The question was the extent to which the client of the retaining lawyer with whom I was asked to work was involved in it.

The client was Dr. Steven Cooperman, who had a flourishing ophthalmology practice in Los Angeles until 1989, when the California Medical Board complained that he had fabricated records and performed unnecessary surgeries. Based on these charges, he agreed to let the board cancel his medical license in order to avoid a forthcoming uncomfortable hearing about the allegations. After leaving his medical practice, he continued to live very well on his accumulated income and from his continuing stock market earnings.

Eventually he contracted heart problems, got divorced, remarried, and decided to add to his already significant art collection by purchasing Claude Monet's "Custom Officer's Cabin in Pourville" and Pablo Picasso's "Nude Before a Mirror," both of which he displayed in one of his two lavish Brentwood California homes. After having the two paintings appraised for $12.5 million he insured them for that amount with the Huntington T. Block insurance agency, which had them reinsured by Lloyds of London. These paintings were stolen from his home in 1992. Meanwhile, because of his luxurious life style Cooperman acquired debts of at least $4 million and was paying $23,000 monthly mortgages on his two homes.

The theft went unsolved for five years until the FBI eventually arrested two lawyers who had been Cooperman's associates, James Tierney and J. J. Little, believing that they had conspired to steal the paintings at Cooperman's direction in order for them to get a cut of the $12.5 million in insurance money that Cooperman would receive after the theft.

Based on a tip from Little's girlfriend, the FBI first arrested Little, who confessed to his role in the theft. The FBI then convinced him to covertly tape-record conversations with Tierney that eventually implicated them both in the crime. Tierney then was arrested and agreed to covertly tape-record nine conversations with Cooperman in 1997, after which Cooperman was indicted on fraud charges for orchestrating the theft of his own paintings (*U.S. v. Steven G. Cooperman* Case No. CR 98-1184-ER).

In March 1999 Cooperman's defense attorney asked me to analyze the following tape-recorded evidence:

- five calls made by J. J. Little to James Tierney on February 4, 10, 12, 13, 16, and their breakfast meeting on February 25.
- one call from Tierney to Cooperman on June 5, two calls on June 6, and one answering machine message left by Cooperman to Tierney on June 7.

The purpose of my linguistic analysis was to help the jury determine on their own whether the tape-recorded evidence was sufficient to implicate Cooperman in the theft of his own paintings or whether Little and Tierney had created this story to cover up a crime that they had committed independently.

BACKGROUND

In the late 1980s Dr. Cooperman had become friends with James Tierney, a former US government attorney who had moved from the East coast to Los Angeles to become a strike force officer. Tierney soon resigned that position to become the lead lawyer for a Hollywood entertainment firm, enabling him to make far more money that he ever had earned when he worked for the government. Cooperman and Tierney liked to invest in the stock market and discuss their successes together.

When he was in his mid-fifties, Cooperman decided to move from Los Angeles to Connecticut in order to continue his friendly relationship with Tierney, who by that time had left his Los Angeles law practice and moved back to the East coast. Cooperman checked out that area in July 1992, and while vacationing with his wife and child at the Jersey shore, he got a telephone call informing him that his two valuable paintings had been stolen from his Brentwood, California, home.

Cooperman quickly returned to Los Angeles and filed a loss claim on his $12.5 million insurance policy. But the insurance company objected strongly, saying that initially the paintings had not been assessed properly and that their actual value was only $2.5 million. The insurer refused to pay Cooperman the amount of his claim, leading Cooperman to sue the insurance company in a civil lawsuit that was ongoing during the investigation of the criminal fraud case described here.

The FBI got no breaks in the art theft case until 1997, when J. J. Little's girlfriend found out about the stolen paintings and blew the whistle on her boyfriend to the police. When questioned, Little admitted that he had the paintings, but he did not know that they had been stolen. He claimed that Tierney gave the paintings to him to hold as a favor to Cooperman so that their value would not be properly assessed during Cooperman's divorce proceedings back in 1992. But the FBI eventually got Little to admit his role in the theft and, in exchange for certain favorable sentencing considerations, he agreed to cooperate with the investigation of Tierney and Cooperman.

In February 1997 the FBI had Little tape-record five telephone calls and one long meeting with Tierney. These tapes produced more than sufficient evidence for the FBI to arrest Tierney. Tierney then confessed that he took the paintings from Cooperman's home on the day Cooperman left for his East coast vacation. Tierney claimed that he gave the paintings to his lawyer colleague from Cleveland, J. J. Little, to hold for him. Tierney and Little had done some high-profile litigation together up to the time that Little's purported cocaine problem led to accusations of suborning perjury and other issues.

Little's four telephone calls to Tierney were mostly about setting up a future meeting with him. Finally on February 13, 1997, Little flew to Los Angeles and taped a ninety minute breakfast meeting with Tierney. Little denied that his girlfriend knew anything about the matter and fished for Tierney to tell him what he should do with the paintings. Little complained many times that even though Cooperman had received the insurance money, he had never paid him for his role in the theft and added that he was worried that the FBI might come knocking on his door. He also threatened to turn

Cooperman in because he had never paid him for secretly storing the paintings. Little was frantic and often irrational during this meeting, while Tierney remained calm and calculating throughout. What the two men said, however, made it very clear that both Little and Tierney were deeply involved in the theft.

Tierney assured Little that the FBI knew nothing about the theft and that there were three alternative scenarios they could follow: (1) turn the paintings over to the authorities now; (2) have the paintings returned anonymously through an intermediary such as an embassy in an overseas country; (3) hang onto the paintings until Cooperman died, which Tierney estimated would be in about five to ten years because of Cooperman's serious heart condition. Tierney reasoned that after Cooperman died they could explain to the FBI that for reasons unknown to them Cooperman had asked Little to store the paintings for him as a favor.

Tierney quickly rejected scenario 1. He considered scenario 2 for a while, but finally rejected it in favor of scenario 3 because it would be a good way, as Tierney put it, for them to get even with Cooperman for not paying them both for their efforts in stealing and hiding the Monet and Picasso.

This tape provided the FBI with abundant evidence to indict Tierney. At this point it was very clear that Little and Tierney were deeply involved in the art theft, but in order to capture Cooperman as the mastermind, the FBI still needed more than the words of questionable witnesses whose reputations were far from reliable or sterling. An indictment of Cooperman would need to be based on dependable evidence that would implicate him as the orchestrator of the theft.

After hearing the tape that Little had made of his conversation, Tierney agreed with the prosecutor to tape-record his future conversations with Cooperman. This investigation followed the commonly used law enforcement technique of first co-opting the more minor players to help capture the major target, in this case Dr. Cooperman. Four months later, in early June 1997, Tierney covertly tape-recorded three telephone conversations with Cooperman, fishing for him to verbally implicate himself in the art fraud.

In a sixteen-minute call on June 5, after twelve minutes of conversation about their stock transactions, for the next two minutes Tierney told Cooperman that Little was going to give the "baseball cards" (his code word for the paintings) to him (Tierney) to hold for him until Little got back from a trip to Luxemburg. Tierney asked Cooperman whether he should tell Little to "drop them off anonymously at the gallery" or do something else with them. To this, Cooperman made what the FBI considered a damaging statement as he told Tierney, "Don't you need dumpsters with everything?" Note that here Cooperman chose the pronoun, "you," rather than "we." Tierney then fished for a pronoun that might bring Cooperman in to the matter, asking him "remember way back you had suggested that I cut them up in little pieces?" Cooperman answered, "yeah, but why not just in the shredder?" Cooperman agreed here that in the past he had advised Tierney what to do with the paintings but he still avoided implicating himself in the theft.

Next, Tierney suggested that maybe Little should just give the paintings back to the insurance company, to which Cooperman said, "I think that is a good idea. Sleeping dogs are best left sleeping." Even though giving the paintings back to the insurance company didn't indicate that Cooperman had orchestrated the theft in the first place, the prosecution also made much of that remark, probably because his "letting sleeping dogs sleep" allowed for the possibility that all three of them should do nothing at all, not just Tierney and Little. Cooperman then dropped the topic and the two men spent the last two minutes of the call recycling the stock market topic.

This call demonstrated that Cooperman must have known that Little had the paintings at that time but he didn't bite on Tierney's fishing efforts to provide him with specific directions about what to do with them. Instead he advised Tierney to stay out of the mess. Since Cooperman didn't admit here that he was involved in the theft, the FBI found it necessary for Tierney to call Cooperman again the next day, June 6 at 7:40 a.m.

This time Tierney tried a different fishing approach, telling Cooperman that he had received a call from a news reporter in Cleveland telling him, "the baseball cards had been recovered." Apparently this was Tierney's coded way of telling Cooperman that Little now had turned in the paintings. Cooperman's response was simply, "Hmm, good." This answer was apparently not what Tierney was fishing for, so he fished again:

TIERNEY: I think that it might not be a bad idea for maybe you and I to, you know, get together and maybe in person and discuss, you know, what should be the best course of action for us.

COOPERMAN: To do absolutely nothing.

TIERNEY: What if I'm contacted by the Feebees? [code for the FBI].

COOPERMAN: Well that's good for them.

TIERNEY: I think it's important that we both are on the same page of the prayer book. So your position is?

COOPERMAN: Don't know from nothing. And you too don't know from nothing.

TIERNEY: He's got no credibility.

COOPERMAN: Look, if he's carrying around dirty needles because of his drug addiction, that's the last thing you want to get involved with.

> If somebody has a dirty needle, they should dispose of it properly in a medical fashion. If they don't, it's their problem. And the main thing is, don't make it yours, you could get stuck with that needle. And then you get the same disease. That's what they taught us in med school at the very beginning. And then you bury the person who gets the disease.

The prosecution inferred that Cooperman's parable of the dirty needles implicated him in the crime. All the rest of this conversation (75 percent of it) was about the new house Cooperman was building in Fairfield, Connecticut. This house was also one of the sources of his current financial problems with his bank. The insurance company had disputed his claim and had not yet paid him on his policy because of dispute over the original allegedly improper assessment of the paintings.

Although it was clear that Cooperman was aware that Little had the paintings, to this point he still hadn't provided an explicit indication that he was involved in the theft. Tierney couched his fishing effort as a request for directives from Cooperman to tell him what to do about his current communication with Little without actually accusing Cooperman of being involved in the theft. Cooperman's advice was that it was none of their business and Tierney should do nothing about it, all the while not admitting that he had any involvement in the matter. Although the prosecution apparently believed that Cooperman was telling Tierney to lie about their involvement, this belief was an inference for which there still was no explicit language evidence to support.

When law enforcement sends agents back for still one more attempt to find what is needed, the defense can understand that the agent hadn't gotten what he wanted up to that time. So on the next day, June 7, the FBI had Tierney call Cooperman once more, this time on the pretext of arranging a face-to-face meeting. This twelve-minute call began with the two men talking for seven minutes about plans for Tierney's visit to Los Angles. Then Tierney introduced the topic of J. J. Little for three minutes during which Cooperman reprised his parable of the dirty needles and repeated that Tierney should not get involved in Little's problem:

COOPERMAN: My feeling is that when you are not involved in something, why get yourself involved in it? And hey, if somebody tries to hook you into it saying, "You do this, you do that," that's their problem. And to make it your problem, it becomes your problem. You know it's up to you to say, "Hey, don't even think about it. Leave me alone." Not that you say it because you're dealing with crazy people. You just don't have any contact. Is the point to try to aggravate you or what?

TIERNEY: What point?

COOPERMAN: In trying to involve you.

TIERNEY: Well, I haven't heard that he's trying to involve me. What I found out was that the art was recovered. I don't know what he's saying.

COOPERMAN: But what difference does it make?

TIERNEY: Yeah, that's true. But if he tries to implicate me—

COOPERMAN: That's ridiculous. Totally ridiculous.

TIERNEY: No, but there's consequences though. If he tries to implicate me, then I could get questioned and—

COOPERMAN: But if you get questioned, what are you going to say? You tell them what you know, which is nothing. You haven't the foggiest idea. And you don't know for a fact if anything he's telling you is true anyway, given somebody's use of cocaine and everything else.

The final two minutes of this conversation recycled the topic of plans concerning Tierney's visit to Los Angeles, with still no admission by Cooperman. Apparently the FBI now needed Tierney to make still another stab at eliciting Cooperman's culpability.

Tierney tried unsuccessfully to call Cooperman two times again the following day, June 7, to plan a time to meet with him, but he failed to reach him. He left messages on Cooperman's answering machine asking him to return his calls and Cooperman returned Tierney's second call on his answering machine saying:

COOPERMAN: As far as the article in the New York Times, yeah I was really surprised, uh, first of all I ain't heard nothing about the paintings getting found and I woulda thought that, you know, maybe since they were my paintings, I was the one who suffered the loss. That I would have been notified that they were found even though I guess I no longer own them, the insurance company owns them . . . I think it's great the paintings were found. As much as I dislike the insurance companies for what they did to me. You know, they can recover something. The paintings are insured, you know, which is great. I thought, like I had said to you, I thought they would show up if ever in Japan, 'cause that's where everybody had been saying is where these things usually go. But I was really surprised. Why they didn't let me know is a little bit puzzling. So be it.

Along with Little's earlier conversations with Tierney, these recorded telephone calls with Cooperman constituted the entire evidence used by the prosecution in its art fraud case against Cooperman. In February 1999 he was formally indicted (*U.S. v. Steven G. Cooperman* No. CR 989-1184) on six counts of conspiracy to commit wire fraud (U.S. 18 § 1343), perjury (U.S. 18 § 1621), and interstate transportation of property converted and obtained through fraud (U.S. 18 § 2314).

LINGUISTIC ANALYSIS

As in the other cases described in this book, I found the best way to view the language evidence is to first see it in its holistic context, beginning with snapshot views of the speech events, schemas, agendas, speech acts, and conversational strategies used by the participants that then could be assembled into a panoramic picture of the entire event. In most such cases, the prosecution focuses on small language units that comprise what they believe to be convincing isolated smoking gun evidence. Sometimes these purported smoking guns can wither away when contextualized by the speech event, schemas, agendas, speech acts, and conversational strategies in which the alleged smoking guns are nested.

SPEECH EVENTS

Since Little had been caught and had agreed to work with the FBI, his role could have only one purpose—to capture Tierney's criminal involvement on tape. Little was quite successful in his effort to implicate Tierney and it led to Tierney's arrest. In the same way, when Tierney agreed to work undercover for the FBI to tape-record Cooperman, his role also could have only that same purpose—to capture Cooperman's criminal involvement and complicity on tape. As in virtually all undercover operations, the strategies of these two cooperating witnesses can be called fishing speech events. This event is somewhat similar to a police interview speech event (Shuy 2013) and even more similar to the confrontation call speech event used by complainants who have made accusations that require more convincing proof than that which the accuser is able to provide to the police (Shuy 2012, 197). Unlike most speech events, the fishing speech event is a continuous effort with few if any discernable separate stages. That is, the fishing effort starts at the beginning and continues until it succeeds or fails. As in most conversations, there are intervening interludes about other topics, but from the perspective of the person doing the taping it remains a fishing speech event throughout.

Targets' perceptions of the fishing speech event can be very different when the conversations begin. They may think of them as friendly or business speech events of some sort, at least unless the callers continuously repeat the same questions.

One defining factor of a fishing speech event is that the targets are unaware that the conversation is being recorded for later listeners to hear. This causes targets to be less cautious about what they say and how they say it. If they admit an accusation, the person doing the taping has succeeded, but when targets are forced to deny the same accusations multiple times, they tend to become suspicious and try to change the topic and end the uncomfortable conversation as quickly as possible. Doing this can become complicated, however, when the accusers and targets are close friends, family members, or business associates. In such conversations, the participants expect politeness and civility. When Little taped Tierney and when Tierney taped Cooperman, no discernable language evidence demonstrated that the targets knew or even suspected that they were being covertly tape-recorded, a condition that lulled the targets into not being concerned or careful about how they talked.

Another defining factor in the fishing speech event is that initially the targets are led to believe that they are in a different speech *fraud?*

event such as a friendly conversation but at first they may not understand that they are not. This confusion causes them to be politely cooperative about the need to remember and discuss the past events they are asked to discuss. But if and when targets begin to suspect the callers' motives, they commonly try to offer pre-closes to end the conversation.

The first analytical step in analyzing Little's meeting with Tierney and with Tierney's telephone calls to Cooperman was to identify the speech events in which these conversations were couched, for doing so could help identify the schemas of the participants and determine the parameters of what they could be expected to say in such speech events. In this case, the fishing speech event topics required linguistic analysis to show how the protagonists couched their topics and how their targets responded.

When Little taped his breakfast meeting conversation with Tierney, very little fishing was necessary. Tierney appeared to understand Little's agenda from the beginning and gave strong indications that he and Little were equally guilty of stealing and harboring the paintings.

Things were very different in Tierney's subsequent calls to Cooperman. In Tierney's first call on June 5, he represented the speech event as a friendly business call about their mutual stock transactions and they discussed this topic for the first three-fourths of the conversation before Tierney finally got around to introducing the topic of Little. His topic switch indicated for him at least that what was at first a friendly business conversation was only a prologue to a more serious fishing speech event. The cover reason for talking about stocks apparently made it difficult for Cooperman to understand that the call was actually about something very different. In the end, Tierney's fishing speech event was successful only to the extent that it established Cooperman's knowledge that Little currently had the paintings in his possession, but it was unsuccessful in establishing that he knew how Little had got them or that he (Cooperman) was involved in the theft himself. His advice to Tierney was to not let Little involve him in his problem and to "let sleeping dogs sleep."

In Tierney's second call on June 7 at 9:15 a.m., he was careful this time to establish his fishing speech event at the beginning of the conversation as he spent the first two minutes on the topic of Little and the paintings. But Cooperman switched the topic quickly to the stock market for one minute until Tierney switched it back to Little again. This battle of the topics lasted only one minute until Cooperman succeeded in switching the topic back to stocks once more. At this point Tierney apparently gave up on his own fishing event and for the final nineteen minutes of the conversation all of their topics were a friendly conversation speech event about Cooperman's new house in Connecticut and his wife's unpleasant demands for how it could be completed and furnished.

Tierney attempted a fishing speech event for the last time at 11:30 on that same morning of June 6. In this twelve-minute call, the first seven minutes were a friendly conversation speech event with topics including Tierney's plans to come visit Cooperman in Los Angeles. Then they switched to their familiar business speech event topics about the stock market. After three minutes of this Tierney managed to get them on the topic of Little again, with Cooperman merely repeating his earlier advice to Tierney to stay out of Little's problem concerning the paintings. At that point they returned to the topic of plans to meet when Tierney would fly to Los Angeles for an ostensible job interview with a law firm there.

Tierney tried hard to wrest control of this speech event, but he met strong resistance from Cooperman, who gave no evidence of catching onto Tierney's real purpose for his calls. On the whole, Cooperman treated the calls as friendly speech event calls from a business partner. Here we have a snapshot of two different speech events operating at the same time, reflecting the simultaneously dueling speech events seen in other chapters of this book and in the bribery cases of Cullen Davis and Billy Clayton (Shuy 2013).

USE

SCHEMAS

As in all conversations, in this case the participants' schemas grew out of their understandings of the speech event they apparently believed they were in. When Little tape-recorded his conversations with Tierney, his language demonstrated that his schema was that Tierney was deeply involved in the art theft, which Tierney's own language revealed to be quite accurate. When Tierney taped Cooperman, his schema could only have been that Cooperman was guilty of fraudulently orchestrating the theft of his own Monet and Picasso paintings in order to collect the insurance money. The important question, however, was whether their conversations actually demonstrated this.

Cooperman's schema may be argued, but his participation while he talked on the phone with Tierney indicates that he thought Tierney was making friendly calls with a touch of business. The language evidence indicates either that he showed a lack of interest in Little's problems or that he was trying to avoid the topic. At any rate, he did not admit his role in the theft even though the prosecution apparently believed that his language provided strong evidence against him. A snapshot view of participants' schemas shows that with the lack of Cooperman's clear and unambiguous inculpatory statements, the government's case had to be built on the questionable words of Little and Tierney along with whatever inferences they chose to make about the language used by Cooperman.

AGENDAS  *useful*

As noted throughout this book, the speech event helps determine participants' schemas and their schemas are given flesh by what they choose to talk about, their agendas. In conversations, speakers don't simply talk randomly. They usually have something on their minds to talk about. What they have on their minds can best be ascertained by the topics they introduce and recycle and by their responses to the topics introduced by the other participants.

Analysis of the agendas in the earlier conversations of Little and Tierney is not relevant here for two reasons. First, they both clearly implicated themselves in the art theft and second, even the prosecution concluded that they did not provide clear, sufficient, and explicit evidence that Cooperman directed them to steal the art for him. If the two men had clearly implicated Cooperman, there would have been less need to get Tierney to subsequently tape-record his conversations with Cooperman. Little had already been arrested and had already agreed to assist the government in capturing Tierney's guilt on tape. Little's only task was to obtain language evidence that Tierney directed him to hide the paintings and that he was not paid for his effort. Little was successful in accomplishing both tasks and when Tierney was arrested, he too agreed to cooperate with the FBI and record his conversations with Cooperman.

Tierney's subsequent conversations with Cooperman made his agenda clear. Their first conversation on June 5 showed the following agenda outline of their conversation. Other than the greeting and closing, this conversation contained twenty-three topic introductions, fourteen made by Tierney and nine by Cooperman. The twenty-three topics can be divided into four themes:

1. stock transactions (3 minutes), with four topics by Tierney and three by Cooperman;
2. Cooperman's move to Connecticut (6 minutes and 30 seconds), with three topics by Tierney and one by Cooperman;
3. news about Little (3 minutes), with six topics by Tierney and three by Cooperman; and
4. recycling the theme 1 stock transaction (1 minute), with two topics by Tierney and two by Cooperman.

Themes 1, 2, and 4 were peripheral to Tierney's goal, which he presented most strongly in theme 3.

In theme 1 Tierney used the undercover agent's common strategy of softening the perception of their targets by embedding their actual goal within legally benign topics such as stock transactions and Cooperman's new home. It is noteworthy that Tierney introduced the only topic about Little during theme 3, in which he reported that "our friend in Cleveland [Little]" was coming to Los Angeles with "baseball cards [the paintings]" to hold for him, but that Little planned to turn them in to an art gallery. To this Cooperman asked if a dumpster or a shredder might be a better thing for Little to do with them and to "let sleeping dogs sleep."

Tierney's second call on June 6 at 7:40 a.m. also contained four themes:

1. news about Little and possible contact by the FBI, with five topics by Tierney and none by Cooperman;
2. stock transactions, with one topic by Cooperman and none by Tierney;

3. a recycling of Tierney's theme 1 about Little, with one topic by each of the men; and

4. Cooperman's new house in Connecticut, with ten topics by Tierney and seventeen by Cooperman.

It is again noteworthy that Tierney, not Cooperman, introduced six of the seven topics about Little. Of special interest in this conversation were the two abrupt topic changes made by Cooperman to both of Tierney's themes about Little. After Tierney introduced the first five topics about Little, Cooperman switched the topic to stock transactions, to which Tierney apparently had little interest because he then switched the topic back again to Little. To this, Cooperman told him only that the last thing Tierney would want to do is get involved with Little, and he then switched the topic back to his house in Connecticut, which lasted through the remainder of their conversation.

Topic switching carries its own contextual meaning. Topic switchers are not interested in the ongoing topic, consider it finished, or are afraid of it. The defense could argue that Tierney's topic about Little held no interest to Cooperman, while the prosecution could argue that he was afraid of it and moved away from it as quickly as possible. There is no way for anyone to read Cooperman's mind about this, but the prosecution's inference is not the only possible way to understand these topic shifts.

Tierney called Cooperman again on June 6 at 11:30 a.m. and once more the conversation had four themes:

1. meeting arrangements, with seven topics introduced by each speaker;

2. stock transactions, with four topics by Cooperman and two by Tierney;

3. Little's forthcoming visit to Los Angeles, with five topics by Tierney and three by Cooperman; and

4.. recycling of stock market transactions, with two topics by each man.

Again it was Tierney who introduced the only theme about Little (theme 3), during which he expressed his fear that Little might rat him out. Note that Tierney did not even mention how Little might implicate Cooperman. Cooperman's topics about Little concerned only how he was a crazy, cocaine-addicted liar, and that Tierney should not be afraid of him.

From the topic analysis above, it is clear that Tierney's agenda was to capture Cooperman's culpability in the art theft on tape. Cooperman's agenda, when he wasn't talking about topics in which he showed more interest—the stock market and his new home—was to assure Tierney that Little was unbelievable and potentially harmless to him.

Agenda analysis views conversations from the perspective of what must be on speakers' minds enough for them to introduce topics about it. This agenda analysis did not support the government's apparent belief that Tierney had captured Cooperman in illegality.

Snapshots of speakers' agendas also show that what is not said can be as important as what is said. Cooperman did not involve himself in the topic of Tierney's fear of being caught. His words indicate that this was Tierney's problem, not Cooperman's. His contributions to the theme of Little and the stolen art consisted of questions to Tierney about why he didn't have the art destroyed and that Tierney now should stay out of the whole affair. This snapshot of agendas indicates that Cooperman knew or had learned at some time that Little had the art in his possession, but it doesn't display his association in that involvement.

SPEECH ACTS

In most conversations, speakers use speech acts such as agreeing, denying, offering, giving opinions, promising, advising, threatening, warning, complaining, giving directives, requesting or reporting information, and giving or requesting opinions. In a case charging fraud, one can expect the speech acts to include many of these as well, for fraud is usually accomplished using some of these speech acts.

As might be expected of a person who covertly records a target, Tierney commonly used the speech acts of requesting Cooperman's advice. Such speech acts could be useful in proving Cooperman's culpability if his advice would have been to do something illegal, but here it didn't.

In the first tape (June 5) Tierney used the speech act of reporting information about Little in ten of his seventeen uses of speech acts. Of his other four speech acts, two were requesting Cooperman's advice about whether or not he should wipe the paintings down if he should decide to turn them in and whether Cooperman wanted to avoid publicity. Two were requests for information about stocks and how Cooperman's move went, and one was a promise to call Cooperman again.

In the second tape (June 6 at 7:40 a.m.) containing forty topics, only seven were introduced about Little and all of these came at the very beginning of their conversation. Tierney introduced the first six and Cooperman's only speech act contribution to this topic was to advise Tierney that the last thing Tierney should do was to get involved with Little in anything. The remaining thirty-four topics were about Cooperman's new house and his lack of financial resources. Seven of Cooperman's speech acts were complaints about his wife. Cooperman's only speech act of promising was that he would send Tierney some money that he owed him from a case they had worked on together in the past. Besides requesting Cooperman's advice three times about what he should do about Little, ten of Tierney's speech acts were requests to Cooperman for information about his new house in Connecticut.

The third and final conversation was at 11:30 a.m. on June 6. Ten of the thirty-five topics were about Tierney's problem with Little, in which Tierney's speech acts were reporting information that he dodged the bullet, had heard that the paintings were recovered, doesn't know what Little is saying, is not going to call Little, and that he feared the FBI might question him. Cooperman's speech acts in his part of the conversation were to request why Tierney should get involved in it, to opine that Little is crazy and is trying to point guilt away from himself, is lying, and is using cocaine. The rest of this conversation consisted of questions by both men relating to their plans to meet on Sunday before Tierney's interview for a job with a Los Angeles law firm (fifteen topics) and five topics by both about how they hope their stocks will increase in value.

The snapshot of the speech acts Cooperman used in this conversation showed that nothing criminal could be adduced.

CONVERSATIONAL STRATEGIES

Often we can find many clues about the intentions of speakers by analyzing the way they use conversational strategies to persuade or elicit information, such as ambiguity, blocking, hit-and-run, withholding important information, contaminating content or quality of the tape, scripting, or inaccurately restating what another person is saying (Shuy 2005). We can also learn something from the way a speaker ignores or dismisses what the other speaker says, because what is not said also can provide important evidence in a criminal case. Another conversational strategy is to lie.

As with the analysis above, there is little need to point out the conversational strategies used by Little as he talked earlier with Tierney because Tierney clearly exposed his own guilt in the art theft throughout their long conversation. On the other hand, their conversations made clear that lying was part of their way of life. They accused others of lying (Cooperman and Little's girlfriend, in particular) and Tierney pointed out that he knew a lot of lawyers who will lie for them. The taped evidence does not make totally clear whether Little originally got the art from Tierney, but Tierney said he would deny this if asked and threatened Little that he would concoct his own "story" if Little ratted on him. At one point in their conversation, Little said, "Well I can lie."

Little didn't need to be ambiguous in order to block what Tierney was saying, or to use the other possible conversational strategies available to him. What they told each other implied Cooperman's involvement, but even the prosecution didn't find this to be adequate proof of Cooperman's guilt, which is why the FBI agents then had Tierney tape-record his own conversations with Cooperman.

Compared with the conversations of Little with Tierney, the conversations Tierney recorded with Cooperman demonstrated that Tierney was a less than adequate undercover operative. While failing to elicit from Cooperman any explicit language that would clearly connect him to the theft, Tierney missed many opportunities to do so. One omission was his almost total lack of the typical conversational strategies used by undercover agents in such cases. But he did use one of them—contaminating the tape with covert sounding language. Twelve minutes into his first call to Cooperman on June 5 Tierney finally brought up Little's pending trip to meet with him in Los Angeles. To contaminate the tape by making this sound covert, Tierney used code words, referring to Little as "our friend in Cleveland" who was bringing "the baseball cards." The problem with this code was that Cooperman gave no evidence of immediately understanding it even though the code was probably obvious and in that sense Cooperman participated in the use of it.

Undercover agents are allowed to lie to targets, and Tierney lied to Cooperman in his second phone call on June 6 at 9:15 a.m., leaving a message on Cooperman's answering machine saying that he just got a phone call from "a reporter in Cleveland" who told him that the "baseball cards" had been recovered a while ago. By that time Cooperman apparently had figured out this simple code, but when he returned Tierney's call on that following day and left a message on his answering machine, Cooperman said, "I was a little surprised. Why they didn't let me know is a little bit puzzling, but so be it," suggesting that he may have thought that it was a genuine news report, or perhaps that Tierney was being dishonest with him.

Curiously, this snapshot of Tierney's conversational strategies revealed that the prosecution's accusation that Cooperman used coded language in these calls was totally in error. It was actually cooperating witness Tierney who used the code every time, although it is likely that Cooperman came to understand it.

SMOKING GUNS

Like most lawyers, the prosecutors pinned their prosecution on smoking gun phrases and expressions that were isolated from the entire language information found in the evidence. In these tapes there were very few smoking guns. Most already have been revealed in the passages cited above.

Cooperman Used Coded Language

On June 5 and June 6, as mentioned above, Tierney used "baseball cards" to refer to the stolen art. Tierney was working for the FBI here and using code made the tapes appear covert. It is true that Cooperman finally tumbled to what Tierney was talking about, but the covert sound of the conversation was entirely Tierney's doing, not Cooperman's, making this smoking gun evidence questionable.

Cooperman Advised Tierney to Destroy the Paintings

This statement is accurate inasmuch as Cooperman likely knew or thought he knew that Little had the paintings in his possession and that Tierney was likely involved, but it did not provide explicit evidence that Cooperman was implicated in the theft, which is what Tierney undoubtedly was trying to establish in his undercover work for the FBI. At any rate, after first suggesting on the June 5 tape that Tierney and Little destroy the paintings, Cooperman quickly changed his mind to advising Tierney to do nothing at all:

> TIERNEY: I think I remember way back you had suggested that I cut em' up in little pieces?
>
> COOPERMAN: Yeah.
>
> TIERNEY: What do you think if I went to a hardware store and I bought like turpentine or paint thinner and wiped 'em down. Would that work?
>
> COOPERMAN: No.
>
> TIERNEY: It wouldn't?
>
> COOPERMAN: Huh-uh. Why not just in the shredder?
>
> TIERNEY: Originally I thought, if I got it back to the insurance people, at least they recoup something, but **you** don't

want the publicity of having 'em recovered and all that other bullshit?

COOPERMAN: I think the idea, sleeping dogs are best left sleeping.

Here Cooperman admitted that at one time in the unspecified past (whatever is meant by "way back") he had suggested that Tierney have the paintings destroyed, but as bad as this may sound, it did not explicitly demonstrate that Cooperman was involved in the theft. Apparently he knew that Little had the paintings, but his concluding idea was that Tierney should do nothing. Note that Cooperman did not say "**we** should do nothing." Nor did Cooperman even respond to Tierney's fishing effort when he used the pronoun "you" to suggest that Cooperman would not want the publicity of having them recovered. Saying nothing usually cannot be considered inculpatory evidence, especially during conflicting speech events with conflicting participant schemas.

Cooperman Implicated Himself When He Told Tierney the Parable of the Dirty Needle

It is necessary to examine the pronouns Cooperman used in this parable on June 6 at 7:40 a.m. (emphasis added):

COOPERMAN: I would think if he's carrying around dirty needles because of his drug addiction, that's the last thing **you** wanna get involved with. The main thing is don't make it **yours**, **you** could get stuck with that needle and then **you** get the same disease. That's what they taught us in medical school from the very beginning.

TIERNEY: Then I guess it applies to life too, right?

COOPERMAN: It applies to all of life, and then **you** put the last nail in the coffin and **you** bury the person who gets the disease.

In their 11:30 a.m. conversation that same day, Cooperman reprised this parable:

COOPERMAN: My feeling on that is when **you're** not involved in something, why get **yourself** involved in it?

Later in that same conversation Cooperman continued:

COOPERMAN: Because **you're** dealing with crazy people. **You** just don't have any contact. And is the point to try to aggravate **you** or what?
TIERNEY: What point do you mean?
COOPERMAN: You know, in trying to involve **you**.
TIERNEY: I haven't heard that he's trying to involve **me**.
COOPERMAN: But what difference does it make?
TIERNEY: Yeah, that's true. But if he does try to implicate **me**—
COOPERMAN: It's ridiculous.
TIERNEY: No, but there's consequences though. If he tries to implicate **me** then, you know, **I** could get questioned.

Although it is indisputable that the English second person pronoun, *you*, can have either a singular or plural antecedent, it is instructive that here Tierney interpreted Cooperman's *you* as a reference to Tierney alone, as is demonstrated by Tierney's subsequent uses of the first person pronouns, *I* and *me*. Neither here nor anywhere else in their conversations did Tierney refer to involvement in the theft with pronouns or other words that included

Cooperman in the theft. Tierney could easily have said "if he tries to implicate **us**" and "**we** could be questioned," but he did not. This is another of those instances in which what is not said is as important as what is said. The prosecutors might infer that Cooperman was tacitly admitting his role in the theft, but their own language evidence does not support that inference.

The prosecutors also made much of Cooperman's agreement with Tierney that this parable refers to "all of life," claiming that the parable intended to tell Tierney that he meant that they should not admit their own guilt but rather let Little take all the blame. In a sense, this interpretation is possible, but since Cooperman did not specifically define the object of the "dirty needle" parable, the prosecution could only infer that his parable was inculpatory.

Reprising the adverbial modifiers that characterize fraudulent language noted in chapter 1, Cooperman showed his power over Tierney in his conversations with him but the degree to which it was unconscientious is less than clear. During his conversations with Tierney he withheld any mention of his own role in the matter but this could hardly be considered deceiving Tierney if they both were aware of the whole story anyway. By being cautious at all times, Cooperman seems to have avoided speaking without belief in the truth. The issue was more about what Cooperman did not say than what he did, leaving the rest to inferences.

INFERENCES AS EVIDENCE

The government's smoking gun snapshots, extracted from the other language evidence, was largely based on inferences. These purported smoking guns appear to be based on the prosecution's inferences about what was said and not said. This doesn't mean that their inferences were wrong. We all have to infer things regularly in our lives, even often. Juries are told to use their best judgments about the cases they hear, which often means that they have to make inferences about the evidence.

The Jury's inferences are often right, as they probably were in this case as well, but it is the linguist's job to point out where the need for inference exists and any of the alternative understandings that inferences may convey. The linguist's only task is to use the tools of linguistic analysis to provide snapshot clues provided by the speech event, schemas, agendas, speech acts, and conversational strategies, and then assemble them into a panoramic picture of the conversations. Linguists point out what was said, how it was said, what was not said, what can only be inferred, and demonstrate to juries those areas in which they are forced to infer. At that point it is up to jurors to make their own ultimate decision by comparing the language evidence with their own inferences about it.

The prosecutor's inferencing process began when he indicted Cooperman based on the recorded language evidence provided by the tapes made by Little and Tierney. The government undoubtedly knew that the words of Little and Tierney were not trustworthy and convincing evidence, because they could have stolen the paintings of their own accord without Cooperman even knowing about it as a possible way of helping Cooperman get the insurance money to relieve his current financial crunch. However unlikely that scenario may have been, the prosecution needed more conclusive evidence, the best being from Cooperman's own language. The tapes that Tierney provided, however, were of questionable value in this, and the jurors were faced with the task of making the decision based on their own inferences.

The following table summarizes the major inferences that the prosecutor and the jury had to make, compared with the actual tape-recorded evidence.

Inference	Language Evidence
Little had the art in his possession	Clear
Tierney was involved in the theft	Clear
Cooperman knew that Little had the art	Clear
Cooperman told Tierney to destroy the art	No, he said to do nothing
Cooperman was involved in the theft	No language evidence
Cooperman used code with Tierney	Tierney spoke the code
Cooperman's parable implicated himself	Unclear

CONCLUSION OF THE CASE

In July 1999, the jury convicted Cooperman on eighteen counts of orchestrating the theft of the Picasso and Monet paintings from his own home. I gave my analysis to the defense attorneys and they may or may not have used it at trial but they didn't call on me to testify as an expert witness. As for the inferences required for conviction, I can only assume that the jury made the same inferences as the prosecutors. It seems likely that since the jury could ascertain from the tapes that Cooperman knew that Little had the paintings, they must have believed that Cooperman orchestrated the theft, which was not the worst inference in the world they could have made.

Before Cooperman was sentenced, he struck a deal with the prosecutor to reduce his sentence by revealing that a powerful New York law firm was involved in kickbacks relating to its many class action suits in which that law firm relied on Cooperman as an expert. Cooperman testified that in the past he had received about $5 million from his arrangement with that law firm. The law firm denied this, of course, and an investigation followed. For his purported help in this, Cooperman received a reduced sentence of 21 months in prison. Without this reduced sentence, he could have been sentenced to from seven to ten years. He was released from prison in July 2003 and died shortly afterward.

[9]

PRICE-FIXING (FRAUD)

The Sherman Antitrust Act of 1870 prohibits business activities such as cartels and monopolies that the government considers anti-competitive. This Act declared illegal "every contract, combination in the form of trust or otherwise, or conspiracy, in restraint of trade or commerce among the several states, or with foreign nations." It is often referred to as a law that would aid the consumer by keeping fraudulently created prices down and therefore help assure a competitive business landscape.

At the time the law was enacted, businesses had been organizing trusts that tried to control the market by suppressing competition, leading to the creation of monopolies in the marketplace that, with no competition, could charge customers whatever they wanted. Economic theory postulates that the public is best served by free competition, not by monopolies or cartels, and that is the issue the Sherman Antitrust Act addressed. The key expressions in the Act were "restraint of trade," "monopolies," and "abusing power unfairly."

Additional legislation followed, including the Clayton Act of 1914, the Federal Trade Commission Act of 1914, and the Robinson-Patman Act of 1936, all of which tried to further prohibit noncompetitive marketing. In short, the Sherman Antitrust Act attacked corporations that agreed with each other (fraudulently) conspired) to inhibit price competition and abused their power unfairly by raising, fixing, or stabilizing prices.

Price-fixing constitutes fraud in several ways. It takes unfair advantage of competitors and customers, an intentional and deceitful practice that deprives the marketplace of something of value. It is an unethical false representation of the product and a perversion of the truth. It constitutes cheating in the strongest sense of the word. One form of price-fixing is called "market allocation," which is charged when competitors agree to not compete with each other in the specific marketplaces and do so by dividing up sales in specific geographic areas.

One example of price-fixing allocation, *The United States v. Michael Andreas, Mark Whitacre, Terrance Wilson, and Kazutoshi Yamada* (Criminal No. 96-CR-762) is described in this chapter.

Until technological advances enabled the use of undercover tape recording, it was very difficult for the government to successfully prosecute corporations that attempted to fix prices in the marketplace. Although the case against Archer Daniels Midland (ADM) executives took some very bizarre twists and turns, it provides a good illustration of how undercover tape recordings brought down the top executives in that company, along with an executive of a Japanese competitor. This case was so unusual, in fact, that it inspired the publication of a book written by Kurt Eichenwald (Random House, 2000) and movie directed by Steven Soderbergh in 2009, both called *The Informant.*

Using a mountain of tape-recorded evidence, the government had little difficulty proving that the ADM and Japanese company executives fraudulently conspired to produce restraint of trade through market allocation and price-fixing. Even though this case did not end well for the defendants, it illustrates how linguistic analysis did what it could to help. But the facts are the facts, and all that the linguistic analysis could do for ADM was to point out a few things that the prosecution may have misinterpreted. Sometimes even things like that can be helpful to defendants at the sentencing phase.

BACKGROUND

ADM is a multimillion-dollar corporation in Decatur, Illinois, that was headed by vice-chairman of the board, Michael Andreas. Its slogan was "supermarket to the world" and its bio-products division, headed Mark Whitacre, was one of the world's largest manufacturers of lysine, an amino acid produced through a fermentation process creating products that farmers use as a protein additive to supplement a diet of corn, thereby ensuring the optimum and proper growth of their swine and poultry.

ADM's problems began in August 1992, when Mark Whitacre reported to Andreas that Japanese lysine-producing competitors were plotting to sabotage ADM. Hearing this, Andreas asked the Central Intelligence Agency (CIA) for help. In September, during the investigation, Whitacre alleged to the CIA that ADM was engaged in the price-fixing of lysine. By December of the same year, Whitacre admitted that he had made up the story about the Japanese sabotage plot and the CIA turned over the investigation of price-fixing to the FBI. Whitacre did not disclose to the FBI or to ADM that all the while he had been fraudulently bilking his own company out of millions dollars during that year. This would be discovered a bit later.

By January 1993 Whitacre had convinced the FBI that he could be a valuable asset to them as their undercover informant in the investigation of price-fixing at ADM and he subsequently tape-recorded his meetings with various individuals. To get the ball rolling, Whitacre told Andreas that a Japanese competitor in the lysine business was accusing ADM of breaking its word on a previously alleged pricing agreement. Two months later, ADM's senior vice president, Terrance Wilson, suggested that the world's leading producers of lysine should form a trade association that could serve as a cover for their secret meetings that were really about ways to control the lysine market through an agreed upon allocation of production and sales.

Executives of some of the major lysine-producing companies had already held meetings in Vancouver and Paris under the auspices of forming this purported lysine trade association before Whitacre secretly recorded an October 1993 meeting between Andreas, Whitacre, and two senior executives of a Japanese agricultural company called Ajinomoto who were apparently trying to reach an agreement about how they could allocate the total production of lysine for the forthcoming year, 1994. His tape recording of this meeting was considered central to the eventual prosecution, for it allegedly set the price-fixing scheme in place. Meanwhile, Whitacre continued to fraudulently bilk ADM, this time out of $220,000 for services he falsely attributed to another company. Whitacre pocketed the money himself and placed it in his secret personal overseas bank account.

The major producers of lysine met again in Tokyo in December 1993 to report to each other their monthly sales figures for lysine, and in March 1994 they met again in Hawaii to swap sales data and to talk further about the proposed lysine trade association that Wilson had introduced a year earlier. At the same time Whitacre continued to bilk ADM with bogus invoices and contracts for which ADM paid two and a half million dollars to a fictitious company that was actually controlled by him. After this he continued to drain ADM's resources and by February 1995 he had authorized payments of $3,750,000 to his own Swiss bank account.

In June 1995 Whitacre's undercover efforts led the FBI to raid ADM's headquarters, where they confiscated a large number of company files. By August ADM finally discovered that Whitacre was an FBI informant and fired him when they also realized that he had been stealing millions of dollars from the company. Whitacre defended the accusation, claiming that this money was part of those "off the books" bonus schemes commonly used by top ADM executives, but ADM vehemently denied that any such scheme existed. Soon after this Whitacre tried to kill himself by inhaling carbon monoxide fumes while he sat in his car with the motor running and the garage door closed. He was rescued, however, and at the hospital he was diagnosed as manic-depressive.

From January 1993 through August 1996, Whitacre's undercover work on behalf of the FBI had amassed over 200 hours of audio and videotape recordings. This tape-recorded evidence, in addition to the confiscated corporate files, resulted in ADM agreeing to pay a fine of 25 million dollars to settle several lawsuits contending that ADM had been price-fixing lysine. Two Japanese companies also agreed to pay 20 million dollars in fines. But even then Whitacre's troubles were not over. In September 1996 ADM sued him for embezzlement.

ADM's troubles were also far from over. After the judgment against ADM, Andreas and Wilson resigned their positions and Whitacre sued the company, contending that he was dismissed for whistleblowing. And in January 1996, the government indicted Michael Andreas, Terrance Wilson, Mark Whitacre, and Ajinomoto executive, Kazutoshi Yamura, for violating section 1 of the Sherman Act, charging them with price-fixing and "entering into and engaging in a combination and conspiracy to suppress and eliminate competition by fixing the price and allocating the sales volumes of lysine offered for sale to customers in the United States and other countries."

Whitacre was also indicted on criminal charges of defrauding ADM of more than nine million dollars. Whitacre pleaded guilty to thirty-seven criminal charges and was serving his nine-year sentence in a North Carolina prison when the government's criminal case against Andreas and Wilson began. At that point, Michael Andreas's lawyers thought they needed some help from a linguist, which is the focus of this chapter.

When the trial started in July 1998, the prosecutors began their case with what they must have believed their strongest evidence, the October 25, 1993, videotape of the meeting attended by the ADM executives Andreas and Whitacre and the Ajinomoto executives Kazutohi Yamada and Hirokazu Ikeda. Because the many telephone calls and other meetings recorded by Whitacre were thought to be less damaging to ADM than this videotaped meeting appeared to be, ADM's lawyers asked me to focus my analysis only on that October 25 meeting.

This October 25, 1993, meeting was the third time the lysine manufacturers had convened under the guise of a trade association. As mentioned above, they had met together twice before, first in Paris and then in Vancouver, under the auspices of the fledgling lysine association. Such associations can have legitimate purposes beneficial to their members as long as they don't become cartels or monopolies that allocate production and thereby control prices in the marketplace. Apparently the earlier two meetings didn't resolve whatever issues were on their agendas, so the October 25 meeting was planned.

Before it took place, Whitacre warned Andreas that the Japanese company, Ajinomoto, was engaged in lysine price-fixing. This apparently bothered Andreas enough to convene this new meeting in order to determine the accuracy of Whitacre's accusation. Andreas invited the Ajinomoto executives to a meeting at ADM's home office in Decatur, Illinois. From Andreas's perspective, not only could such a meeting flush out whether or not Whitacre's suspicions were accurate, but it also could lead to a discussion about both company's current and future plans for producing and distributing lysine. Andreas admittedly didn't know much about the Asian companies that were in the lysine business and he told Whitacre that he hoped to find out more about them from Ajinomoto, the leading Asian company in that business. By this time Whitacre had already signed on with the FBI and he covertly tape-recorded the meeting.

SPEECH EVENT

Unlike common business speech events relating to sales and purchases of a product or service, this speech event followed the general outline of a particular type of business meeting whose aim is to merge interests in a business plan that would be beneficial to both companies. This type of speech event typically has four stages:

The Merged Interests Speech Event

1. Identify the problems shared by both parties and how the companies might proceed in their future business in light of existing or potential competition with each other and other companies.
2. Discuss and clarify the dimensions of the problems identified.
3. Negotiate alternative approaches suggested during the meeting.
4. Agree or disagree about how to proceed in the future.

This was the third time lysine manufacturers had met on this topic. Their conversation began with a considerable amount of discussion about companies with which Ajinomoto was associated in various products besides lysine and some talk about the lysine business in general. The four speech event stages provide a snapshot illustrated by the following sequence of excerpted statements made by the participants during the course of the meeting about the quantity, relationships, optimal growth, and distribution of shares:

1. Problem: how Ajinomoto and ADM can compete and grow in the lysine business in light of existing or potential competition from three Korean lysine-producing companies.

   IKEDA: We talk about quantity.

   YAMADA: Let's talk about the lysine association . . . can we agree about quantity?

   WHITACRE: We talked about this in Paris.

2. Dimensions of the problem: the relationship and effect of producing lysine in light of (1) other products the participant's companies produced, such as MSG, soybean meal, and others; (2) the amount of lysine currently produced by competing companies such as Cargill, Staley, Orsan, and others; and (3) any potential legal problems involved in such competition.

   ANDREAS: Our goal is to expand the marketplace capacity.

   ANDREAS: The volume of competitors is the same as three years ago.

   ANDREAS: If nobody builds any more capacity, everybody will be full. We'd have 70% of the capacity . . . too much.

   IKEDA: We will try to elaborate the figures, then compromise.

   IKEDA: In Vancouver we tried for agreement on quantity.

   IKEDA: We have to agree, then persuade our friends

   WHITAKER: Let's put down what we agree on.

   ANDREAS: If we agree on what the other people are doing, we know what the marker is.

ANDREAS: The question is who gets that growth?

ANDREAS: The question is how do we share growth?

ANDREAS: The question is, how much of the growth do you want?

ANDREAS: The question is whether they'll agree to how much more they'll do in the next year.

3. Negotiation of alternatives: the amount of growth based on volume of production that would be optimal for the five companies producing lysine.

ANDREAS: Do Kyowa, Miwon and Cheil agree to 2, 2, and 2?

ANDREAS: I suggest that you tell them they can have 2,000 tons more in 1994 and we get the rest between you and us.

ANDREAS: Why don't we say we've agreed that growth will be 14,000 tons or more?

ANDREAS: Tell 'em ADM has agreed to increase volume by 5,000 tons based on 15 growth.

ANDREAS: If they don't agree, our number's liable to be over 5 . . . we'll grow to 20,000 instead of 5.

YAMADA: I don't know if others 100% agree to give major part to ADM to contain ourselves to 5,000 ton of growth in 1994, providing the market is stable.

IKEDA: Rather easy to agree to this figures among four companies.

WHITACRE: As long as it's 68 plus growth.

ANDREAS: As long as they know what we're doing.

4. Agreement: the distribution of market shares among the competing companies producing lysine.

WHITACRE: So on volume you're gonna propose 67,000 tons plus growth.

IKEDA: Plus, uh, uh, to substantial growth . . . and we see if they agree, yeah.

The first two stages of this merged interests speech event were at least marginally legally benign, for the sharing of general information about the field is not considered illegal. But stage 3 gave clear indication of moving away from merely reporting amounts of past production to each other toward allocating their production, and although no agreement about distributing market shares was reached in stage 4, their conversation introduced the possibility that such agreement might be reached at some time in the future.

To bring an indictment, the government needed to get their agreement to conspire, which did not take place during this snapshot view of the merged interests speech event.

SCHEMAS

In very guarded business conversations like this one, indirectness plays an important role in disguising schemas. Such indirectness can be exacerbated when the conversation is between speakers of different languages, and mutual understanding is even more problematic when the native language and politeness culture of some of the participants is Japanese. Recall that Andreas entered the meeting with Whitacre's unsupported report that Ajinomoto was already fixing the price of lysine.

Andreas's language indicated that his schema at the start of the meeting was to determine whether or not Whitacre's accusation was true. Since it would be difficult for Andreas to come right out and ask Yamada whether his Japanese company was fixing lysine prices in Asia, he had to take a more indirect route. One way to do this would be to let the Japanese executives talk about how to expand the "market capacity" for lysine, especially in the Asian area that included the three Korean competitors. Andreas's second schema was that he could gain the support of the Japanese participants, who gave evidence through their language that they also were trying to find ways to agree about how to expand their "market capacity" and "share growth" in relation to that of the competition in Korea. So far, the conversation was fairly consistent with what might be expected in a legitimate meeting of a lysine association and nothing explicitly illegal had taken place.

Consistent with a predictable lysine association meeting, Yamada opened the conversation by seeking Andreas's expert advice about various companies with which Ajinomoto was already associated or was planning to associate. Andreas offered his opinions about many of these companies while at the same time was learning from Yamada about the Korean lysine competitors with whom Andreas was admittedly unfamiliar.

After about an hour into the conversation, Ikeda and Yamada finally revealed their own schema by introducing the topic of possible mutual allocation of the production of lysine. At that point Andreas's schema for the meeting changed quickly from his initial schema of learning more about the Korean companies to the Ajinomoto executives' schema of allocating lysine production in a way that would lead to the "benefit of both ADM and Ajinomoto." At that point, Andreas took charge of the conversation and expressed his opinions about what that allocation ought to be. Yamada and Ikeda politely posed some hypothetical objections, but these were not strong enough to encourage Andreas to think that they seriously opposed his suggestions. At that point the schemas of Andreas and Yamada appeared to be in harmony about the meaning of the vague terms, "expanding market capacity" and "sharing the growth."

Once they got to that point, Whitacre's schema supported that of Andreas and Yamada, but he obviously held another very different schema as well. Since he was covertly recording the meeting, his primary and probably only schema was that all the participants would reach the point of planning the illegal act of price-fixing, for after all, that was what the FBI had engaged him to expose. But when the FBI agents reviewed the tape of this meeting, they were apparently frustrated that the participants had talked about allocation but had not reached any agreement about how to do it. The prosecution needed that agreement in order to bring a successful indictment.

In summary, Andreas's language indicated that his initial schema for this meeting was to learn about his Korean competitors from executives of the Japanese company, Ajinomoto. Yamada's language indicated that his initial schema for this meeting was to obtain Andreas's opinions about various companies with which Ajinomoto was as currently associated or about to be associated. Up to that point their conversation was characteristic of a legally benign lysine association. But the initial schemas of both men changed when Ikeda introduced his schema that the two companies should find ways to allocate production of lysine. The schema snapshot of this meeting contributed to the developing possible guilt of the participants, but it didn't quite reach it.

AGENDAS

The meeting lasted from 9:00 a.m. to 1:30 p.m., except for a short lunch break during which the ADM and Ajinomoto executives dined separately. The government's 243-page transcript revealed many topic introductions that can be categorized into six major themes. Each theme contained many related topics and responses. Space does not permit a complete topic/response analysis here but a brief summary of the themes follows.

Theme 1: Relationships with Other Companies

Yamada introduced theme 1 by asking Andreas what he thought about his company's relationships with Amylum, Orsan, Cargill, Staley, and LaFarge in terms of lysine and other products such as MSG, corn, citric acid, and soybean meal. Andreas provided his knowledge about the companies and their executives, at one point responding:

> ANDREAS: My only problem with Cargill is if they enter the lysine business, but we can live with any partners you select because of the need to expand the market. You can make the best judgment how to keep the market on steady ground.

Although Cargill was a major U.S. competitor in lysine, Andreas was amenable to Ajinomoto's future association with that company because, as he put it, this could "help expand the market." Andreas explained to Yamada that he doesn't understand the Asian competition as well as Yamada does and would like his information and advice about the ability and capacity of the Korean companies, Kyowa, Miwon, and Cheil.

Theme 2: The Market Situation and Possible Compromise

Yamada introduced theme 2, about ways to "persuade better market situation," eventually clarifying this to mean achieving a possible agreement about each company's quantity of production and hinting at the idea of allocating sales volume. Andreas responded with purportedly helpful advice about the companies with which Ajinomoto was currently related or with whom they planned to buy or merge, but to this point he did not respond to Yamada's vague and indirect hint that they allocate volume of sales.

It was Ikeda who first suggested what he called "compromising" about how much should be allocated to the five companies:

YAMADA: We're trying to persuade better market situation. Can we agree about quantity?

ANDREAS: The market is larger than most think. In three years everyone will run out of capacity. It's a matter of controlling that capacity. Our goal is 3 or 4 years to expand the marketplace capacity. The volume of competitors is the same as 3 years ago. The only change is lower prices. We have the most capacity in the business—9,000 tons a month. The market shrank for our competitors like Cargill but our business is still bigger than before Cargill entered the market. Our goal is to establish ourselves and keep everybody else out. 70% growth is too much but we don't want to shrink.

IKEDA: We will try to elaborate the figures, then compromise. The question is how much for 5 manufacturers. We have to agree, then persuade our friends. They want not your right to have bigger figures for 1994.

It is unclear what Andreas meant by his vaguely stated "controlling that capacity," but it is common practice for corporations to try to beat their competitors and in a sense to "keep everybody else out." To this Ikeda suggested that they "elaborate" their figures and compromise about them.

Theme 3: Market Growth over Past Three Years

Theme 2 led to Ikeda's introduction of theme 3 in which they agreed to "elaborate" their figures and share their estimates of their own company's production and sales of lysine over the past two years, presumably as a way to determine how Ikeda's idea of "compromise" might be put into action. Andreas responded by briefly "elaborating" ADM's figures:

ANDREAS: ADM was 218 in 1992, 245 in 1993.

Theme 4: Growth Predictions for Next Year

Next the conversation moved from "elaborating" their figures for past years to Ikeda's new topic introduction of "estimating" figures for the coming year. Ikeda introduced theme 4 by requesting predictions of growth and production of lysine for 1994. Whitacre, who had been fairly silent to this point, now jumped in and suggested that they write down on paper what they agree on for the coming year, perhaps because he may have thought Andreas was not quite on the same page with Ikeda at that point in the discussion.

Since Whitacre was secretly tape-recording the meeting, he also needed to be able to document any explicitly illegal discussion and having the figures written down could provide good support for this. Whitacre's covert contribution here appeared to be that of trying to nudge Andreas into the idea of allocation:

> IKEDA: You have any idea of quantity for 1994? We estimate your sales smaller.
> WHITACRE: We estimate your sales smaller too. Let's put down what we agree on.

Theme 5: Sharing Market Growth

Andreas took Whitacre's bait and introduced theme 5, which was the critical part of this meeting. Andreas began by asking questions about Ikeda's suggestion concerning how they could "share growth" between ADM, Ajinomoto, and the three Korean companies. Encouraged by Whitacre and without being explicit, Ikeda promoted the idea that the two companies could work together to control the Asian market by allocating shares of the growth among themselves and the Korean companies.

Based on this tape alone, it is unclear whether Andreas harbored Ikeda's apparent agenda intention all along, but with the encouragement nicely set up by Ikeda and Whitacre, Andreas now seized the opportunity and offered specific suggestions. Supported by Whitacre, Andreas took the lead by first suggesting, then virtually demanding that ADM and Ajinomoto get the lion's share while the three Korean companies would be allocated smaller chunks of the lysine business:

> ANDREAS (TO YAMADA AND IKEDA): The question is how much growth do you want? The question is whether they'll agree to how much more they'll do in the next year?

Now fired up, Andreas concluded with a threat:

> ANDREAS: If they don't agree, our number's liable to be over 5. We're willing to contain ourselves to a 5,000-ton growth in 1994, providing the market is stable.

Whitacre, taping the meeting, naturally supported Andreas in this, for it suited the purpose of his FBI undercover role:

> WHITACRE: If not, we go up to 20. Let 'em think we're smaller than we really are. If the market grows 15, we get half.
>
> ANDREAS: The question is, how do we share the growth? How much of the growth do you want? The question is,

whether they'll agree to how much more they'll do in the next year. Do Kyowa, Miwon, and Cheil agree to 2, 2, and 2?

IKEDA: I cannot say if they agree or not.

To this, Andreas put on his hat of "chief-executive-in-control" and grew even more explicit:

ANDREAS: I suggest that you tell them they can have 2,000 tons more in 1994 and we get the rest between you and us. Why don't we say we've agreed that growth will be 14,000 tons or more. They add 2,000 tons apiece and we split the rest.

But Yamada was still not convinced:

YAMADA: Miwon wants to increase it proportionally. They say ADM eats all the growth for past 2 years. And now is trying to absorb all the growth.

WHITACRE: We created the growth.

YAMADA: Very difficult to convince them.

WHITACRE: Tell them anything. It will be a problem when numbers are submitted.

Whitacre's contribution, "tell them anything," supported his ongoing undercover need to bring the smell of deception into the exchange. He continued his support for deceiving the Koreans while Andreas insisted that the other companies should know what they were doing. At that point Andreas reprised his warning and at the same time insisted that the Koreans be aware of the whole procedure. Yamada was still not convinced that the Korean companies would agree to the allocation. Meanwhile, Whitacre continued to suggest that they deceive them:

> ANDREAS: If they don't agree, our number's liable to be over 5. We'll grow to 20,000 instead of 5.
>
> YAMADA: I don't know if others 100% agree to give major part to ADM to contain potential capacity.
>
> WHITACRE: They don't need to see real numbers.
>
> ANDREAS: We're willing to contain ourselves to a 5,000-ton growth in 1994, providing the market is stable.
>
> WHITACRE: If not, we're going up to 20. Let them think we're smaller than we really are. If the market grows 15, we get half.
>
> ANDREAS: As long as we understand each other, present it however you want. As long as they know what we're doing.

Theme 6: Closing and Invitation

After a brief lunch period Yamada introduced theme 6, which brought the meeting to a close. He invited Andreas to come to Japan for another meeting in which he could try to convince the three Korean companies himself, to which Andreas agreed:

> YAMADA: Mr. Andreas to Japan? Invite you officially.
>
> ANDREAS: If that would establish more trust in the industry.

This meeting ended with Andreas being clear about what the stage 4 market shares should be for ADM, Ajinomoto, and three Korean producers of lysine, but with the Ajinomoto executives not agreeing that this goal could be accomplished. Doing so would require future meetings to get that agreement, which apparently is why Yamada invited Andreas to Japan for the next one. It was also why the FBI, after reviewing this tape, decided that another meeting was needed to try to get an agreement on tape.

The snapshot of the agendas of this meeting indicated that it was the Japanese executives who introduced the topic of allocation. Even though there was a considerable amount discussion about how lysine could be allocated, the participants did not end the meeting with agreement to do it.

SPEECH ACTS

The predictable speech acts in price-fixing include advising, offering, agreeing, objecting, reporting information, opining, complaining, warning, threatening, and requesting information and opinions. The major legal concerns are agreements and objections. Yamada requested Andreas's help about various companies he was considering buying or was associating with and Andreas advised Yamura about their strengths and weaknesses and how to deal with them. Andreas reported information about ADM's plans and threatened what might happen to the Korean lysine producers if they wouldn't comply with his as yet unmade proposition. Whitacre supported what Andreas advised and reported, but also agreed with Yamada about their need to decide how production of lysine should be allocated. Yamada and Ikeda advised that they allocate lysine production, but offered polite objections to whether or not the three Korean companies would accept a lower allocation.

The most important speech act of this meeting, agreeing to allocate lysine in the marketplace, was not made by either party. For the purpose of my analysis of this conversation, I pointed out to the defense attorneys that it contained no speech acts of an agreement. The FBI also realized that the agreement was missing and instructed Whitacre to arrange future meetings of the lysine association, including one that eventually took place in Hawaii, where Whitacre finally orchestrated a scene on videotape in which the participants clearly voiced their speech act of agreement.

CONVERSATIONAL STRATEGIES

There were very few of the conversational strategies that commonly occur in undercover operations, possibly because the person doing the taping, Whitacre, did not appear to need to employ the available strategies of ambiguity, camouflaging, interruption, and others. He did suggest that they withhold information from the Korean companies, but he didn't even need to camouflage the topic of possible price-fixing because Ikeda had introduced it explicitly. The Japanese participants' frequent use of Asian indirectness might qualify as an ambiguity strategy, but if so, it appeared to have no strong effect on the meeting, possibly because Andreas didn't even seem to notice it.

SMOKING GUNS

The primary linguistic finding relating to this conversation demonstrated that no agreement had been reached about how to allocate lysine production and sales.

Second, Andreas did not introduce the idea of price-fixing by mutual allocating lysine in the marketplace. After lengthy talk about the lysine business, allocation was clearly introduced and promoted by Ikeda and Yamada. In the legal context, the fact that it was not Andreas who brought it up could be used by the defense to demonstrate his lack of predisposition to fix prices. His purported goal for the meeting, as shown by the language he used as the conversation began, was to learn more about his Korean competitors from the two Ajinomoto executives, although, of course, it is not possible to know what else was on his mind. Even if Andreas was not predisposed to commit an illegal act, it could not be disputed that Ikeda and Yamada provided that opportunity with a strong assist from Whitacre. Andreas then enthusiastically embraced that opportunity in theme 5 of their meeting. There was little hope for a claim of entrapment here, since without being coerced and with very little prompting Andreas clearly and eagerly bit on Ikeda's suggestion to allocate lysine production.

Third, the major smoking guns cited by the government were uttered not by Andreas, but by Yamada and Ikeda:

- We're trying to persuade better market situation.
- Can we agree about quantity?
- We will try to elaborate the figures, then compromise.
- We have to agree, then persuade our friends.
- It's rather easy to agree to this figure among 5 companies.
- I don't know if others 100% agree to give major part to ADM to contain its potential capacity.

These statements were indisputably clear evidence of their desire to allocate the production of lysine, but the group lacked an agreement to do so. If it were not for the later meeting in which the same men agreed to allocate production, this October 25 meeting offered some small possibilities for Andreas's defense. For example, if he was predisposed to allocate, the taped evidence did not demonstrate it. Nor was there agreement to conspire at this point, although it certainly came in their later meeting in Hawaii.

In most undercover operations, the opportunity to commit a crime is provided by the agents, as in bribery cases (Shuy 2013) and in solicitation to murder cases (Shuy 2014). In this investigation the role of undercover operative, Mark Whitacre, was relatively minor. He encouraged deception, as noted above, but it was Ikeda and Yamada, in their culturally indirect manner, who provided the opportunity for Andreas to bite on their allocation plan. Whitacre's main role was to suggest that the two companies commit to paper their current figures as a way of predicting next year's production, which could put specificity on what previously had been rather vague and general talk. He also supported Andreas once he bought into the possibility.

Smoking gun statements by Andreas included the following:

- In three years everyone will run out of capacity. It's a matter of controlling the capacity.
- Our goal is to establish ourselves and keep everyone else out.

If these statements were all that the government had on Andreas, the defense may have been able to make somewhat of a case. But there was more:

- The question is, who gets that growth?
- The question is, how do we share the growth? How much growth do you want?
- The question is whether they'll agree to how much more they'll do in the next year.
- Do Kyowa, Miwan and Cheil agree to 2, 2, and 2?
- They can have 2,000 tons more in 1994 and we get the rest between you and us.
- Tell them ADM had agreed to increase volume by 5,000 tons based on 15 growth.
- Why don't we say we've agreed that growth will be 14,000 tons?
- They add 2,000 tons apiece and we split the rest.

- If they don't agree, our number's liable to be over 5. We'll grow to 20,000 instead of 5.
- We're willing to contain ourselves to a 5,000 ton growth in 1994.
- As long as we understand each other.
- As long as we know what we're doing.

Andreas posed these contributions as questions and hypotheticals, not quite enough for the prosecution to charge him at this point. Even taking into consideration the snapshots of the speech event, schemas, agendas, speech acts, and conversational strategies, it was simply not possible to derive a linguistic analysis of these smoking gun expressions that could indicate anything other than that Andreas agreed to go along with Ikeda's plan to decide on how to allocate the production of lysine in such a way that both companies could benefit financially. The plain fact was that even though Andreas did not introduce the idea of allocation himself, he fully embraced the opportunity that Ikeda and Yamada offered to him.

Andreas's defense attorney suggested to me the possibility that Andreas simply may have been stringing the Japanese executives along in what has been called the "blowing theory defense." Since I had seen this defense theory offered and then shot down in flames several times before, I tried to discourage the attorneys from even trying it. Congressmen Richard Kelly's defense attorney tried to use it in his 1980 Abscam bribery case. Congressman Ozzie Myers also claimed that he was "just blowing" to the undercover agent in his bribery trial in that same year. The juries in both cases quickly rejected these defense theories. Nevertheless, I examined the language evidence for any clues to Andreas's efforts to deliberately deceive the Japanese executives and found none. Whether or not Andreas was lying or "blowing" to the Japanese executives, the speech event structure of negotiating a potential merged business agreement was very much evident. As far as I know, Andreas's lawyers then abandoned that idea. It's a desperately weak defense approach used only when there is nothing else to go on.

Other linguistic contributions in this case were to help the defense attorneys clarify a few passages of the tapes in which the government's transcript was simply wrong. One example was a passage in the meeting described above in which the government claimed Andreas was agreeing to a deal to allocate when he said, "we're gonna deal here." The dispute over this passage occurred possibly because at that point the two speakers overlapped each other. After listening many times to a tape loop of this passage on the highest quality equipment available, I concluded that the transcript should have said:

> YAMADA: As long as the end results come out that way.
> ANDREAS: We're not gonna deal here.

Andreas began his utterance, "We're not," as Yamada was saying "end results," and then Andreas paused slightly before he continued, "gonna deal here:" His "gonna" overlapped with Yamada's "way," but his last two words, "deal here," were not overlapped, probably causing the government's transcriber to hear it as Andreas saying "we're gonna deal here" as his complete utterance. When I charted the written representation of the spoken utterance in such a way that it indicated sequential time, the passage looked like this:

> UNIDENTIFIED: As long as the end results come out that way.
> ANDREAS: We're not gonna deal here.

This isn't the only evidence that Andreas was disagreeing with the other speaker. His intonation pattern also supported his negativity. Using lines to indicate pitch height in his utterance, I represented

Intonation

the sentence as shown above, showing that his intonation pattern supported his negativity to the other speaker's utterance.

Andreas stressed "we're not" and "deal" to indicate his separation from the other speaker's idea about who would be doing what. During my years of working in the area of language and law I've found that negatives are among the most difficult items for transcribers to detect, not only in overlapped speech, but also even in the speech of a single audible speaker. Contracted negatives are often the most difficult, but full negatives seem to be almost equally problematic for transcribers who are untrained in phonetics and who lack experience dealing with overlapping speech.

RECAP AFTER THE MEETING

In undercover operations it is common practice for the person wearing the recorder to activate it before meeting with the target and to let it keep running after the meeting ends until such time as it is possible to turn it off or disconnect it without being noticed by the target. It is also common for the prosecution to ignore those later recorded portions and not bother to make a transcript of them. This case was a bit different, however, because Andreas was Whitacre's main target, causing him to keep the tape running as he and Andreas left the meeting room and started home in their car. Whitacre let his tape-recording continue because apparently he was trying to capture anything else Andreas might say to inculpate himself. This enabled Whitacre and the prosecution to discover what Andreas thought had taken place, a kind of recap of how he understood what happened during the meeting. Selected portions of their conversations follow:

> WHITACRE: They made it complicated, didn't they?
>
> ANDREAS: It sure didn't take much to get 'em there.
>
> WHITACRE: You made it very clear. We're not gonna go any lower than where we're at. Bottom line is, they're satisfied with where we're at.
>
> ANDREAS: Yamada said the way we're going to explain it is that we're giving you more market share to keep you from utilizing that big capacity. They were prepared to give us more market share, more of the growth . . . more than our share of the growth before we walked into that room. . . . He said, we give you more growth because we're trying to keep your capacity down. So it's kinda like a bribe, you know.
>
> WHITACRE: What he's saying they're taking us 54 to 67 in order to keep our 150,000 tons at bay.
>
> ANDREAS: I told Yamada we'll limit our growth to 5,000 tons or we won't. Take your pick. It'll either be 5 or 25. You don't think they'd be stupid enough now to go from 73 to 87 do you? They know it'd wreck the market.

This recap enabled the prosecution to verify that Andreas did not misconstrue the indirectness of Yamada and Ikeda. It was clear that he understood that down the road an eventual deal could be made to control ADM's capacity to produce more growth and to possibly monopolize the market. That Andreas compared Yamada's strategy with a bribe did not help his case one bit.

SUMMARY OF THE LINGUISTIC
ANALYSIS

So if this linguistic analysis couldn't help Andreas's case, why should I go into detail about it? One important point is that the retaining attorneys are always in control of the evidence they give the experts to analyze. Since it was their decision to ask me to review only the October 25, 1993, tape-recorded conversation, there was nothing I could do about the many other phone calls and meeting tapes in evidence. My universe for analysis was only that single crucial conversation. I can't get into the minds of the lawyers as to why they gave me only that one tape, but experts analyze only that which is provided to them. It was my impression when I accepted this assignment that if my analysis could clarify matters in this one conversation, it might possibly be of use to the retaining lawyers. As it turns out, my analysis didn't really help much other than to alert them about where the weaknesses in their case might be. But I didn't consider this a failure on my part. The expert's analysis can be only as useful as the data permits.

Sometimes linguistic analysis works for defense attorneys and sometimes it tells them only where their cases are weak or hopeless. In this case I could demonstrate how the language of the speech event was legally benign up to a certain point, during which vague expressions used in isolation such as "expand marketplace capacity," "build more capacity," "growth," "better market situation," and even "quantity" could be understood to be business jargon expected of corporate executives. But when "growth" became "share the growth," and "how much growth do you want," the discussion became problematic for Andreas. It is easy to understand how businesses would like to "keep everybody else out" as long as this is accomplished legally through sheer business or marketing skills, but when "keep everybody else out" and other terms are contextualized in discussions of allocation, the meaning of otherwise mere business jargon can take a very uncomfortable turn for the defense.

The snapshot of speech event analysis showed that the meeting followed the structure of one type of business speech event that started out legitimately but turned into something very different when the Japanese executives introduced the topic of allocation. The linguistic contribution to the defense here was that it was not Andreas who turned that speech event around. The down side of this, however, was that Andreas took advantage of the opportunity of Ikeda's changed direction and appropriated it as his own. This could demonstrate Andreas's lack of predisposition to allocate and fix prices, but this mattered little when he subsequently took charge of developing this new direction in the conversation.

In many criminal investigations it is common for the agents to provide the opportunity for the targets to either agree or disagree with the idea of having someone murdered or accepting a bribe. If the agents coerce or otherwise use outrageous techniques that influence their target unduly, this provides the defense an opportunity to claim entrapment. But such was not the case here. The surrogate agent, Mark Whitacre, did not even need to push or coerce the Japanese executives to introduce the topic of allocating lysine. They did it on their own accord and without Whitacre's strong urging and with Andreas eagerly following suit.

The snapshot provided by the analysis of the participants' schemas also was worth examining but in the end this analysis also could not go very far toward helping the defense. We can never know what internal schema Andreas had in his mind, but his spoken language evidence in this conversation indicated that at first it was to learn from the Ajinomoto executives more about his Korean competitors in the lysine business. If that was his only schema, my analysis might have been helpful to his case. But after Ikeda and

Yamada put allocation on the table, Andreas converted his previously articulated schema to theirs and he then took over the direction about how to accomplish it.

The snapshot analysis of agendas was similarly unhelpful to the defense. After the initial theme of discussing other companies and executives, Yamada turned to his own apparent agenda of allocation by saying he was "trying to persuade better market situation" by controlling the overall quantity of production of lysine. This appeared to convert Andreas's agenda to Yamada's, and from that point on he took charge of the finding ways to allocate by "sharing the growth." Even though the meeting concluded with no clear agreement about how to accomplish this with the Korean competitors, the damage was done. Andreas's language showed that he willfully and knowingly wanted to join the conspiracy to do this.

The snapshot offered by speech act analysis provided only one possibly helpful point for the defense. The participants made requests, advised each other, suggested solutions, and finally gave the appearance of being unified in their need to convince the Korean companies to cooperate with their allocation plans. Andreas made no objections or denials to this theme after the Japanese executives introduced it. The most important speech act, however, was the lack of their agreement about allocating lysine during this conversation.

Unlike most other conversations surreptitiously recorded by an agent, it was not necessary for Whitaker to use the available conversational strategies found in some undercover operations. The targets were so willing to discuss how to allocate lysine that he didn't need to push or coerce the idea.

These rather meager linguistic contributions left the examination of the smoking gun expressions as potential help for the defense. One alleged smoking gun was destroyed by careful analysis of the overlapped speech, but it was a small grain of sand on a very large beach. Of marginal assistance to the defense was my agenda analysis showing that the most critical initial smoking guns were uttered by Yamada and Ikeda and not by Andreas. Another was the lack of any speech act of agreement at the end of the discussion.

I describe this case only because it illustrates how linguistic analysis can work in price-fixing cases. Even though such analysis can't alter the actual language evidence, the defense attorneys thought it might be worthwhile to see what they might learn from it. Once I submitted my analysis to them, my role obviously was over. They were disappointed but not surprised that I couldn't find more that was helpful to their cases, but they said they used my analysis wherever they could during the trial. Sometimes that's all linguistic analysis can offer.

Reprising the adverbial modifiers that characterize fraudulent language as noted in chapter 1, Andreas appeared to exercise his power unconscientiously over his apparently willing Japanese colleagues. Both Andreas and Whitacre withheld, concealed, and misrepresented information and they both knowingly deceived and acted surreptitiously. It is equally clear that they spoke without belief in the truth of what they said. Not a pretty picture.

CONCLUSION OF THE CASE

The three-year investigation of ADM concluded in July 1999, when Andreas and Wilson were convicted at trial for their roles in the global conspiracy to fix the price of lysine. The prosecutor characterized Wilson as the mastermind of the conspiracy but made it clear that Andreas gave the final approval. Both received sentences of 24 months in prison and fines of $350,000.

Whitacre, was not present at the trial because he was already serving a nine-year prison sentence for stealing millions of dollars from ADM. He was also convicted and sentenced to twenty additional months in prison. He complained bitterly about this, saying that the government would have had no case without his cooperation, which seems to have been a somewhat bizarrely accurate complaint that the government rejected.

Sometimes linguistic analysis can provide only marginally helpful assistance to the retaining defense attorneys. This was such a case.

[10]

THE EFFECTIVENESS
OF LINGUISTIC ANALYSIS
IN FRAUD CASES

Determining whether or not law cases result in a favorable verdict for the retaining lawyer's client is not an effective way to evaluate the usefulness of the linguistic analysis provided in these or any other cases. The outcome of a case is the lawyers' sole responsibility no matter how useful the linguists' assistance might have been. However, in the cases described in this book a comparison of the outcomes with the prosecution's charges may be able to offer some small and tentative insights into the possible effectiveness of the linguistic consulting and reports given to the retaining attorneys.

As was noted in each of the eight fraud cases described here, I was not asked to provide linguistic expert witness testimony at trial, so there was no way to assess the effectiveness of this. In fact, two of the cases were, at best, long shots for the defense lawyers, who probably suspected from the beginning that it was unlikely that their clients could get a favorable verdict. After a jury found Andreas (chapter 9) guilty of knowingly and willfully price-fixing, the judge sentenced him to twenty-four months in prison and a $350,000 fine. Similarly, a jury found Cooperman (chapter 8) knowingly and willfully guilty of fraud and the judge sentenced him to twenty-one months in prison. In both cases the prosecution used additional inculpatory information that went beyond the language evidence and it alone was probably strong enough to make these verdicts predictable.

As the analysis in chapter 9 shows, there was relatively little that linguistic analysis could do to support Andreas other than that which pointed out that his language in the only conversation I was given to analyze did not demonstrate his predisposition to commit the crime and that the participants did not agree to allocate lysine during that meeting. On the other hand, it also showed that Andreas knowingly bought into the idea of allocation as soon as the Japanese participants introduced that topic. Andreas then took over the conversation and plotted how the two companies could conspire to fix prices in the marketplace. In the face of that evidence, there was no way that any linguistic analysis could be of much benefit to his defense lawyers. This case is a good example of the way retaining lawyers do not always ask their experts to analyze all of the evidence. In a later taped conversation, all of the participants clearly agreed to fix the price of lysine.

In Cooperman's fraud case (chapter 8) linguistic analysis was able to demonstrate that the tape-recorded language didn't produce any evidence that he was knowingly and willfully guilty of orchestrating the plot to have his own paintings stolen so that he could reap the benefits of the insurance policies he held on them. On the other hand, it showed that Cooperman knew that Little currently had the paintings in his possession. The jury possibly inferred his guilt from what was said on those tapes along with additional physical evidence of his guilt that went beyond the tape-recorded conversations.

It's clear that the linguistic analysis in these two cases couldn't provide very much help to the defense lawyers, but this was not entirely the fault of the analysis because the prosecution also had additional non-recorded evidence pointing to their guilt. Linguistic contributions are limited to only the language evidence, and there wasn't very much of it that could be helpful to the retaining lawyers in these two cases.

In contrast, linguistic analysis sometimes can provide some help to defense lawyers during their subsequent negotiations with prosecutors for obtaining reductions in the charges made in indictments. In three of these eight cases the defense lawyers were somewhat successful in negotiating pleas relating to most but not all of the charges. Valentine (chapter 7) pleaded guilty to only one of the three counts of knowingly and willfully committing securities fraud and was given a four-year prison sentence. Burkhardt (chapter 6) also pleaded guilty to only one of the prosecution's three counts of knowingly and willfully conspiring to launder money, resulting in his forfeiture of $1.5 million and various properties. The sentence his lawyers were able to negotiate, however, did not require him to serve any prison time. Hsu's attorneys (chapter 5) were able to persuade the government to drop ten of the eleven charges against him in exchange for his guilty plea to only one charge of knowingly and willfully attempting to steal trade secrets, for which he received what his lawyers described as a slap on-the-wrist fine of $10,000 with no probation or prison time. They reported that Hsu agreed to the plea in order to get out of this country as quickly as possible and save the expense and trauma of a trial. In these three cases, the linguistic analyses possibly could have made modest contributions to the defense attorneys when they negotiated their fairly favorable plea agreements.

The remaining three of these eight cases resulted in even more favorable results for the retaining attorneys. The jury found Smith (chapter 2) not guilty on all the government's charges of knowingly and willfully conspiring to make false statements and committing wire fraud. Similarly, the jury acquitted Heroux and Miklasevics (chapter 3) on all charges of knowingly and willfully conspiring to make false statements in violation of EPA regulations. The attorneys in Cohen's (chapter 4) case of knowingly and willfully conspiring, aiding and abetting, and violating the Foreign Corrupt Practices Act convinced the court to dismiss his case before the trial even started.

In all of these cases I shared my linguistic analysis with the retaining attorneys, who likely used it in their briefs and negotiations with the prosecutors. It is not possible to know how useful this linguistic analysis actually was, but it offered some help to the defense in all the cases except those of Andreas and Cooperman, which posed exceptionally difficult problems of their own making.

Providing linguistic analysis of the language evidence to attorneys may be the best way for linguistic experts to be useful to retaining lawyers. In my opinion, Plan A is always to try to educate the retaining lawyers in the linguistic analysis and provide suggestions about how they can use it themselves, while Plan B is to testify at trial. The retaining lawyer's decision about which plan to use depends, among other things, on how effective the linguists are in explaining their analyses to them and, among other things, how well those lawyers can understand it and use it most effectively.

Plan A is consistent with what Solan expressed very well in his article, "Linguistics Experts as Semantic Tour Guides" (1998). He explained that lawyers do not generally know what linguistics is, probably because it is a relatively unknown, small discipline, containing only about 4,000 members of the Linguistic Society of America in contrast with about 800,000 US lawyers whose focus is naturally on the law rather than how language is used as evidence in their cases. Although Solan's point was that linguists can serve as tour guides when they are called as expert witnesses, his idea seems to be equally relevant for linguists to serve as tour guides to retaining lawyers even if they decide not to use those linguists at trial.

The wheels are probably grinding in the minds of some readers who still may wonder why it requires a linguist to help untangle the language evidence in these eight fraud cases when competent lawyers may have been able to try their cases without any linguistic help at all. No doubt some of them can. This question is one that judges often ask when linguists are proffered as experts in law cases. Perhaps some lawyers have the training and skills to go it alone, but most do not and I suspect they believe that linguists who specialize in the structure of language sounds, grammar, semantics, pragmatics, speech acts, discourse, and variation can explain their analyses more cogently than they can.

One problem is that lawyers, no matter how brilliant they may be, are less likely to be able to think about and conceptualize the language evidence in the way linguists do, and therefore they are not likely to be able to come up with the linguist's analysis in the first place. In many of the cases I've worked on in the past three and a half decades, the lawyers who called me said that they thought something was odd about the language evidence but they couldn't put their finger on what it was. Past examples of this include defense attorneys for the Abscam Investigations of bribery defendants Kenneth McDonald, Harrison Williams, the defense lawyers for the Brilab Investigation defendant Billy Clayton, and the US attorney who headed the impeachment of Federal Judge Alcee Hastings (all discussed in Shuy 2013). The same can be said about the defense lawyers in the murder cases of T. Cullen Davis, Stephen Allen, Mohammed Arshad, and Beverly Monroe (all discussed in Shuy 2014).

Some defense attorneys have their own reasons for using expert witness linguists at trial. For example, in a solicitation to murder case in Dundee Scotland (Shuy 2014), the defense lawyers suspected that something was wrong with the undercover officer's part of the tape-recorded conversation and with the defendant's responses, but they couldn't determine what it was. After I gave them my analysis, they decided that they didn't think they would be able to explain it very well when they cross-examined government witnesses. In addition, they said they thought that using an expert witness linguist could be more effective way to convey this crucial information in their direct examination. They told me that if they used my analysis by themselves in cross-examining the government's witnesses, it would not look like it was a vital part of their defendant's case. They reasoned that if linguistic testimony became a major part of their direct case, it could have more power because the defense would be taking the offensive rather than merely reacting from a defensive crouch.

Another question that some judges raise when linguists are proffered for expert witness testimony is that their linguistic analysis would be too difficult for jurors to understand and therefore it would be a waste of the court's valuable time to permit them to testify. This poses a paradox for expert witnesses of all specializations. When we make our linguistic analysis of the evidence clear and understandable, it may look so obvious and simple as to suggest that the same analysis easily could have been presented by the lawyers without the help of an expert. Even worse, it can look like simple common sense rather than making technical linguistic principles clear. Paradoxical or not, linguists need to make their testimony and reports easy to understand. It's not a matter of dumbing down their work. Rather, it's a matter of finding ways to make it clear to those who are not so trained. Doing this is often not easy for academic scholars who are more accustomed to trying to impress colleagues with their erudition when they speak at their academic conferences. Nevertheless, this is what linguists need to do and this book is one effort to show how it can be done in cases related to fraud. It remains rather clear, however, that we linguists apparently have not made our potential contributions clear enough about such things.

I have worked on many cases, including the ones described in this book, in which the analysis was clear enough that the retaining lawyers appeared to be able to use it themselves without my testimony. As mentioned earlier, their decision depends on many factors, however, including the ability of the lawyer to absorb the analysis properly and completely, on the judge's impatience about hearing still another witness in what may be an already very long trial, and on the potential negative effect on a jury when the defense case seems so hopeless that the lawyer appears to be required to depend on using outside experts to try to save the day.

Some judges also opine that since the language evidence is in English and the average person such as a juror speaks English natively, there is no particular need to have an expert in linguistics come and explain the language evidence to them. Nothing could be more inaccurate. Expert linguists are trained in the theory, research, and practice of linguistics, using specialized tools that other fields, including law, do not normally know or have accessible. It seems odd to linguists that the courts readily accept experts in medicine, engineering, psychology, and other specialties, knowing that these experts have ways of seeing the evidence that the average person lacks. In contrast, linguistic specialization and expertise often remains invisible to the courts.

Still another common objection to linguistic expertise made by the courts is that linguistic testimony might usurp the function of the jury. Note the conditional verbs that some judges use when they say "might usurp" or "could usurp" or "appears to usurp." And when they proclaim that it "would usurp" or "will usurp," they answer the question before it is fully investigated, sometimes even without a voir dire of the expert. It seems reasonable that total outsiders, non-advocates to the proceedings such as expert witnesses, should be able to provide as much objectivity and neutrality as they can to aid the jury as it considers issues about which lawyers on both sides are admittedly and necessarily advocates. It would seem that a non-advocate's genuine objectivity might be appreciated in such cases.

If the retaining lawyers follow Plan A and use their linguistic experts as tour guides and use the linguistic findings by themselves, they can avoid these common objections made by some judges about why a lawyer needs to use a linguistic expert witness or that using one might contaminate the jury. This is not to say, however, that linguists should never testify at trials. Sometimes retaining lawyers decide that Plan B is the best avenue to take. Lawyers are, after all, the experts in how to try their own cases.

Whether linguists testify or not in law cases of any type, including fraud cases, it's probably good for them to begin by emphasizing the goals and analytical procedures of linguistic analysis, which I have found to be the same goals and analytic procedures found in virtually all types of cases that involve large amounts of spoken language evidence. The linguist's task is help lawyers, judges, and juries better understand what the language evidence does and does not say and how they can observe the language clues that provide a panoramic picture built by individual snapshots of the conversations based on tools that most lawyers, judges, and juries don't know about.

As all of these eight cases demonstrate, the speech event is the first snap shot to point out, because it is the first clue that guides the speakers in what they are permitted and expected to say. As some of these cases demonstrate, targets may believe they are in one speech event while the agents try to convert it into their own very different speech event. Conflicting simultaneous speech events can produce odd sounding language that may be difficult for lawyers, judges, and juries to figure out or, depending on their own schemas, that they may not even think sounds very odd.

Even when targets come to realize that they are in a different speech event than the one promoted by undercover agents, their language can provide important clues to their schemas about the agents' speech events, and this provides a different snapshot of the whole communication. When the schemas of the targets' and agents' are different, they usually produce talk that demonstrates how their schemas influence their conversational agendas, as revealed by the topics they bring up (or topics they don't bring up) and the structure of their responses to the topics brought up by the other participants. I repeat that there is no way for anyone to reach into the speakers' minds, but the topics they introduce and recycle are likely to provide the most helpful reflections of their conversational agendas. Their topics and responses provide the best window to discover this, thereby providing still another snapshot of the entire body of language evidence.

Additional meaning can be found in the snapshot of speech acts that the participants use. Fraud cases require speech acts of promising, admitting, giving directives, reporting and requesting information, accusing, complaining, advising, offering, agreeing, and denying, with the further requirement that all of these have to be accomplished felicitously. In some instances, these speech acts are made indirectly, requiring the listener to infer what they really mean or to not understand them at all. Seven of the eight fraud cases described in this book give evidence of this, the exception being the Andreas case in chapter 9.

Additional reflections of the intentions of speakers and listeners can be discovered in the way certain conversational strategies are used. Because ambiguity is a major source of conversational misunderstanding, when agents sometimes use it in a way that causes listeners (as well as later listeners such as prosecutors and juries) to infer meaning the result can be dangerous, because inferences often have the possibility of being wrong. Undercover agents have been known to use ambiguously worded statements as a common undercover technique in their investigations of fraud, as can be seen in chapters 2 through 7. The ambiguity strategy is one of their essential tools in fishing for a target to produce an inculpatory response. Other such strategies in the fraud cases described in this book include the hit-and-run strategy, the strategy of withholding information that the target would need in order to fully understand the issues involved, the contamination strategy of putting certain information on the tape even though it is not relevant to the investigation but nevertheless gives the appearance of impropriety, and the strategy of interrupting or otherwise blocking targets from finishing utterances that might appear to be benign rather than inculpatory (Shuy 2005).

This leads us to the place that most prosecutions begin—the smoking gun expressions that are believed to reveal the defendants' knowing and willful fraud. As noted in the cases in this book, such smoking guns seem to stand out and thus they receive the primary attention of both the prosecution and the defense. Humankind loves to find quick and easy answers and in much of the government's evidence found in criminal investigations, smoking guns fit that bill quite nicely. For prosecutors, smoking guns are a godsend. For defense attorneys, they are deadly. A large part of their attractiveness to prosecutors is that smoking guns are not very work-intensive. They stand out sharply for all to see, giving the strong impression that they now resolve the case and that nothing more needs to be done.

Prosecutors are perfectly right about the smoking gun evidence found in many cases. For example, in the Abscam case of Ozzie Meyers the US Congressman responded to the agent's bribe offer with, "Where I could be of assistance is on private bills . . . you need influence. . . . We use our influence. . . . I know the right people. . . . I'll be in the man's corner a hundred percent. I'll deliver"

(Shuy 2013, 71). No linguistic help could prevent Meyers from going down in flames. But not all cases are that transparent.

Other criminal cases provide much less clear evidence that the purported smoking guns were what the prosecutor thought they were. For example, in the narcotics case of automobile executive John DeLorean, the prosecution believed DeLorean's agreement that "investment is a good thing" in his final meeting with the agent was true smoking gun evidence that he was willing to invest the remaining funds of his sinking business into the agent's drug operation. Analysis of the discourse throughout the sixty-four tape-recorded meetings demonstrated otherwise. In the context of the entire set of conversations, DeLorean had always used the word, "investment" to refer to investors buying stocks in his company, never to his investing in the agent's drug scheme. When it was pointed out that there was contextual evidence in the alleged smoking gun passage that DeLorean continued this pattern, the government's smoking gun died a painful death (Shuy 1993, 2013).

The prosecution is not alone in regarding smoking guns as serious. Defense attorneys fear them as much as the government loves them. One of the first things defense lawyers report when I begin to work on their cases is that certain passages of the tapes are "very troublesome." Inevitably these are the smoking guns. Sometimes linguistic analysis can show that they are not smoking guns at all and sometimes that they really are. When they are, the only advice the linguist can give is for the lawyer to try to get the best plea bargain possible.

Although genuine smoking guns are deadly for the defense, many alleged smoking guns can be understood by contextualizing them within the entire body of the language evidence. Good examples of this can be found in virtually all of the cases described in this book, but the cases of Cohen, Hsu, Smith, Heroux, and to a lesser extent those of Valentine and Burkhardt amply illustrate how purported smoking gun evidence can evaporate when seen within the context of the speech event, the schemas evidenced by the participants, the topics they choose to introduce (or choose not to introduce), their responses to the topics introduced by others, the felicity of the speech acts used by both parties, and the conversational strategies of ambiguity and others used by the agents.

There is no way to whitewash an actual crime, and especially not by using linguistic analysis. Linguists do not make such a claim. Some years ago I was called by a lawyer who had heard about my participation in other criminal cases. When he asked me to "work my magic" on his client's bribery case, I sensed immediately that his client was in deep trouble. When I later analyzed the language evidence, I discovered that there was absolutely nothing that could be done for this client, at which point my relationship to this case ended abruptly, for there was no possible "magic" to be offered. His client had apparently knowingly and willfully committed a crime. Linguists can't change the actual language evidence, but they can describe and explain what it is with tools that most lawyers don't have.

Sometimes, as in six of these eight fraud cases, this may have been somewhat helpful to the defense; other times, as in the other two cases, not so much, even though it was possibly somewhat useful for them to know where the language evidence demonstrated that their clients had serious problems.

Friends and colleagues have asked me why I would want to work on a case in which the clients are guilty. First of all, guilt or innocence is the concern of the court alone, not that of the retained experts. It is up to the lawyers on both sides to make their cases. The linguist only analyzes the language evidence and tells them what it can and cannot do for them. And this is what this book tries to demonstrate.

REFERENCES

Austin, J. L. 1955. *How to Do Things with Words*. Cambridge, MA: Harvard University Press.

Bartlett, Frederic. 1932. *Remembering: A Study in Experimental and Social Psychology*. Cambridge: Cambridge University Press.

Black's Law Dictionary. 2004. Edited by Bryan A. Garner. St. Paul, MN: Thomson West.

Bloomfield, Leonard. 1933. *Language*. New York: Henry Holt.

Bok, Sissela. 1989. *Lying*. New York: Vintage Books.

Bolinger, Dwight. 1980. *Language: The Loaded Weapon*. London: Longman.

Buller, D. B., and J. K. Burgoon. 1994. "Deception: Strategic and Non-strategic Communication." In *A Strategic Interpersonal Communication*, ed. J. A. Daly and J. M. Wiemann, 191–223. Hillsdale, NJ: Lawrence Erlbaum.

Eggington, William. 2008. "Deception and Fraud." In *Dimensions of Forensic Linguistics*, ed. John Gibbons and Teresa Turell, 251–264. Amsterdam: John Benjamins Company.

Eichenwald, Kurt. 2000. *The Informant*. New York: Broadway Books.

Ekman, Paul. 1985. *Telling Lies: Cures to Deceit in the Marketplace, Politics, and Marriage*. New York: Norton.

FBI Undercover Operations: Report on the Subcommittee on Civil and Constitutional Rights of the Committee on the Judiciary. House of Representatives, 98th Congress, 1984.

Galasinski, Dariusz. 2000. *The Language of Deception*. Thousand Oaks, CA: Sage Publications.

Garner, Bryan A. 1995. *A Dictionary of Modern Legal Usage*. New York: Oxford University Press.

Goffman, Erving. 1974. *Frame Analysis*. New York: Harper.

Grice, H. P. 1975. "Logic and Conversation." In *Syntax and Semantics*. Vol. 3, *Speech Acts*, ed. Peter Cole and Jerry Morgan, 113–128. New York: Academic Press.

Gudjonsson, Gisli. 1993. *The Psychology of Interrogation, Confessions and Testimony*. New York: John Wiley & Sons.

Gumperz, John. 1982. *Discourse Strategies*. Cambridge: Cambridge University Press.

Gumperz, John, ed., 1990. *Language and Social Identity*. New York: Cambridge University Press.

Hansel, Mark, and Cheryl Ajirotutu. 1982. "Negotiating Interpretations in Inter-Ethnic Settings." In *Language and Social Identity*, ed. John Gumperz, 1–21. Cambridge: Cambridge University Press.

Heymann, Phillip. 1984. "Undercover Operations (36-39)." Report of the Subcommittee on Civil and Constitutional Rights, 98th Congress, 2nd Session, 36–39. Washington, DC: U.S. Government Printing Office.

Husserl, Edmund. 1965. *Phenomenology and the Crisis of Philosophy*. New York: Harper & Row.

Hymes, Dell. 1972. "Models of Interaction of Language and the Social Life." In *Directions in Sociolinguistics*, ed. John Gumperz and Dell Hymes, 35–71. New York: Holt, Rinehart and Winston.

Jones, Eugene. 1916. *Manual of Equity Pleading and Practice*. Washington: J. Byrne and Company.

Landau, Sidney. 1989. *Dictionaries and the Art and Craft of Lexicography*. New York: Cambridge University Press.

Levinson, Stephen C. 1983. *Pragmatics*. New York: Cambridge University Press.

Merriam Webster's Collegiate Dictionary. 2003. 11th ed. Springfield, MA: Merriam-Webster Incorporated.

Miller, Gerald R., and James B. Stiff. 1993. *Deceptive Communication*. Newbury Park, CA: Sage Publications.

O'Barr, William M. 1982. *Linguistic Evidence: Language, Power, and Strategy in the Courtroom*. New York: Academic Press.

Patton, G. W. 1972. *A Textbook of Jurisprudence*. Oxford: Clarendon Press.

Puzynina, J. 1992. *Language in the World of Values*. Warsaw: Panstwowe Wydawnictwo Naukowe.

Saussure, Ferdinand de. [1924] 1983. *Course in General Linguistics*. Edited by Charles Bally and Albert Sechehaye. LaSalle, IL: Open Court.

Searle, John. 1969. *Speech Acts*. London: Cambridge University Press.

Searle, John. 1983. *Intentionality: An Essay in the Philosophy of Mind*. London: Cambridge University Press.

Sherzer, Joel. 1989. "Namakkke, Sunmakke, Kormakke." In *Explorations in the Ethnography of Speaking*, ed. Richard Bauman and Joel Sherzer, 263–282. Cambridge: Cambridge University Press.

Shuy, Roger W. 1993. *Language Crimes*. Cambridge: Blackwell.

Shuy, Roger W. 1998. *The Language of Confession, Interrogation, and Deception*. Thousand Oaks CA: Sage Publications.

Shuy, Roger W. 2005. *Creating Language Crimes*. New York: Oxford University Press.

Shuy, Roger W. 2008. *Fighting Over Words*. New York: Oxford University Press.

Shuy, Roger W. 2010. *The Language of Defamation Cases*. New York. Oxford University Press.

Shuy, Roger W. 2011. *The Language of Perjury Cases*. New York: Oxford University Press.

Shuy, Roger W. 2012. *The Language of Sexual Misconduct Cases*. New York: Oxford University Press.

Shuy, Roger W. 2013. *The Language of Bribery Cases*. New York: Oxford University Press.

Shuy, Roger W. 2014. *The Language of Murder Cases*. New York: Oxford University Press.

Solan, Lawrence. 1998. "Linguistics Experts as Semantic Tour Guides." *Forensic Linguistics* 5 (2): 87–106.

Tiersma, Peter. 1987. "The Language of Defamation." *Texas Law Review* 66 (2): 303–350.

Tiersma, Peter. 1990. *Legal Language*. Chicago: University of Chicago Press.

Tyler, Stephen R. 1978. *The Said and the Unsaid*. New York: Academic Press.

Whitney, William Dwight. 1867. *Language and the Study of Language: Twelve Lectures on the Principles of Linguistic Science*. London: N. Trubner and Company.

INDEX

Abscam investigation 273, 286, 295
agendas 5, 42–43, 53, 64, 71, 92, 107,
    123–139, 169–190, 196–197,
    203–205, 236–239, 262–269, 279
aiding and abetting 88, 115, 145, 285
Ajirotutu, Cheryl 9
Allen, Stephen 286
ambiguity 13, 18, 34, 44, 48, 49, 54, 65, 70,
    107, 143, 194, 205–212, 291
Andreas, Michael 252–256
Archer Daniels Midland 251–283
Arshad, Mohammed 286
Austin, J. L. 21

Bank Secrecy Act 156
Bartlett, Frederic 7
Bloomfield, Leonard 6
blowing theory 273
Bollinger, Dwight 11
Bok, Sissela 11
Brilab Investigation 286
Buller, D. B. 23
Burgoon, J. K. 23
Burkhart, Karl 157–192, 284, 292

camouflaging 143, 212–216
Clayton Antitrust Act 13, 252
Clayton, Billy 235, 286
coded language 127, 184, 243
Cohen, Yochanan 88–110, 285, 292

communicative competence 6
conspiracy 16, 27–28, 30, 55, 56, 66, 82,
    88, 113, 119, 144, 154, 168, 194, 231,
    251, 255, 279–280
conversational strategies 9, 23, 44–46,
    65–66, 70, 85, 105–106, 143–144,
    150, 175, 183, 189, 192, 204–221,
    242–245, 290
Cooperman, Steven 221–250, 282–285
Criminalizing conversations 112, 204,
    216–219

Davis, T. Cullen 235, 286
DeLorean, John 292

Economic Espionage Act 112
Eggington, William 11
Eichenwald, Kurt 254
Ekman, Paul 11
Environmental Protection Agency 24, 56, 287
espionage 113
Espionage Act of 1917 112

Federal Bureau of Investigation
    safeguards 47, 163, 204
Federal Trade Commission Act 251
fishing strategy 38, 43, 50, 53, 64, 66–69,
    77, 94, 98–104, 187, 190, 226–227,
    231–234, 291
Foreign Corrupt Practices Act 24, 87–91, 285

Foreign Military Sales Program 26
fraud
  academic 1
  corrupt foreign practices 87–88
  dictionary definitions 14–18
  environmental 55–84
  Federal statute 12
  government contract 2, 26–55
  insurance 2, 221–250
  money laundering 155–192
  Ponzi scams 1, 3
  price fixing 251–281
  publishing 1
  resource conservation 56–86
  securities 3, 193–220
  trade secrets 111–154

Galasinski, Dariusz 11, 23, 193
Goffman, Erving 7
Grice, H. P. 8, 108, 172
Gudjonsson, Gisli 93
Gumperz, John 6, 32, 165

Hansel, Mark 9
Hastings, Alcee 184, 286
Heroux, Kenneth 56–86, 287, 295
Heymann, Phillip 120, 163
hit and run strategy 9, 45, 104, 106–108,
  175, 241
Hsu, Kai-Lo 115–154, 284
Husserl, Edmund 20
Hymes, Dell 6, 165
hypotheticals 85, 105, 183, 260, 270,
  273, 278

industrial espionage 111, 114
inferences 20, 49, 82, 85, 147, 148, 151–153,
  163, 190, 215, 236, 247–249, 290
intentionality 8, 20, 21, 170
interviewing strategies 84
intonation 274–275

Jones, Eugene 15, 16

Kelly, Richard 273

Landau, Sidney 14, 16
Lanham Act 113

Leonard, Robert 88
Levinson, Stephen 20
lying 11, 12, 15, 19, 20, 241–242, 273

McDonald, Kenneth 286
Miller, Gerald 11
money laundering 24, 87, 88, 91, 155–159,
  168–170, 188
Money Laundering Control Act 156
Monroe, Beverly 286
Myers, Ozzie 273, 294

O'Barr, William 19
objections by judges 288–290

Patent Act 113
Patton, G. W. 13
police interview procedures 93–94
power 16, 18–19, 109, 208, 218, 252, 280
predisposition 8, 92, 116, 120, 122, 158,
  162, 165, 171, 209, 270, 278, 283
price fixing 13, 24, 251–281
  defined 252
  market allocation 253, 272
Puzynina, J. 11

recap evidence 275–276
Resource Conservation and Recovery
  Act 56–110
Robinson-Patman Act 251

schemas 5, 7–8, 41, 62–63, 90, 122–123,
  167–170, 200, 235, 260–262
securities fraud 193–220
Sherzer, Joel 6
Shuy, Roger W. 7–9, 11, 14, 20, 23, 32, 62,
  65, 121, 128, 143, 163–165, 169, 170,
  178, 184, 188, 189, 205, 212, 232,
  235–236, 241, 271, 286, 291, 292
Searle, John 9, 14, 21
Sherman Antitrust Act 13, 251
Smith, David 26–55, 284, 292
smoking guns 5, 10, 35, 46–54, 71, 104,
  107, 142, 144–150, 169, 187, 189,
  199, 204–231, 243–249, 271–275,
  291–292
snapshots 5, 24, 41, 71, 89, 144, 153, 167,
  190, 191, 197, 204, 239, 247, 273

softening 237
Solan, Lawrence 285
speech acts 5, 9, 10, 43, 64–65, 105,
    134, 139–143, 148–150, 187–188,
    203–204, 240–241, 269–279,
    290–293
speech events
    business evaluation speech event 7, 61–62
    business progress speech event 32–42, 47
    business transaction speech event 32,
        90–91, 109, 120–122, 141, 164–166,
        172–174, 198
    defined 6–7
    fishing speech event 231–235
    merged interests speech event 257–260
    stock sale speech event 197–200
Stiff, James 11

Taxol and Pacilitaxel 115–153
testifying vs. consulting 7, 86, 163, 190,
    282, 287–288
Tiersma, Peter 13, 20
topics 8, 31, 35, 36, 45, 49, 63–64, 67–69,
    71, 77, 78, 89, 92–109, 123–149,

170–186, 196–203, 226–241,
    257–270, 278, 283, 290, 293
transcript 45, 262, 274
trolling operation 120, 158, 264
Tyler, Stephen 20

undercover operations 3, 9, 30, 32, 42–49,
    66, 88–152, 157–178, 195–218,
    231–243, 252–279, 286, 290, 291
Uniform Trade Secrets Act 113
U.S. Drug Enforcement Agency 158
U.S. House of Representatives Committee
    on the Judiciary 163
U.S. Foreign Military Financing
    Program 26
U.S. Social Security Administration 21

Valentine, Mark 194–220, 284, 292

Whitacre, Mark 253–280
Whitney, William Dwight 5
Williams, Harrison 286
withholding information 22, 44, 45–46,
    54, 72, 143, 144, 241, 291